Making home

Contemporary American and Canadian Writers

Series editors
Nahem Yousaf and Sharon Monteith

Also available
Thomas Pynchon   Simon Malpas And Andrew Taylor
Jonathan Lethem   James Peacock
Mark Z. Danielewski   Edited by Joe Bray and Alison Gibbons
Louise Erdrich   David Stirrup
Passing into the present: contemporary American fiction of racial and gender passing   Sinéad Moynihan
Paul Auster   Mark Brown
Douglas Coupland   Andrew Tate
Philip Roth   David Brauner

Making home

Orphanhood, kinship, and cultural memory in contemporary American novels

Maria Holmgren Troy, Elizabeth Kella, and Helena Wahlström

Manchester University Press

Copyright © Maria Holmgren Troy, Elizabeth Kella, Helena Wahlström 2014

The rights of Maria Holmgren Troy, Elizabeth Kella, and Helena Wahlström to be identified as the authors of this work have been asserted by them in accordance with the Copyright, Designs and Patents Act 1988.

Published by Manchester University Press
Oxford Road, Manchester M13 9PL
www.manchesteruniversitypress.co.uk

British Library Cataloguing-in-Publication Data
A catalogue record for this book is available from the British Library

ISBN 978 0 7190 8959 6 hardback
ISBN 978 1 5261 5607 5 paperback

First published 2014
Paperback published 2021

The publisher has no responsibility for the persistence or accuracy of URLs for any external or third-party internet websites referred to in this book, and does not guarantee that any content on such websites is, or will remain, accurate or appropriate.

Typeset
by Frances Hackeson Freelance Publishing Services,
Brinscall, Lancs

Contents

	Series editors' foreword	*page* vii
	Acknowledgments	ix
	Introduction	1
1	Orphans and American literature: texts, intertexts, and contexts	10
2	From captivity to kinship: Native American orphans and sovereignty	40
3	Literary kinships: Euro-American orphans, gender, genre, and cultural memory	83
4	Family matters: Euro-American orphans, the *bildungsroman*, and kinship building	126
5	At home in the world? Orphans learn and remember in African American novels	169
	Coda	214
	Bibliography	225
	Index	250

Series editors' foreword

This innovative series reflects the breadth and diversity of writing over the last thirty years, and provides critical evaluations of established, emerging and critically neglected writers – mixing the canonical with the unexpected. It explores notions of the contemporary and analyses current and developing modes of representation with a focus on individual writers and their work. The series seeks to reflect both the growing body of academic research in the field, and the increasing prevalence of contemporary American and Canadian fiction on programmes of study in institutions of higher education around the world. Central to the series is a concern that each book should argue a stimulating thesis, rather than provide an introductory survey, and that each contemporary writer will be examined across the trajectory of their literary production. A variety of critical tools and literary and interdisciplinary approaches are encouraged to illuminate the ways in which a particular writer contributes to, and helps readers rethink, the North American literary and cultural landscape in a global context.

Central to debates about the field of contemporary fiction is its role in interrogating ideas of national exceptionalism and transnationalism. This series matches the multivocality of contemporary writing with wide-ranging and detailed analysis. Contributors examine the drama of the nation from the perspectives of writers who are members of established and new immigrant groups, writers who consider themselves on the nation's margins as well as those who chronicle middle America. National labels are the subject of vociferous debate and including American and Canadian writers in the same series is not to flatten the differences between them but to acknowledge that literary traditions and tensions are cross-cultural and that North American writers often explore and expose precisely these tensions.

The series recognises that situating a writer in a cultural context involves a multiplicity of influences, social and geo-political, artistic and theoretical, and that contemporary fiction defies easy categorization. For example, it examines writers who invigorate the genres in which they have made their mark alongside writers whose aesthetic goal is to subvert the idea of genre altogether. The challenge of defining the roles of writers and assessing their reception by reading communities is central to the aims of the series.

Overall, *Contemporary American and Canadian Writers* aims to begin to represent something of the diversity of contemporary writing and seeks to engage students and scholars in stimulating debates about the contemporary and about fiction.

Nahem Yousaf
Sharon Monteith

Acknowledgments

Making Home is a collaborative and co-written study by three scholars who have worked closely together with the book from its inception to its completion. We have brought to this work a shared background in American literary studies, our specializations within this field, and our knowledge of other areas such as gender studies and memory studies. In our exploration of orphanhood and kinship, we have been able to draw upon insights accrued during Elizabeth Kella's previous work on representations of ethnic communities in American fiction; Maria Holmgren Troy's earlier research on American domesticity, as well as her work on memory, trauma, and genre; and Helena Wahlström's research on representations of American families, particularly fatherhood and masculinity. Collaboration and collective writing of chapters have broadened and deepened our study. More than the sum of its parts, the dynamic of the project has taken us into new territories in terms of the writing process and enabled us to ask new, or at least different, questions about literary American orphans making home.

Time to write, together as well as apart, is absolutely essential in order to carry through a book project such as *Making Home*. A generous three-year grant from the Swedish Research Council has provided research time and, at times, opportunities for the three of us to work together in the same location despite our geographically dispersed academic homes. We are grateful to Helge Ax:son Johnson's Foundation for giving Liz Kella and Helena Wahlström a travel grant to the British Library, where they worked together for two weeks in 2008. We also spent two weeks together in the British Library in 2009 thanks to a grant from the Magnus Bergvall Foundation. Maria Holmgren Troy would like to express her gratitude to the School of English, Film,

Theatre, and Media Studies at Victoria University of Wellington, New Zealand, where she worked on the book project as a visiting scholar for two and a half months. We also want to acknowledge the editor of *American Studies in Scandinavia* for granting us permission to reprint excerpts from two articles that appeared in that journal in 2010 and 2011, as parts of Chapters 2 and 5.

About halfway through the project, we arranged an international symposium on representations of family at Uppsala University, in conjunction with a full-day workshop in which Caroline Levander and Marianne Novy offered feedback on first drafts of three chapters. The generous, thought-provoking, and productive comments and questions we received from them helped us strengthen the focus of *Making Home*. Funding for the symposium was granted by the Royal Swedish Academy of Letters; support was also provided by the Centre for Gender Studies and the English Department at Uppsala University. The Swedish Research Council kindly helped fund the workshop with an additional grant. We would also like to thank Donald E. Pease for taking the time to discuss the project. Thanks are also due to all who have offered constructive comments and suggestions at conferences, symposia, and seminars throughout the project, and to the team at Manchester University Press and external readers. Our most heartfelt thanks go to the series editors, Sharon Monteith and Nahem Yousaf, who acted as ideal readers of our book manuscript and helped us improve and refine it beyond what we could have achieved on our own. Finally, thanks to all our loved ones, near and far.

Introduction

'You little orphant,' he'd said when we were young. 'Who said you get pork chop for dinner? That's for the *real* children.' (Erdrich, 1984: 249)

Orphans abound in American literature. The stories they tell are gripping ones of vulnerability and survival, exclusion and inclusion, individuality and collective identity, the trials of the past and the possibilities of the future. Complex, even contradictory figures, capable of signifying conflicting social, psychological, and cultural conditions and desires, literary orphans mark profoundly charged sites of multiple meanings. Defined as a child or young person who has lost one or both parents through death, abandonment, or removal, orphans are without family, but they are nevertheless fundamentally constituted by their relation to family. For these reasons, we suggest, literary orphans are uniquely capable of fulfilling a range of narrative functions important to imagining family and, due to the conceptual connections between family and nation, to imagining America. American literary production from the 1980s onwards has generated new investments in literary representations of orphans and orphanhood, and American novels by Native American, Euro-American, and African American authors have made prominent use of orphan figures to think and re-think difference within and beyond the family and the nation.

Making Home argues that the trope of orphanhood has again become relevant in the late twentieth and early twenty-first centuries as shifts in the American social, political, and literary landscape have produced a sense of crisis but also a strong sense of possibility. Beginning in the 1980s, the academy underwent significant transformations as a result of struggles concerning multiculturalism and gender politics. The so-called canon wars triggered debates on aesthetic value, the meaning of culture and history, and hegemonic American identity that in various ways argued for the accommodation of difference in understandings of 'American' in the academy, but also in the nation at large. At the same time, feminist critiques of patriarchal families, as well as actual changes in family patterns, disrupted cherished notions of the nuclear family ideal, paving the way for new forms of kinship and home. We propose that in these times of perceived crisis and urgency – marked by the new social movements of the 1980s and 1990s as well as the US response to international terrorism after 2001 – the orphan has become an increasingly significant literary figure, particularly useful for explorations of what it takes to make home in the USA.

Orphans are mobilized anew by contemporary writers to explore a time of change, social upheaval, and crises in national identity. Our study builds on scholarship that explores the connection between national crisis and the trope of orphanhood. Diana Loercher Pazicky's *Cultural Orphans in America* (1998) examines orphanhood in earlier periods of crisis, from Puritan times through the mid-nineteenth century. In the US after the Revolution, Pazicky argues, the 'true children/citizens' inside the national family – those men (often with dependent families) who owned land – gained power and legitimacy from the exclusion of those who were other – primarily the poor, the enslaved, the racial or cultural 'other.' Pazicky terms such excluded groups *cultural orphans*, defined as 'groups of marginalized racial, religious, and ethnic outsiders – Negroes, Indians, and immigrants – who represented difference' (*ibid.*: xiii).[1] Whatever group or groups were 'orphaned' at different junctures in American history, the processes of scapegoating, displacement, and marginalization 'enabled the "children" to protect their identity within the family of the colony or the republic' (*ibid.*). We place the contemporary novels we discuss in *Making Home* in relation to the perceived crises in American unity and identity that have emerged in the last two decades of the twentieth century and the first of the twenty-first.

The cultural work that literary orphans perform today, we propose, responds to and intervenes in social and discursive challenges to American identity in an era of new social movements, culture wars, minority and gay rights, alternative families, globalization, and terrorism. We attempt to show the ways that contemporary American novelists use the orphan as a figure of difference in order to interrogate normative definitions of family and nation, and to sketch their possible re-formulations. In doing so, writers draw on, extend, alter, or disrupt earlier literary representations of orphans, families, and the USA. Literary orphans of the last several decades, we argue, function as a means to examine the conditions and limits for incorporating difference into the American family and, by extension, into the American nation, conceived in an increasingly multicultural and global fashion. In the works we examine, then, orphans become agents in making new kinds of home.

Making Home investigates contemporary novels as sites of cultural memory – in terms of genres, intertextual allusions, and their relationship to a national literary canon. Cultural memory is a helpful concept because the novels we investigate engage aesthetically as well as socio-historically with relationships between the past, the present, and possible futures. While cultural memory is closely related to ideology in that it contributes to the formation of a nation's cultural values and meanings, as Bakhtin observes: 'A genre lives in the present, but always *remembers* its past ... Genre is a representative of creative memory in literary development' (Bakhtin, 1984: 106). Bakhtin regards genre as a way of viewing the world, as '"form-shaping ideology" – a specific kind of creative activity embodying a specific sense of experience' (Morson and Emerson, 1990: 282–3), which impacts both authors and readers. We argue that orphan figures are pivotal to the ways that contemporary novels engage and reaccentuate genres as cultural memory. Moreover, orphans in American literature have specific national inflections, since orphanhood is a privileged trope in discourses on American identity.

The orphan has been a central figure in the formation of a national literary history in the USA, for example in the figure of the American Adam, and in the canonization of Mark Twain's *Adventures of Huckleberry Finn* (1884). In the earliest specifically American genres of captivity narratives and slave narratives, acknowledged in the late twentieth century as important literary texts, orphanhood and family have a central place. We argue that contemporary writers who are interested in expanding the canon to incorporate cultural difference use the orphan figure to explore alternatives to US hegemony. In other words, contemporary texts revisit the literary tradition through this figure. The figure of the orphan, because of its strong position in canonical American literature and criticism, allows US writers to insert themselves into that tradition but also to revise or even reject it, at times mobilizing the resources of alternative expressive traditions to make visible points of commonality and critique. Hence, the literary orphan functions both to reflect upon and to shape aspects of collective memory in the USA.

Another crucial reason for investigating fictional orphans is that they embody an intrinsic ambiguity, conjuring ideas of both family and familial loss, of both inclusion and exclusion. Such ambiguity gains particular significance when social protest and civil rights activism problematize cherished connections between nation, race, and family, and when feminist and queer challenges trouble the nuclear family ideal, the mythical force of which is supported by institutions and practices as well as embedded in a national imaginary. The orphan figure clearly activates normative ideas about the nuclear family. At the same time, it is a mechanism for denaturalizing family and exploring alternatives to that norm. This duality is visible in the ways orphans are used in contemporary fictional meditations on national belonging. Alternative kinship formations that the orphan inhabits, therefore, signify on both familial and national levels.

In its focus on the ways that literary representations of orphans speak to the changing realities of American national and multicultural identity in an increasingly global context, *Making Home* examines literature in the light of contemporary social realities – including child welfare in the USA. If children have historically become orphans by losing one or both parents through death or abandonment, voluntary or coerced, child removal is a form of state intervention which, even when grounded in benevolent ideas about the best interest of the child, deprives children of their birth parents, either temporarily or permanently. Modern adoption practices, while creating new familial relationships, may also separate children from their birth parents, especially when adoption records are confidential. These issues are the focus of the research that we draw upon to position fictional texts in specific historical and cultural contexts, especially the history of orphans, orphanages, foster care, and kinship formation in the USA. What we analyze, however, are fictional representations of children and teenagers who have lost one or both birth parents, due to any of the above processes. Including children with one parent in the study is motivated in part by the manner in which these figures are represented; a sense of psychological, social, or symbolic orphanhood may be elaborated, and sometimes sustained, sometimes transcended, or worked through. This broad application of the term is not a comment on parental loss, single-headed households, or lived family relations, but allows us to capture the range of imaginative artistic responses to the urgent concerns of family and nation.

Making Home analyzes orphans in a broad selection of contemporary novels by Native American, Euro-American, and African American novelists. Observers and scholars have identified the actual and, more importantly, the imaginary dynamics between these groups as key to the formation of a hegemonic American identity since Toqueville – precisely that identity that became unsettled and shaken in the years immediately prior to and contemporary with the novels we study.[2] Despite demographic and cultural changes in the USA, including the rise of transnational and transracial adoption as well as trends in cross-ethnic, transatlantic, and hemispheric studies, understandings of making home in the USA continue to be informed by ideas of racial differences between these three groups. Our selection includes novels by Native American writers Linda Hogan and Leslie Marmon Silko, Euro-American writers Michael Cunningham, Jonathan Safran Foer, Kaye Gibbons, John Irving, Barbara Kingsolver, and Marilynne Robinson, and African American writers Octavia Butler, Jewelle Gomez, and Toni Morrison.

The triangulation of Native Americans, Euro-Americans, and African Americans that has historically been central to narratives about American identities also informs the structure of this study. In part this is motivated by the awareness that families, orphans, and fictions have different histories, and have been variously treated, included, or excluded in narratives about America. While at first sight the structure of this study may seem to reinscribe difference between these groups, it facilitates the crossing of boundaries between them, because themes and tropes of orphanhood, as well as the final outcomes for orphan figures, cross ethnic divides.

Just as the literary orphan is rich with the possibilities of multiple meanings, so the novel has a unique capacity for incorporating multiplicity and difference – different voices, different times and places, different discourses and, above all, different genres, including oral traditions. The dialogic character of the novel and the flexibility and scope of the form[3] make room for varied positions and trajectories for orphan protagonists. The chapters in *Making Home* explore contemporary orphan tales in relation to genres, among them the captivity narrative, sentimental fiction, the *bildungsroman*, speculative fiction, and the historical novel. At the same time, we show a range of imaginative efforts to envision differences from genre traditions, and to suggest the spaces at least partly outside of these traditions from which some writers operate. For example, we find that some texts by Native American writers bear the strong imprint of practices of captivity and child removal, but substantially alter the conventions of the captivity narrative – that quintessentially 'American' genre – in order to envision different forms of freedom and community. Similarly, conventions of the vampire novel are disrupted when female African American vampire orphans make new family through blood exchanges, and the Euro-American orphan boy complicates conventionally gendered boundaries between sentimental fiction and the picaresque novel.

Making Home extends scholarship on literary orphans in new directions: it investigates orphans in a multiethnic selection of American literature; it addresses representations of orphans in literature for adults; and it focuses on orphans in contemporary fiction. Research in childhood studies demonstrates that literary representations of children and notions of childhood are historically and culturally specific.[4] This insight is important to our investigation of the historically and culturally specific meanings of orphanhood in late twentieth- and early twenty-first-century fiction, when, for instance, the term 'orphan' re-emerged in the orphanage debate of 1994 and the Twin Towers Orphan Fund after September 11, 2001.[5] Characters designated, and sometimes self-designated, as 'orphans' become central to quite a few twenty-first-century American novels, such as Kaye Gibbons's *The Life All Around Me by Ellen Foster* (2006), Hannah Tinti's *The Good Thief* (2008), Toni Morrison's *A Mercy* (2008), and Tim Gautreaux's *The Missing* (2009). However, these novels are set in earlier periods; the 1690s in Morrison's novel, the nineteenth century in Tinti's, the 1920s in Gatreaux's, and the 1970s in Gibbons's, thus relegating orphanhood to the American past. For many critics 'orphan' is above all a nineteenth-century term; Huckleberry Finn, Ragged Dick, and Rebecca of Sunnybrook Farm are instantly recognizable protagonists from the nineteenth-century and early twentieth-century heyday of orphan tales, studied by scholars of this period.[6] The few book-length studies on orphanhood and alternative kinship in twentieth-century American literature typically concern works that were published before the period we focus on in *Making Home*.[7]

Finally, this study is distinct from, but engages with, scholarship on adoption as a social practice, and on adoption in literature. In 2005 Marianne Novy assessed that orphanhood had been studied more than adoption in literature, but the current surge in adoption studies, which has gained impetus from trends in international and transracial adoption, makes a re-examination of literary orphanhood a timely undertaking. While the adoptee until recently has been a strictly binary figure, oriented primarily either toward birth parents or adoptive parents and presuming, as Novy notes, 'only one set of parents' (2001: 1), we argue that the orphan figure marks a site of difference and carries a multitude of potential meanings and familial outcomes. Our focus on orphanhood rather than adoption in *Making Home* allows us to explore a wider range of kinship work in texts which take on complex identity issues, including multiculturalism, transnationalism, and literary history. Our work intersects with recent studies on transracial and/or transnational adoption that include examinations of fiction published after World War II, when transnational adoption in the USA (other than US/Native American) can be said to most forcefully emerge.[8] Mark C. Jerng's *Claiming Others: Transracial Adoption and National Belonging* (2010) and Cynthia Callahan's *Kin of Another Kind: Transracial Adoption in American Literature* (2011) view transracial adoption in literature as registering socio-political concerns such as multiracial identity, mixed-race families, and naturalization of racial, familial, and national identity. *Making Home* contributes to this conversation from a decisively literary angle, focusing on the role played by children and teenagers who have lost or been deprived of parents, in twentieth- and twenty-first-century literary explorations and redefinitions of 'home' in terms of family, nation, and national literature. By analyzing the ways in which contemporary novels both incorporate and resist gendered and raced literary conventions, elaborate on meanings of orphanhood in symbolic as well as actual terms, and explore kinship beyond the nuclear family and/ or adoption, this study offers new insights.

Chapter 1, 'Orphans and American literature: texts, intertexts, and contexts,' places our study in the context of earlier research on American orphan figures in literary history and criticism. Elaborating on the central notions of cultural memory and multiculturalism, and on literary and socio-historical contexts, we lay the groundwork for our subsequent analyses of Native American, Euro-American, and African American orphan figures. Chapter 2, 'From captivity to kinship: Indian orphans and sovereignty,' explores how Native American orphans in contemporary novels are imagined in relation to the near mythical pattern of the Indian captivity narrative; we view captivity as an 'orphaning practice,' for in accounts from Puritan times onward captivity involves forcible removal of the captive from his or her cultural family. Our analyses of *The Bean Trees* (1988) and *Pigs in Heaven* (1993) by Barbara Kingsolver, *Solar Storms* (1995) by Linda Hogan, and *Gardens in the Dunes* (1999) by Leslie Marmon Silko suggest that these authors use the Indian orphan figure to interrogate the possibilities and limitations of American nationhood and Native sovereignty.

Chapter 3, 'Literary kinships: Euro-American orphans, gender, genre, and cultural memory,' investigates the narrative and ideological functions of white Euro-American orphans. In analyses of Marilynne Robinson's *Housekeeping* (1981), Michael Cunningham's *Specimen Days* (2005), and Jonathan Safran Foer's *Extremely Loud and Incredibly Close* (2005), we argue that orphans challenge the American family and, by extension, a hegemonic national identity that privileges white men. These novels both invoke and critique the US canon by elaborating on the quest motif and the mythic figure of the American Adam, and by writing themselves into genres that have housed orphans in American literary history: novels of development, sentimental or domestic novels. Chapter 4, 'Family matters: Euro-American orphans, the *bildungsroman*, and kinship building,' focuses on John Irving's *The Cider House Rules* (1985), and Kaye Gibbons's *Ellen Foster* (1987) and *The Life All Around Me by Ellen Foster* (2006), novels that, we suggest, remember earlier American and English novels to revise the conventions of the *bildungsroman* and challenge its conventional gender boundaries. In the process, the novels describe the kinship building of the protagonists, who develop complex understandings of kinship ties and a consciously affirmative stance on the value of 'alternative family.' Chapter 5, 'At home in the world?: Orphans learn and remember in African American novels,' offers analyses of African American orphans in Octavia Butler's *Fledgling* (2005), Jewelle Gomez's *The Gilda Stories* (1991), and Toni Morrison's *A Mercy* (2008). These writers employ genres like the vampire novel and the historical novel of slavery to move beyond established paradigms of the modern black family. A transnational tendency affords a different inflection on questions concerning home, family, and nation; these novels also imagine feminist, queer, and multicultural forms of kinship that move beyond the nuclear family. However, these forms of kinship are not presented in exclusively utopian terms, for the novels explore the limitations as well as the possibilities of non-normative kinship and transracial, and even trans-species, adoption. Using the literary figure of the orphan, all of these works offer new insights into making home in the USA and in American literature.

Notes

1 Like Pazicky, we sometimes use the term 'Indian' to refer to Native North Americans. Though 'Indian' is clearly a white construct which downplays the diversity and particularity of Native identities, the term has been recuperated by Native American writers and critics today. Throughout this book, we use the terms 'Native,' 'Native American,' 'indigenous,' and 'Indian' quite interchangeably in reference to pan-Indian issues and questions of cultural representation. We identify specific tribal affiliations when these are known and relevant to the discussion.
2 See Natasha Zaretsky on American debates on family decline and national decline 1968–80 (2007). See also Andersen (1991) and Farrell (1999).
3 See Bakhtin (1981).
4 See, for example, Kincaid (1998), Levander (2006), Levander and Singley (2005), Nelson (2001), and Sánchez-Eppler (2005).
5 An MLA search using the word 'orphan' and the phrase 'American literature' yields nine hits for 1980–89, forty for 1990–99, and forty-one for 2000–09, while an MLA search on 'orphan' and 'American' yields ten hits for 1980–89, forty-one for 1990–99, and forty-nine for 2000–09. Both searches, which partly overlap, indicate the increased use of the word orphan in academic discourse in the 1990s as well as in the twenty-first century.
6 See for instance Baym (1993), Lewis (1955), Nelson (2001, 2003), Singley (2011), and Weinstein (2004).
7 See Valerie Loichot's *Orphan Narratives* (2007), Christopher Nealon's *Foundlings* (2001), and Singley's *Adopting America* (2011).
8 See Adam Pertman, executive director of the Evan B. Donaldson Adoption Institute, on how the 'adoption revolution' is transforming American families and the nation (Pertman, 2011). For an incisive discussion of American adoption of Chinese girls and of the emerging (auto)biographical genre of the parental adoption narrative, particularly in terms of Emily Prager's *Wuhu Diary* (2001), see Judie Newman (2007: 58–73).

1

Orphans and American literature: texts, intertexts, and contexts

> The word 'orphan' suggests being cut off from society, abandoned and alone; its opposite conjures visions of family, connectedness, roots, belonging – all subsumed in the image of home. (Porter, 2003: 101)

Orphans in contemporary US novels gain significance in relation to earlier American literature and the history of orphanhood in the USA. This chapter therefore situates our study in both literary and socio-historical contexts, focusing on earlier discussions of the American orphan figure in literary and social history and elaborating especially on literature as cultural memory. We trace the central position of orphans in nineteenth-century American literary history as it has been constructed in the twentieth century; orphans have played major roles in a dominant white male tradition in criticism, but also in gendered and ethnic challenges to that tradition. Previous critical discussion of orphans typically focuses on children's literature, or on nineteenth-century literature, but nevertheless offers useful insights into the historically shifting roles and cultural work of orphan characters, linked to social and political developments in the USA. We also address ideas of the orphan, childhood, and family, and how these ideas operate in social and academic debates over multiculturalism, the US canon, and national belonging. These contexts are an important basis for our subsequent analyses of orphanhood, kinship, and cultural memory in contemporary American novels featuring Native American, Euro-American, and African American orphans.

Orphans, literature, and cultural memory

'[R]emembering the past' is not just a matter of recollecting events and persons, but often also a matter of recollecting earlier texts and rewriting earlier stories. (Erll and Rigney, 2006: 112)

Novels are multifaceted sites of cultural memory – through their employment of genres, their relation to a national literary canon, and their intertextuality. Pierre Nora's concept of 'sites of memory' is useful for examining how textual and material places become a focus of collective remembrance as well as of historical meaning. Such an emphasis on processes in the constitution, maintenance, development, and shifts in these sites of memory supports our view of individual novels as dynamic arenas for the transmission of cultural images and knowledge, for creative revisions of history and identity, and for visions for the future.

As a carrier and shaper of dominant cultural memory as well as counter-memory,[1] literature both reflects and influences constructions of national and group identities. Following the new social movements of the 1970s and subsequent changes in the academic and cultural fields, scholars and intellectuals have criticized 'official' US history as a skewed (mis)representation of the past, serving to characterize particular groups as inferior, insignificant, or making them invisible. The work of recovering, restoring or (re)creating 'alternative' histories has become a priority. Literature plays a pivotal role in these endeavors, as can be seen, for instance, in the works of Linda Hogan, Jewelle Gomez, and Toni Morrison that we examine here. In this context, novels may help shape the collective memory of groups, and also challenge or renegotiate the collective memory of the nation. Indeed, as Barbara Misztal summarizes, 'Collective memory is not only what people really remember through their own experience, it also incorporates the constructed past which is constitutive of the collectivity ... Thus, the notion of collective memory refers both to a past that is *commonly shared* and a past that is *collectively commemorated*' (2003: 13). Importantly then, collective memory consists of historical knowledge as well as 'experience, mediated by *representation of the past,* that enacts and gives substance to a group's identity' (*ibid.*: 15, emphasis added), whether this group is conceptualized as the family, the ethnic community, the nation, or a transnational alliance. The term 'rememory,' coined by Toni Morrison in *Beloved* (1987), signals precisely this blend of psychological memory and cultural remembrance, and has since been linked to intertextuality and the 'replaying of selected images' to realize 'an imaginative recovery of the historical past' (Mitchell, 2002: 12).[2]

Works of literature instantiate cultural remembrance through the use of intertextuality. As Astrid Erll and Ann Rigney note, the recollection of texts from earlier periods can be an integral part of cultural remembrance and discussions of canon formation can be 'revisited as exemplifying the ways in which societies squabble over which foundational texts deserve commemoration or not' (2006: 112). *Making Home* focuses on the period from the 1980s through the early twenty-first century, a period marked by fierce struggles over the racialized and gendered biases of the literary canon. The novels in this study do engage with canonical works, but also with particular critical traditions. In Chapter 3 we pay specific attention to the development of US literary-critical traditions as a form of cultural memory to which novelists have recourse. Intertextuality – which can be thought of as a means to maintain cultural memory, even when it functions to express criticism of earlier texts – is explored throughout the study. We foreground the ways contemporary novels implicitly or explicitly 'remember' earlier texts: critically, nostalgically, or ambivalently. Our investigation also responds to Shelley Fisher Fishkin's call for criticism that addresses how issues like 'influence, exchange, appropriation, "homage," intertextual dialogue, "signifying," "capping," borrowing, theft, synergy, and cross-fertilization' (1995: 455) are used to write contemporary texts across different racial and ethnic categories.

The novels examined in *Making Home* employ a number of different genres, including the captivity narrative, the *bildungsroman*, speculative fiction, and the historical novel.[3] That these fictions refer to, or revisit, other written texts or oral traditions raises questions about the role of genre as a medium of cultural remembrance. Genres play a crucial part in the mediation of situations and events, as these are remembered over time, and may achieve a near mythical force, as can be seen, for instance, in the case of the captivity narrative in US culture. Bakhtin argued that genres are form-shaping ideologies, with both aesthetic and ideological dimensions. We find that in the genres considered, orphan figures have a strong effect on ideological meanings, but also on aesthetic ones, not least in the manner in which memory is narrated and thematized.

Our selection of novels foregrounds memory and remembrance in the characterization of orphan protagonists and, sometimes, in the structure of the narration. Literary orphans, like real orphans, have different degrees of access to one form of collective memory: familial memory.[4] Some of the orphans in the novels that we investigate suffer from lack of knowledge, or from trauma or amnesia, which blocks or limits access to memories of their own or their family's past, as in Hogan's *Solar Storms*, Marilynne Robinson's *Housekeeping*, Jonathan Safran Foer's *Extremely Loud and Incredibly Close*, Kaye Gibbons's Ellen Foster novels, Octavia Butler's *Fledgling*, and Morrison's *A Mercy*. Acts of individual remembrance are arguably most distinctly represented in the novels with a first-person narrator-protagonist, but memory and its links to history are explored in all the novels.[5]

Orphans in American literary history and criticism

> Images of orphanhood have pervaded the American imagination ever since the colonial period ... [W]hatever shape the orphan assumes, the figure signals identity formation, not only individual but cultural.
> (Pazicky, 1998: xi)

Many investigations of orphans in fiction focus on children's literature, and on white orphan heroines and heroes from Rose Campbell in Louisa May Alcott's *Eight Cousins, or the Aunt-Hill* (1875) and Mark Twain's *Tom Sawyer* (1876) to Lemony Snicket's Baudelaire orphans in *A Series of Unfortunate Events* (1999–2006). Most literary analyses of orphans, though, focus on the late nineteenth and early twentieth century. Scholarship to date demonstrates not only that 'the displaced child is an omnipresent rhetorical trope in American writing of this period' (Nelson, 2003: 5), but also that the orphan in children's literature performs certain kinds of cultural work – emotional, social, political – that shift over time.

In the late nineteenth century, the orphan's function is often didactic, facilitating the production of lessons about proper middle-class values, or good citizenship. The orphan is an apt figure for teaching moral lessons to the young. Classic American children's books advocate 'positive thinking, and redemption through naivitë' (Griswold, 1992: 19), and orphan protagonists, from Horatio Alger to Superman, 'exude competence, decency, and a near magical ability to fulfill society's needs' (Nelson, 2001: 54–5).[6] The positive characteristics of the orphan child – especially the male orphan child – are personality traits that resonate with nationalist myths of individualism and self-creation.

Nevertheless, orphans in children's literature are not static but flexible, and scholars have linked representations of orphans to shifting cultural perspectives on childhood and dependency. They relate these representations to social reform and institutional concern with child welfare, to the production of responsible citizens, or to shifts in conceptions of the child's social role.[7] Claudia Nelson observes that in the nineteenth century 'the figure of the self-sufficient orphan who earns by honest toil all the benefits he receives from his parents embodies the sturdy independence and the upward mobility that Victorian America persistently valorized' (2006: 83). The meanings of orphan figures change between the late nineteenth century, when children helped expand the labor capacity of a family, and the early twentieth century, when they fulfilled the emotional needs of adults. In this latter period, Nelson summarizes, the orphan's 'proper "work" was presented as the spiritual and emotional uplift of adults' (2003: 7), but there was also an 'increased interest in the desires and feelings of the young' (2001: 55).[8]

The orphan in nineteenth-century children's literature has also been analyzed in terms of the character's function as social and political critique. Critics have shown how literary orphans underscore society's failure to provide for parentless and poor children or demonstrate the arbitrary and unequal distribution of the benefits of familial belonging (Harde, 2008: 65–6; Nelson, 2001: 54). In early twentieth-century books, representations of orphans from the past were used to reassure contemporary readers 'that even when children's lives are changed in fundamental and dramatic ways, love will be present' (Nelson, 2006: 81). In her readings of more recent fictions featuring internationally adopted children and children of divorced parents, Nelson foregrounds two major functions of the orphan child character: the emotional work to reassure and love, and the political work to incorporate these children into conceptions of American family.

Orphans have also played a major role in a dominant tradition of literary criticism as well as in challenges to that tradition. In this context, there are two significant strands that feature the Euro-American orphan, with which the contemporary novels that we examine engage. In one strand, the orphan is male; it includes many works by male writers that were canonized at the beginning of the twentieth century. The other strand centers on a female orphan and includes novels written by women writers that were suppressed, forgotten, or disparaged from the end of the nineteenth century until well into the second half of the twentieth when they were re(dis)covered by feminist critics. In both of these literary traditions, the orphan confirms and promulgates pivotal American values such as individual agency and pluck. A greater emphasis often lies, however, on individualism and on escapes from the constraints of middle-class family life in the stories of the male orphan.

The male orphan in nineteenth-century American fiction carries meanings closely linked to ideas about American national identity. In a comparative reading of *Great Expectations* (1861) and *Adventures of Huckleberry Finn* (1884), Hana Wirth-Nesher observes that although orphans abound in British fiction, their connotations are different from those of American orphans: 'While English literature has no shortage of orphans, they are usually on a quest to find a place for themselves in society rather than arranging for a romantic exit' (1986: 261). Like many critics, then, she links American boy orphans – the epitome being Huckleberry Finn – to resistance against family, and a reinforcement of individualism. From Huck onwards, fictional orphan boys have been positioned in opposition to family as well as 'sivilization,' rather than moving towards their 'right' family. In Chapters 3 and 4, we explore how Foer's and John Irving's boy protagonists challenge this traditional image of the male American orphan.

In Twain's novel, Huck's freedom takes shape in direct and telling contrast to Jim's enslavement, demonstrating how the freedom essential to American identity is a privilege of race as well as gender. Many critics, including Toni Morrison in *Playing in the Dark* (1992), have demonstrated how American national identity depends upon ideological connections between whiteness and freedom. Hence, in what is considered classic nineteenth-century American literature, the male orphan child is white, and his whiteness is a condition for his representativeness as an archetypal American within the context of a racist culture. Diana Loercher Pazicky highlights and problematizes this connection between male orphanhood, race, and national as well as personal identity, in her discussion of Frederick Douglass's autobiographies: '[these] accounts begin by linking the separation from his family to various forms of dehumanization. Slavery not only made Douglass an orphan but robbed him of a personal and historical identity' (1998: 180). She characterizes Douglass's development as one from 'orphanhood to self-fatherhood' (*ibid.*: 186). While separation from family is cast in very different terms for the enslaved black orphan than for his free white literary counterpart, Douglass's self-fatherhood is an important aspect of American masculinity. The male orphan thus reinforces ideas about a specifically American masculinity,[9] and the white male orphans in the nineteenth-century literary canon can be read as embodying masculine ideals constitutive of national identity. Natty Bumppo, Ishmael, and Huck Finn, although by no means identical heroes, share existential orphanhood as a formative force directing their adventures, which involve homosocial contexts and individual journeys towards new geographical territories. Male orphans in classic American literature often follow strictly gendered trajectories, which lead them from restriction to freedom, in the process reinforcing a masculine ideal typical of settler cultures, marked by self-reliance, strength, and industry. Freedom of movement along the Mississippi River, or across the American landscape of prairie or sea, is also typical for these male orphans and sets them apart from female orphans. Moreover, they typically resent and reject middle-class values as imbued with the ideals of domesticity, traditionally gendered feminine in American culture. In Chapter 3 we analyze Robinson's *Housekeeping* as an exploration and renegotiation of these gendered characteristics, but also of those typically ascribed to the female American orphan.

In contrast to the male orphan's heightened individualism and love of freedom, the female orphan's main aim is to form bonds with people around her and to find, or perhaps rather create, a home, as do Gerty in Maria Cummins's *The Lamplighter* (1854) and Ellen in Susan Warner's *The Wide, Wide World* (1850). There are two main variations in the nineteenth-century Euro-American female orphan tale: when the novel begins she is either a 'poor and friendless child,' or she is a 'pampered heiress who becomes poor and friendless in mid-adolescence' (Baym, 1993: 35). In either case, she has to prove her worth through her own efforts and character, her own agency. In the end, the white female orphan often finds or creates a new sympathetic home, or is reunited with her 'true' family; in short, what we often see in these novels is a reconstitution of white middle-class family life (Pazicky, 1998: 149–77). While these novels, like those featuring male orphans, value independence, individual agency, hard work, and honesty, the orphan heroines who demonstrate these qualities typically end up in middle-class families – through marriage, recovery of lost family, or 'sympathy' with a new family.[10] This female orphan is an apt representative of Real Womanhood, the 'all-American girl' of mid nineteenth-century literature. For Frances B. Cogan, this version of womanhood values female self-reliance and survival, in contradistinction to the virtue of 'passivity' that Barbara Welter emphasizes in her study of nineteenth-century True Womanhood in the USA (1989: 152).[11] A Real Woman could work outside the home, although her proper place was indisputably in the home. Thus, the all-American girl is part of the discourse of domesticity that helped form white bourgeois identity in the US in the nineteenth century. Anti-patriarchal – but not necessarily feminist or radical – the discourse of domesticity provided a framework in which nineteenth-century white women could think about their world and possibly improve it (Romero, 1997: 19–20). Yet, this ideology was fraught with contradictions, obscuring class differences and drawing attention away from the polarizing construction of racial difference at the time (McHugh, 1999: 35–6). Privileging gender difference, the discourse of domesticity ignored the racialization of women's agency and ambitions.

The black female orphan as protagonist is an important figure in Harriet E. Wilson's *Our Nig; or, Sketches from the Life of a Free Black* (1859) and Harriet Jacobs's *Incidents in the Life of a Slave Girl* (1861), as well as in the contemporary American novels that we discuss in Chapter 5. Wilson's Frado and Jacobs's Linda Brent, for example, problematize nineteenth-century white middle-class notions of womanhood, whether True or Real, and expose their reliance on race and class privilege (Carby, 1987: 40–61; Romero, 1997: 27–8). A significant common trait is the protagonists' lack of or limited access to domesticity in the sense of a home of their own, or a home for their families. As cultural as well as literal orphans, both Frado and Linda Brent are painfully aware of this deprivation, as well as the ways that the discourse of domesticity derived from the privileged conditions of white middle-class women in the nineteenth century.[12]

Twentieth-century critical traditions have largely reinforced the gender differences represented by the white male and female nineteenth-century orphan figures. In the mid-twentieth century, the male literary orphan's escape from family, and hence from history, was foundational to the idea of the American Adam formulated by R.W.B. Lewis. Lewis's argument is familiar: *The American Adam* (1955) constructs an American myth of constant regeneration based on nineteenth-century canonical American literature. It defines American literary history and American identity in strictly masculine terms, for in this setting of new beginnings and no past, the American Adam emerges as the primary embodiment of American identity, 'an individual emancipated from history, happily bereft of ancestry, untouched and undefiled by the usual inheritances of family and race' (1955: 5). The American Adam, for Lewis, is a man directed only towards the future, and 'happily' so. Although Lewis recognizes some of the problems connected to the recurrent use of this figure in American literature, the optimism of the American Adam's innocence and forward thrust remains palpable. Robinson's *Housekeeping*, Michael Cunningham's *Specimen Days*, and Morrison's *A Mercy*, we suggest, may be read as commenting on aspects of this figure.

The symbolic orphanhood of the American Adam is a condition for redemption that validates the frontier individualism and democracy of James Fenimore Cooper and Walt Whitman, the non-conformity of Henry David Thoreau, Nathaniel Hawthorne, and Herman Melville, and the knowledge attained, or just missed, by Henry James's characters. It is, in effect, because he is an orphan – and because the orphan is male – that the protagonist of classic American writing is free to fashion his own identity, to create his own destiny, and, in so doing, to realize national myths including that of the American Dream. Though the American Adam is not referred to explicitly as an orphan, he is one according to the critical tradition established in the 1940s and 1950s. The male orphan is made central to the construction of American literary history as well as to the construction of a heroic American cultural identity. In criticism of nineteenth-century canonical literature in the early phases of American Studies as a discipline and methodology, then, the male, white orphan often functioned and began to be acknowledged as a means to bolster ideas of national identity.

Events of the 1960s and 1970s, however, profoundly altered this view of national identity, and of the Adamic figure seen to personify it. Referring to 'the murderous violence that has characterized recent political life,' Richard Slotkin observed in 1973 that 'the conception of America as a wide-open land of unlimited opportunity for the strong, ambitious, self-reliant individual to thrust his way to the top … has blinded us to the consequences of the industrial and urban revolutions and to the need for social reform and a new concept of individual and communal welfare' (2000: 5). Turning a critical eye to the social, political, economic, and psychological regeneration on the westward-moving American frontier from 1600 to 1860, Slotkin demonstrates that 'the means to that regeneration ultimately became the means of violence, and the myth of regeneration through violence became the structuring metaphor of the American experience' (*ibid.*: 5). His analyses of literature, genres, and fictional heroes expose the violence against others, particularly Native Americans, that American heroes must perform in order to fulfill the logic of a mythic American identity. Positive notions of kinship as interdependency, it might be added, are fundamentally at odds with the masculine myth of American identity that Slotkin extrapolates on and critiques. Slotkin's study treats Native Americans primarily as symbolic figures whose characteristics alter in response to the changing needs of colonists and settlers. Countering the projections and stereotypes of Indians generated by Euro-Americans remains important. In Chapter 2, we focus on how Native American writers use Indian orphans to counter the idea of regeneration through violence with an indigenous alternative of regeneration through kinship, exemplifying that shift via detailed study of two novels.

Slotkin's critique challenged many values associated with the American Adam, but did little to counter the masculinist bias of American literary criticism, which continued to gender domesticity, sentiment and sentimentality as feminine. In American literary criticism in the early twentieth century, scholars positioned sentiment/ality as exclusively feminine, and therefore unworthy of critical attention. It was typically described as 'emotional,' 'anti-intellectual,' and even 'simple-minded' (Chapman and Hendler, 1999: 4). As Mary Chapman and Glenn Hendler assert, 'by constructing American masculine stereotypes such as the anti-domestic American Adam or the individual loner/revolutionary, critical master narratives like Mathiessen's and Lewis's have masked the continued presence of sentimental men in American culture and letters' (*ibid.*: 5). Such masking has sustained both a critical focus on certain types of male characters, and a critical blindness to the possibility that the sentimental genre may indeed house male as well as female orphans. In this study, we move beyond the conventional gendered assignation of sentiment and domesticity in our explorations of contemporary orphan stories, such as Oskar's struggles to 'feel right' in Foer's novel and Ruth's rejection of domesticity in Robinson's *Housekeeping*.

In 1978, some twenty years after the publication of Lewis's *American Adam*, Nina Baym published her ground-breaking feminist study *Woman's Fiction* in which she analyzes a number of nineteenth-century American novels by women that feature female orphans. These novels 'chronicle the "trials and triumph" ... of a heroine who, beset by hardships, finds within herself the qualities of intelligence, will, resourcefulness, and courage sufficient to overcome them' (Baym, 1993: 22). Most of these novels had not been included in earlier twentieth-century constructions of American literary history; if mentioned at all they were typically dismissed as domestic or sentimental novels, and therefore inferior. Both the genres and the concepts of domesticity and sentimentalism have been thoroughly re-examined and re-evaluated over the last few decades, but they were unambiguously disparaged when Baym's study was published. Baym questioned the neutrality of literary criteria, finding in them 'a bias in favor of things male,' including 'an exquisite compassion for the crises of the adolescent male, but ... [impatience] with the parallel crises of the female' (ibid.: 14). Published only a few years after Baym's study, Robinson's *Housekeeping* concerns itself exclusively with female crises and relegates male characters to the margins of the female narrator's story. The novel also makes a powerful bid for inclusion in the national literary canon as well as in a feminist tradition.

As Baym points out in the 1993 introduction to the second edition of her book, in 1978, '*Woman's Fiction* was part of a general academic countermovement through which scholars in various disciplines were beginning to retrieve, as best we could, the lost work that we believed was part of our heritage' (ibid.: xii). Feminist literary scholars are among those who have continued this recovery work. An influential example of African American feminist scholarship in the context of the revision of American literary traditions is Hazel V. Carby's *Reconstructing Womanhood* (1987). Carby shows how racial and class biases inherent in what had become known as 'the cult of True Womanhood' are dissected and problematized by nineteenth-century African American women writers including Harriet Wilson and Harriet Jacobs. In a volume of essays on black and white nineteenth-century women writers called *The (Other) American Traditions* (1993), editor Joyce W. Warren observes, '[w]hereas the dominant tradition portrays the male individualist in flight from society, the women writers did not visualize a world without society ... [W]hile the dominant masculine tradition focused on the insularity of the individual, the women writers portrayed characters that were enmeshed in a community of interpersonal relationships' (Warren, 1993: 11). American literary history today includes multiple works by, and critical studies of, women writers and writers of color.[13] But as Fishkin and many other critics point out repeatedly, the influence of feminist and minority studies can be measured by the extent to which 'American literature' can still be made to signify literature by white (male) authors in mainstream criticism.

Both male and female nineteenth-century literary orphans have had a dual function, serving both to reinforce and to critique American society, normative family constellations, and women's domestic roles.[14] This critical function, we argue, is even more pronounced in contemporary American novels that feature orphan characters. However, although feminist and other critics have subjected the American Adam to a great deal of criticism, this figure and the values of independence and freedom he represents remain central to American literature and American literary studies. We discuss this figure along with intertextual interventions into canonized literary and critical traditions in Chapter 3.

Orphans, history, and ideologies of family and nation

> It is that fundamental belief – it is that fundamental belief: I am my brother's keeper. I am my sister's keeper that makes this country work. It's what allows us to pursue our individual dreams and yet still come together as one American family. (Barack Obama, Democratic Convention Keynote Speech, Boston, July 27, 2004)

Analogies between family and nation, such as those used by Barack Obama in his 2004 Democratic Convention speech, are far from new. They have been drawn at least since J. Hector St. John de Crevecoeur and Thomas Paine, who envisioned eighteenth-century America as a child in need of liberation from its oppressive parent: England. In *Common Sense* (1776), Paine observed, 'But Britain is the parent country, say some. Then the more shame upon her conduct. Even brutes do not devour their young, nor savages make war upon their families ... ' (ibid.: 63). In the context of parental tyranny, orphanhood is an infinitely preferable condition. Pazicky summarizes that, 'the young nation shifted its filial allegiance from the parent country to the Founding Fathers, [and] orphanhood seemed to represent an opportunity for self-creation rather than a loss of identity' (Pazicky, 1998: xv). Thus, the association between family and nation, and between orphanhood and freedom, begins its deep entrenchment in American culture in the Revolutionary era.

Ideological connections between family and nation appear to be a defining feature of most, if not all, modern nations. The modern nation state is conceived in familial terms, as a 'natural' association rather than a political community. As Benedict Anderson has shown, nations are imagined political communities and may be conceived of in terms of kinship relations. Family rhetoric helps to shape, naturalize, and thereby justify forms of social and political organization. In other words, the concept of family is intimately connected with social and political forms of inclusion and exclusion. The strong link between orphanhood and national identity, however, appears to be particular to the USA: Pazicky suggests that 'the nature of American historical development left its own distinctive imprint upon the orphan trope' and that tropes of orphanhood 'tended to erupt at times of challenge and crisis' (ibid.: xiii) – particularly at times of perceived crisis in national unity and identity.

Socio-historically, orphans began to be a social issue in the Revolutionary era, when Indian wars, epidemics, natural disasters, and the replacement of family labor with slave labor and indentured servants created many dependent children (ibid.: 59). In the 1800s, orphanhood was a 'fact of life,' for half of all children lost a parent by the age of twenty and, in 1900, '20 to 30 percent of all children lost a parent by age fifteen' (Mintz, 2004: 157). In addition, orphanhood in the 1800s was strongly affected by the casualties of the American Civil War, by migration, increasing urban poverty, and major epidemics.[15] The erroneously dubbed 'orphan trains' of the late 1800s and early 1900s removed large numbers of predominantly white, poor children, most of whom had at least one living parent, from crowded urban centers to rural areas in need of labor.[16] In the first half of the twentieth century, when children lost parents to influenza epidemics and as a result of the searing poverty of the Great Depression, destitute children depended upon their wits, luck, charity, and charitable organizations – particularly orphanages – for their survival. The term 'orphan' became less common when the institution of the orphanage began to decline with the Aid to Dependent Children Act, passed in 1935, partly in response to the many reports of dire conditions in orphanages. Subsequently, residential institutions were transformed into 'group homes or treatment facilities' for orphans, foster children, or children exhibiting anti-social behavior (Mintz, 2004: 159).

However, orphans have never gone away. The term orphan figured briefly in the 'orphanage debate' in the 1990s, and after 9/11 the word 'orphan' occurs in, for instance, the Twin Towers Orphan Fund (TTOF) – contexts to which we return in Chapters 3 and 4. As Susan Faludi has shown, the aftermath of 9/11 in the USA involved normative discursive formations of national identity and familial stability that centered on a reactionary positioning of men as father figures and heroes, and women as 'girls' and victims in need of rescue. Patriotic post-9/11 media discourses also relied heavily on the figure of the child, particularly of the little girl.[17] Children orphaned in the attacks have been especially important figures, and children born after their fathers' deaths in the attacks have been continuously exploited by the media.[18] According to an article in the *Observer* published one year after September 11, 2001, the number of orphans created by the 9/11 attacks was 1,300 (Templeton and Lumley, 2002).[19] The TTOF was immediately set up in order to support these orphans, and according to its website the fund supports more than 1,000 children in eighteen states and territories. On a practical level, this fund helps relatives of the victims of the attacks of September 11, 2001. On a symbolic level, however, it also constructs orphanhood as a national concern, by configuring these particular orphans as a group that deserves special attention. Orphanhood in post-9/11 US culture may thus be connected to special status and national priorities.

Definitions of orphanhood are also important in the context of transnational adoptions. The US Immigration and Nationality Act of 1952, which regulates the immigration of adopted children into the USA, defines an orphan as a child under sixteen 'who has no parents because of the death or disappearance of, abandonment or desertion by, or separation or loss from both parents. An orphan is also a child whose sole or surviving parent has forever and irrevocably released him or her for adoption and emigration because that parent cannot properly care for the child' ('Adoptions', 2010). Additionally, a child may become an orphan if the state, for any reason, assumes custody of the child. Parents may voluntarily relinquish their parental rights, or the state may permanently deprive them of these rights under conditions ranging from desertion, neglect, or material inability to provide for the child.

This extended definition references new social forms of orphanhood, recognizing that the state, as well as a parent, sometimes orphans children by legally removing them from parental custody, usually placing them in foster homes or residential care. Such measures of removal have been disproportionately carried out by child welfare authorities in non-white families. In 1958, for example, the Child Welfare League of America and the Bureau of Indian Affairs collaborated to facilitate the adoption of Native children by white families deemed more suitable to child-raising.[20] In the 1970s, just prior to the publication of the literary works in our study, critical investigations into the stark overrepresentation of Native children in the domestic adoption pool found that the adoption rate of these children was considerably higher than the adoption rate of non-Indian children (Bouvier, 2006: 105), and that 90 per cent of Indian placements were in non-Indian homes (Satz and Askeland, 2006: 54).[21] These and other facts revealing that adoption together with other forms of Native American child removal could reasonably be referred to as a form of cultural genocide led to the passing of the Indian Child Welfare Act of 1978. This unique piece of legislation affirms tribal jurisdiction over child custody, adoption, and welfare, and it aims to protect 'the best interests of Indian children' and to promote the stability and security of Indian tribes and families.

The National Association of Black Social Workers (NABSW) also foregrounded the idea of cultural genocide in its position paper of 1972, arguing for 'racial matching' in adoption practices in order to preserve a cultural heritage among black children and to better equip them for the realities of growing up in a racist society.[22] Racial matching was a dominant practice from the 1970s through to the 1990s, when the 1994 Multiethnic Placement Act (MEPA) made it illegal for federally funded agencies to delay or deny adoption or foster-care placement on the basis of race. A subsequent amendment, the Interethnic Adoption Provisions (IEP) of 1996, strengthened this legislation, making racial considerations in placement practices illegal. These legislative changes responded in part to the negative outcomes for children with extended time in foster care, in part to pressures from proponents of transracial adoption. Yet, the controversy surrounding transracial adoption continues today. Critics observe that calls for 'racial blindness' overlook the fact that the overwhelming majority of racial matching – white parents with white or non-black children – is not referred to as such.[23] Although African American children are removed from their families to a disproportionate degree, black children in foster care continue to have lower chances of adoption than white or non-black children, and this continues since the abolition of racial-matching policies. According to Dorothy Roberts, the majority of those who adopted black foster children in 1993 were 'middle-aged Black women who are relatives or foster parents of the child' (2003: 172). An assessment of US transracial adoption, noting the difficulty of obtaining reliable statistics, observes that decades after the MEPA-IEP and even after the enactment of the Fostering Connections to Success and Increasing Adoptions Act of 2008, adoption agencies face difficulties in finding permanent families for children in care, and African American children are still disproportionately represented among such children and among those seeking adoption (McRoy and Griffin, 2012: 45). Transracial adoption activates concerns about the value of sameness and difference, the worth of assimilationist and multiculturalist strategies and goals. The novels we examine here mobilize the orphan as a figure of difference in order to interrogate such complex issues.

Central to all definitions of 'orphan' is the fact that an orphan is a child, and recent developments in childhood studies clearly show that childhood is a historically specific cultural construction. Scholars in the humanities and social sciences, influenced by Philippe Ariès's 1962 study *Centuries of Childhood*, have increasingly come to understand childhood as a socially constructed category. As Caroline Levander and Carol Singley write, 'the child is not only born but made – not only a biological fact but a cultural construct that encodes the complex, ever-shifting logic of a given group and therefore reveals much about its inner workings' (2005: 4). In nineteenth-century America at least three very different conceptions of the child were at play: 'Calvinist conceptions of "infant depravity" and the inherent sinfulness of children, Lockean conceptions of childhood as a "blank slate" upon which parental authority must write, Romantic visions of the child as natural and as innocent as nature vied and mingled with each other' (Sánchez-Eppler, 2005: xviii). Karen Sánchez-Eppler also points out that '[t]he histories we do have of American childhood tell of the gradual and uneven transformation of cultural attitudes toward children, which increasingly cast children as distinct from adults, their specialness valued in emotional rather than economic terms' (*ibid.*: xvii). Some earlier notions of childhood still linger in common understandings about children as special human beings, although American childhood today is configured as primarily marked by vulnerability.

The specific links between vulnerability and the child in the US context have been explored by, for instance, Gillian Brown, Ian Hacking, and James Kincaid. In *Endangered Children* (1997) sociologist LeRoy Ashby examines the history of American understandings of children and childhood, and their impact on child welfare, law, and social policy from colonial times to the late twentieth century. Regarding the particular ways in which the image of the American child is constructed, Levander and Singley observe that 'the United States is distinctive in the ways it has seized upon the image of the child in opposition to that which is constructed or institutionalized, and in the extent to which it has promoted the child as a force of resistance as well as innocent vulnerability' (2005: 4). How, then, do such contemporary conceptions of the American child as innocent and vulnerable, but also as an agent constituting 'a force of resistance,' inform representations of orphans in American novels?

Helpful for our explorations of literary orphans is Levander's scholarship on the American child that focuses on what she calls 'the child's signifying responsibilities' (2006: 16). She finds these responsibilities particularly rich because of the way that the figure of the child can contain opposites: it suggests a natural, essential, or basic form of identity, 'an innocent, natural self seemingly unmarked by social categories' (*ibid.*: 6), at the same time as the child by definition embodies a potential for change, development, and transformation *away* from childhood. This ability of the child to carry contradictory meanings, we suggest, is comparable to the signifying powers and responsibilities of the orphan figure.

If one signifying responsibility of the child is the potential for maturity, one of the orphan's is the potential to be integrated into a family; the term 'orphan' is one that makes sense primarily in the context of family. As Laurin Porter observes in *Orphan's Home*: 'The word "orphan" suggests being cut off from society, abandoned and alone; its opposite conjures visions of family, connectedness, roots, belonging – all subsumed in the image of home' (2003: 101). By this logic, the condition of orphanhood evokes the possibility of adoption into a family or home, and indeed, what Marianne Novy calls 'the adoption plot' figures prominently in literature because it 'dramatize[s] cultural tensions about definitions of family and the importance of heredity' (2001: 2). Moreover, she writes, 'representing adoption is a way of thinking about the family, exploring what a family is, that is at the same time a way of thinking about the self, exploring distance from the family' *ibid.*: 2).[24] Literary representations of orphanhood invite considerations of similar and overlapping issues. As Pazicky's study shows, and as we argue in this book, orphanhood can be a way of thinking about nation as well, not least since discourses of family and nation are so interdependent and entangled in the US.

Throughout the late twentieth century, the white, middle-class, male-headed nuclear family ideal, which had ideologically established the boundaries for 'healthy' forms of intimate relations and served as an index for the 'health of the nation' came increasingly under critical scrutiny. Concerns about the dissolution of images of national unity were interwoven with – and even expressed as – concerns about the decline of the family. 'In the 1970s,' Natasha Zaretsky argues, 'much of the public debate around the family had revolved around whether the institution of the family was becoming obsolete' (2007: 241). Concern about the alleged decline of the American family signals anxieties about single parents, homosexual families, ethnic relations, and the impact of feminism, and other new social movements, on the definitions and meanings of family life in the US.[25] Though most Americans still claim they wish to live in a family (Strach, 2007: 9) and little suggests that family as a social unit is threatened, rhetoric about the 'downfall' of the traditional family ideal masks the reality of familial diversity in the USA, and downplays the fact that, for many people, the demise of that ideal may prove more liberating than threatening. As critiques of the white, nuclear, male-headed family developed further in the 1980s and 1990s, and the diverse composition of families became newly visible, the important question was raised: 'what, in the end, makes a family?' (Zaretsky, 2007: 241). *Making Home* highlights the wide range of answers to that question, seeing the orphan figure as important to the projects of making home in different families and in a multicultural nation.

'Family,' it is clear, means many things to many people, demonstrating how dependent the term is upon social and cultural context. The American family in its actual and ideal forms has generated a body of scholarship, with historical and sociological studies over recent decades revealing how the meaning of family, like that of childhood, has undergone significant transformations.[26] Stephanie Coontz writes that forms of family in early America 'were forged from the interactions and clashes' between the three groups we discuss: 'the politically, economically, and militarily dominant Euro-American colonizers; the indigenous Native Americans, and the Africans brought by Europeans first as indentured servants and then as lifetime slaves' (2008: 5). In another important critical investigation of American ideas about family, Coontz observes that families in the past were expected to be functioning economic and social units. Only in the late nineteenth century were people 'urged to make the nuclear family their central repository of loyalty, obligation, and personal satisfaction' (2000: xviii). In that era, the white middle-class family ideal served as a norm that African American women writers had to negotiate with special care, as we have noted. The idea of separate public and private spheres, then so central to gendered roles in white families, was challenged by the new ideals of companionate marriage and masculine domesticity in the early twentieth century.[27] The nuclear family ideal, still so familiar today, is yet another transformation in forms of kinship.

Indeed, the white 1950s ideal of the nuclear family composed of the male breadwinner, female homemaker, and biological children existed only as a short-lived social phenomenon for just a couple of decades after World War II.[28] In other words, late twentieth- and early twenty-first-century conceptions of 'traditional families' are always based on an understanding of the patriarchal nuclear family that is largely a myth: the model that contemporary families risk being measured against – and found lacking – is, as Coontz (2000) puts it, 'the way we never were.' Critics have estimated that by the mid-1980s less than 10 per cent of American families corresponded to the nuclear ideal (McCarthy, 1997: 1). In spite of the factual rarity of nuclear families, their assumed superiority and normative power continue to hold sway in different arenas, including contemporary American politics and culture. Coontz puts it succinctly: 'Despite ever mounting evidence that families of the past were not as idyllic and families of the present not as dysfunctional as they are often portrayed, many political leaders and opinion makers in the United States continue to filter our changing family experiences and trends through the distorting lens of historical mythologizing about past family life' (2000: xi).

What Coontz calls the 'nostalgia trap' of the American family ideal remains powerful. Families structured otherwise than according to the nuclear pattern – including queer kinship relations and what Kath Weston calls 'families we choose' – are still termed 'alternative.' This designation underscores the normative power of the nuclear ideal that continues to operate into the twenty-first century.

The normative power of this ideal, Patricia Hill Collins observes, 'lies in its dual function as an ideological construction and as a fundamental principle of social organization' (1998: 63). Hierarchies of gender and age are naturalized in the concept of the 'traditional' family, and these hierarchies intersect with racial hierarchies, enabling race relations in the USA to be explained over and again in terms of family ideals.[29] Indeed, Collins claims that because 'racial ideologies and practices [are] so reliant on family for meaning, family writ large becomes race' (ibid.: 65). Levander reinforces aspects of Collins's analysis in her study of the idea of the child in American national identity, observing that the concept of nation 'continues to be understood within the founding context that the child provides' (2006: 7). This context is the powerful discourse of family – mother country, fatherland, 'patria,' and child – which offers a variety of imaginative kinship positions within the national family. A sense of identity and belonging is instilled in citizens, Levander aserts, 'by recreating accustomed family relations and extending the nation's founding image of the child to transform those diverse individuals within its physical boundaries into a collective entity committed to creating and upholding a shared civic environment' (ibid.: 7). The child is a trope that naturalizes the nation through its strong referential bond to family, and that ultimately 'races' the nation as well.

The largely mythical family ideal has produced very real effects in the social and political realms, contributing, for instance, to the pathologization of black families at different points in US history. Much of this pathologization is based in the understanding that the absence of men and the domination of women as heads of household indicate social dysfunctionality. Daniel Patrick Moynihan's 1965 government report entitled *The Negro Family: The Case for National Action*, known as the Moynihan Report, is often attributed a leading role in establishing the pathological deviance of African American families and gender relations in the national consciousness. Although scholars before Moynihan had asserted that the black family was beset by problems, as Candice M. Jenkins observes, the report stresses that the black family structure is 'the underlying cause of racial oppression – rather than ... an unfortunate effect of it' (Jenkins, 2007: 65). Moynihan's analysis of 'emasculated' black men is clearly informed by patriarchal assumptions about the desirability of a male-headed nuclear family. In Chapter 5, we discuss subsequent scholarship that views female-headed households and other family structures in terms of resilience, for such family structures have been prevalent. Cynthia G. Hawkins-León notes that in 1973, 44 per cent of African Americans lived in an extended family situation, as opposed to 11 per cent of whites. Additionally, one third of African American families headed by a woman over sixty-five include children who have not been legally adopted (Hawkins-León, 1997: 210–11). Dorothy Roberts also cites the high rate of unwed motherhood, but observes that 'the rate of fatherlessness among whites has reached what it was among Blacks three decades ago' (2003: 63), with the result that at the turn of the last century more babies are born to single white mothers than single black mothers. Nevertheless, perceived and actual differences from the white, patriarchal imagery of the family have been rendered suspect at strategic moments in political and cultural discourse.[30]

The nuclear family ideal has also influenced government treatment of Native families and children. As James G. White and Sarah Michèle Martin observe, the Indian Adoption Project of the 1950s and 1960s was the first national project conceived to remove an entire child population from their native cultures, as hundreds were placed into white homes. In Minnesota, around one in four Indian children below the age of one was taken from an Indian home and adopted by non-Indians. Grounds for removal was basically that Indians did not conform to non-Indian child-rearing practices. Other such statistics for the 1970s support the conclusion that 'the American Indian family was being separated at a rate greater than any other culture in the United States' (White and Martin, 2008: 298).

In a complex and changing context of racialized kinship norms and forms, American literature almost obsessively investigates family structures and their impact on individual and national identity.[31] Cindy Weinstein argues that '[o]ne might even think of the question – what is a family – as quite literally, a cultural *idée fixe* in which the family is constantly trying to be "fixed," as if it were in need of definitional repair, as if idea and practice have become unhinged' (2004: 19–20). Literary orphans have a privileged position in contemporary efforts to rethink family and nation and to perform purposeful explorations of non-normative kinship forms. If the white child-in-family works discursively to consolidate familial and national identity, as Levander has argued, the orphan, regardless of race, is suspended outside of family, and can thus be used by writers to interrogate this consolidation. The novels we investigate therefore depict a wide range of familial relations, and we address American familial diversity, even though the nuclear family ideal haunts a number of the narratives.

The way that the word 'orphan' conjures images of home points in at least two directions. On the one hand, the status of orphanhood can be said to reinforce a normative definition of the nuclear family, regardless of the fact that this ideal matches neither white American social realities of the last half century, nor the social realities of African Americans or Native peoples. On the other hand, orphanhood is a condition that effectively marks a radical disconnection from family, and thus encourages thinking beyond a nuclear family model. Indeed, the very concept of orphanhood is challenged by kinship networks of various kinds. Morrison's *A Mercy*, Silko's *Gardens in the Dunes*, Robinson's *Housekeeping*, and Irving's *The Cider House Rules*, for instance, each depict very different types of homes for orphans and different types of homecomings. In the chapters that follow, we examine the place of orphans within various and alternative family relations.

Although far from all the orphan characters in the novels we examine are adopted, adoption practices certainly hinge on definitions of certain groups of children as orphans, and hence adoptable. As noted, transracial adoption practices in the USA – especially since the 1970s – have been critiqued. The racial implications of transnational adoption have also been problematized in studies that demonstrate that it is more than a post-World War II phenomenon. While Mark C. Jerng's *Claiming Others* 'resituates transracial adoption from a mid-to-late twentieth-century story to a historical phenomenon with roots deep in the formation of national and racial identity' (2010: xxxvi), Cynthia Callahan's *Kin of Another Kind* observes that '[b]efore World War II, transracial adoption was legally forbidden but very much alive in literature and unsanctioned practice' (2011: 2). Both Callahan and Jerng see transracial adoption in literature as intimately related to anxieties over the definition of racial and national identity and to historical crises around race relations. In fiction, transracial adoption 'allows authors to address these issues in relation to a much broader sweep of concerns: multiracial identities, mixed-race families, social change following the civil rights movement, tribal autonomy, and immigrant identities' (*ibid.*: 25). As Jerng observes: 'Transracial adoption appears most prominently in literature, public discourse, and social practices during precisely some of these large-scale national traumas focused on the formation of its citizenry and the question of national and racial belonging: Native American removal; slavery and emancipation; the height of Jim Crow/segregation; and the Korean and Vietnam wars' (Jerng, 2010: xii).[32] Chapters 2 and 5 discuss examples of transracial and even trans-species adoption, whereas Chapters 3 and 4 explore racialized boundaries to understandings of kinship as idea and lived practice.

In non-literary discourses surrounding adoption, stresses Claudia Castañeda, the 'mutability of the child figured as a body in process makes it eminently appropriable; not yet fully formed, it has no prior being that must be displaced and then re-placed. It only has to become, according to taste' (2002: 108). This perceived mutability, combined with what Levander calls the 'seemingly authentic, pre-social self with which the child has become exclusively equated by the late eighteenth century' (2006: 6), has dubious echoes in late-modern discourses concerning transracial or transnational adoption. The notion of eminent appropriability runs counter to indigenous notions of kinship, and according to some, promotes cultural imperialism. Castañeda calls for changes in representations of the parentless child which might resist the dangers of essentializing and deracinating the child in order to 'refuse the simple "availability" of children for adult visions of the future' (2002: 108). As Castañeda aptly demonstrates, the orphan child becomes central in visions for mixed-race families and, by extension, for a multicultural America.[33]

Orphanhood and American multiculturalism

> We are orphans, standing on the blank page of America, waiting to be acknowledged. (Barbara Chase-Riboud, 1989)[34]

In today's commonsensical usage, multiculturalism can have a purely descriptive function. Used first in 1941, though, it came into more widespread use from the late 1960s to describe the USA as home to many cultures as well as to mark the factual demographic changes in the racial and ethnic composition of US citizenry. Over 30 per cent of the US population today is made up of racial minorities, and estimates vary as to *when*, not *whether*, whites will cease to be the numerical majority. In this use of multiculturalism, culture and race tend to be conceptually conflated, or at least intertwined.

David Theo Goldberg explains that multiculturalism is a term with a history that begins in opposition to monoculturalism, an institutional ideology that 'not only purports to universalize the presuppositions and terms of a single culture, [but] likewise denies *as culture ...* any expression that fails to fit its mold of "high culture"' (1994: 5). The 'one' of the US motto, *E pluribus unum,* was emphasized in the core values of majority culture and in the hegemonic melting-pot model of assimilation. Against this ideological construction, the Civil Rights Movement and other new social movements in the 1960s 'signaled a shift from the prevailing assimilative standard to the new one' (*ibid.*: 6), first of integration, then of pluralistic multiculturalism: 'Multiculturalism and commitments to cultural diversity emerged out of this conflictual history of resistance, accommodation, integration, and transformation' (*ibid.*: 7). Multiculturalism proposes the recognition of differences between groups, as opposed to the erasure of differences, as a requisite for a more just society. Such a model ascribes value to heterogeneity, and insists upon cultural autonomy, integrity, and sometimes sovereignty.

However, multiculturalism is also vulnerable to reservations about separatism, incommensurability, essentialism, and the unintentional perpetuation of unjust social categories. Critiques along these lines flourished in the so-called 'Culture Wars' and 'Canon Debates' of the 1980s and 1990s when, for example, Allan Bloom's *Closing of the American Mind* (1987) advanced the idea that the new openness of US university education and curricular reform had only deleterious effects, and when Harold Bloom's *The Western Canon* (1994) defended aesthetic standards for literary study as opposed to social interests. Multiculturalism has also been rejected by some critics because it promotes the premise that 'all cultural differences are equal in value' and hence is counterproductive for anti-racist struggle (Harrington quoted in Alcoff, 1998: 23). Still others see multiculturalism as incoherent because attempts to define distinct cultures inevitably collapse into the very racialized categories they seek to avoid. Christopher Douglass makes this point in his 2009 study of multicultural literature, as does David Hollinger in *Postethnic America: Beyond Multiculturalism* (1995), in which he proposes a cosmopolitan rather than multicultural ideal.

In creative response to both the critiques and the advances of multiculturalism, the field of American Studies has broadened and, indeed, been transformed, even challenged. Jay Prosser charts the development in the 1990s of a New American Studies, which 'radically and interrogatively' (2008: 4) traversed different contexts, reading across national, disciplinary, and historical contexts. Recognizing the USA as key to globalization processes, current and historical, has spurred scholarship on transnationalism, migration, alliances, intersections, borders, and border crossings of all kinds. Taking account of the multicultural, international, and global dimensions of American literature and culture, as well as of linguistic diversity and acts of cultural translation, has led scholars such as Caroline Levander to ask, 'Where is American Literature?'[35] In tracing literary beginnings and tracking literary adaptations over space and time, the notion of unique national origin and of an original work become unsettled.

Throughout the 1990s and 2000s, the possibilities of the postethnic, postracial, and postnational have flourished, not least with the election of Barack Obama to the US presidency in 2008, and his re-election in 2012. But these possibilities have far to go before they are realized. Practices such as the massive US surveillance of communication networks through the PRISM program, leaked in 2013, give the lie to postnational ideals. The routine racism that arguably informs at least some of the resistance to Obama's leadership, the debates over legislation such as Arizona's ban on ethnic studies, and tragic events such as the highly publicized shooting of the unarmed black youth, Trayvon Martin, in Florida in 2012 and the acquittal of his killer suggest that the USA is still a place where race and ethnicity matter very much, even as the global and US financial crisis illuminate stark class differences. Thus, multiculturalism continues to be relevant and to have an effect on literary production. It is clear that multiculturalism 'takes seriously the desire of groups to conserve group identity and existence' (Sundstrom, 2008: 102), and the questions that this raises about tradition and change, domination and oppression, and essentialism and constructivism in identities and cultural production make up much of the literary landscape of the orphan figures we examine in the following chapters.

The USA is a nation largely constituted by racial encounters, and the social construction of race continues to have important social, material, and ideological consequences. *Making Home* focuses on the broad categories of Native, African American, and Euro-American orphans, and we call attention to processes of racialization because we understand constructions of race and racialized identity to play a constitutive role in the USA – in spite of what Ronald R. Sundstrom calls 'the unrequited American desire to escape the encompassing burden of race' (*ibid.*: 2). We use 'Euro-American' to refer to white orphans, well aware of the historical shifts in ascribing 'whiteness' to various groups of European immigrants (Jacobson, 1999: 14; Alcoff, 1998: 9), but also aware of the twentieth-century consolidation of whiteness in the USA in contrast to Native Americans and African Americans: whites 'owe their now stabilized and broadly recognized whiteness *itself* in part to these nonwhite groups' (Jacobson, 1999: 9). The white and Euro-American orphan also has a specific history in the USA.

The fact that genetic and biological definitions of distinct races do not hold does little to diminish the power of 'race' or its material and ideological consequences: 'Race may be a social construction without biological validity, yet it is real and powerful enough to alter the fundamental shape of all our lives' (Alcoff, 1998: 8). Processes of racialization contribute to the social mechanism that Michael Omi and Howard Winant referred to in 1986 as 'racial formation' in the USA. The place of race in social justice, as well as in literary scholarship, has been hotly debated throughout the period we examine. Especially since the 1990s, essentialist ideas about both 'blackness' and 'whiteness' in US literature have been complicated. Many literary critics have observed the prevalence of hybridity and the lack of 'purity' in genres and texts to argue instead that American culture has always been multicultural.

Yet, histories are also specific to particular demographic groups, and fictional representations of orphans are linked to these histories in complex ways. Questions concerning cultural diversity and social justice are clearly activated by the particularly vexed relations Native and African American children have had to the conditions of orphanhood. Historically, children from these groups have been orphaned through removal in a disproportionate manner due to oppressive government and social policies, from the 'peculiar institution' of slavery that deliberately sought the destruction of family and kinship ties, to Indian boarding schools, to practices of child removal and adoption. In contemporary times, Native and African American children remain overrepresented in statistics on adoption and foster care.[36] Meanwhile, they remain underrepresented in the literary canon, and therefore we find compelling reasons to explore how, if at all, these histories and these conditions inform literary representations of orphans of color by Native American, African American, and Euro-American writers. At the same time, the whiteness of white orphans needs to be 'made strange' (Dyer, 1997: 10) by being made explicit. Sarah Ahmed summarizes, 'We still need to describe how it is that the world of whiteness coheres as a world, even as we tend to the "stresses" in this coherence, and the uneven distribution of such stress' (2007: 165). Although historians and cultural and literary critics, including David Roediger, George Lipsitz, Ruth Frankenberg, Sharon Monteith, Valerie Babb and Grace Elizabeth Hale, have stressed the racialized character of whiteness, as well as its dependency on racial 'others,' the taken-for-granted whiteness of 'Americanness' has not yet been eradicated.

In Chapters 3 and 4, we link the contemporary white fictional orphan to a whitened American literary history, and address the ways that whiteness intersects with gender and class. In Chapters 2 and 5 we focus on how contemporary novelists mobilize and reclaim Native and African American orphan figures to interrogate issues of cultural identity, cultural survival, cultural regeneration, and alternative futures that are sometimes at odds with, sometimes reflective of, 'the American way.' We focus on representations of orphans from three racialized groups, building on the work of Slotkin, Morrison, Pazicky, Owens, Levander, and other scholars who have found these groups to be of fundamental importance to the emergence, continuation, and complication of an American national identity, as well as of a national literature, even as the boundaries of such a literature continue to be challenged.

In other words, we explore what signifying functions are assigned to orphans of color and to white orphans in literary discourses about American identities. Although, in American culture, 'poor, disabled, or orphaned children or children of color occupy marginalized positions in relation to more idealized versions of childhood' (Levander and Singley, 2005: 5), nevertheless the imaginative recreation of such marginalized positions in literature presents unique perspectives. These perspectives are inscribed in novels that activate and sometimes reinvent specific genres – notably the sentimental novel, the captivity narrative, speculative fiction, the historical novel, and the *bildungsroman* – thereby envisioning orphans intertextually with these genres and with literary history.

Notes

1 George Lipsitz defines counter-memory as 'a way of remembering and forgetting that starts with the local, the immediate, and the personal.' It 'forces revision of existing [and dominant] histories by supplying new perspectives about the past. Counter-memory embodies aspects of myth and aspects of history, but it retains an enduring suspicion of both categories. Counter-memory focuses on localized experiences with oppression, using them to reframe and refocus dominant narratives purporting to represent universal experience' (1990: 213).
2 What Angelyn Mitchell highlights is the traumatic and forgotten aspects that make 'rememory' an apt term for discussing the memory work of people and communities who have been written out of, or under-read in, 'official' histories.
3 Carol Singley considers the adoption novel 'a subset of the Bildungsroman, which developed with the rise of the middle class and its attendant questions of birthright and belonging' (2011: 11).
4 The term collective memory was first used in the 1920s by sociologist Maurice Halbwachs, who argued that all memory is socially framed by people's remembering in different groups. For an excellent discussion of family memory as a kind of collective memory, see Erll (2011).
5 In imagined 'acts of recollection,' literature offers illustrations of and insights into individual remembrance and 'cultural knowledge about how memory works for individuals and groups' (Erll and Rigney, 2006: 113).
6 Singley also highlights this redemptive quality of adoption in nineteenth-century American literature (2011: 10–11).
7 See, for instance, Harde (2008), Mills (1987), Nelson (2001), Sanders (2008), and Taylor (2009).
8 Mills (1987) traces a development in representations of orphans, from Eleanor H. Porter's sunny Pollyanna in 1913 to the bitter orphans in more social-realistic books of the 1960s, and argues that these shifts reflect changes in social attitudes toward child development.
9 See Kimmel (2006).
10 For a discussion of sympathy in these novels, see Weinstein (2004).
11 June Howard brings up problems with Welter's model, especially later critics' uncritical use of it (2001: 233).
12 See McHugh (1999: 35–59) on the formation of the discourse of domesticity in terms of nation, gender, race, and class. See also Romero (1997).
13 One example of a more inclusive literary history is the collection of essays in Jay Prosser's edited volume *American Fictions of the 1990s* (2008).
14 See for instance Nelson (2003) and Weinstein (2004).
15 See Mintz (2004) for a good historical overview.

16 Charles Loring Brace's Children's Aid Society (CAS) shipped approximately 100,000 children from New York City to foster homes in New York and other states between 1854 and 1917. Other charitable and social organizations were also involved in child relocation projects, seeking a solution to urban poverty for vulnerable children and to labor needs in rural areas in the west. See e.g. O'Connor (2001), and Holt (1994).
17 The widely publicized image of a little girl sitting on the shoulders of a man in an all-male crowd is one example (Levander, 2006: 22), and Oliver Stone's film, *World Trade Center* (2006) foregrounds a toddler girl in the arms of her police officer father as its final image of restored order and hope for the future.
18 See Faludi (2007: 96).
19 Problematical terms such as 'half-orphan' or 'double orphan' have been used to describe children who have lost one or two parents. Ultimately, these modulations signal the difficulties of, as well as the felt need for, precise terms.
20 See, for example, Vernon B. Carter (2009), Briggs (2012), or Holt (2001) for discussions of the Indian Adoption Project. See also Duthu (2008) on The Indian Child Welfare Act (150–5).
21 Adoption and removal rates vary considerably by state. See David Fanshel's *Far From the Reservation* (1972) for an early influential account of transracial adoption, and see Briggs's (2012) discussion of the lead-up to the 1974 hearings preceding the passage of the Indian Child Welfare Program (ICWA).
22 The NABSW modified its position in 1994 to support transracial adoptions in certain situations (McRoy and Griffin, 2012: 41).
23 Dorothy Roberts argues that 'the literature advocating the elimination of racial considerations in child placements focuses on making it easier for white people to adopt black children,' primarily by making it easier for states to permanently terminate parental rights, creating 'legal' or 'unnatural' orphans (2003: 167). See also Ruth McRoy and Amy Griffin (2012) on the outcomes of MEPA-IEP See Briggs (2012) on 'crack babies' and adoption reform.
24 Novy's work on the literature of adoption foregrounds adoption rather than the condition of orphanhood, primarily because most adoptees in the USA have not lost their birth parents through death (Novy, 2005). Like Novy, we find that adoption plots function as meditations on issues that extend far beyond family politics, but we focus on orphans, in the broad sense of the term, in order to explore *all* the options – even those which do not lead back to family.
25 For critique and problematization of such concerns see Margaret Andersen (1991), Betty G. Farrell (1999), and Zaretsky (2007).

26 Examples are sociological studies by Andersen (1991), Judith Stacey (1998), and Therborn (2004), cultural studies like *Rethinking the Family* edited by Barrie Thorne and Marilyn Yalom (1992), and the anthropological work of Kath Weston.
27 For historical studies on masculinity and domesticity in that period, see LaRossa (1997) and Marsh (1990).
28 See Andersen (1991), Coontz (2000), or Hawes and Nybakken (2001). Although there is an idealized image of the Victorian nuclear family, O'Connor has pointed out, this is an anachronistic view that underplays the Victorian family's 'elasticity in terms of its capacity both for incorporating others – kin and strangers – and for dispensing with its own offspring' (2001: 97).
29 See also Candice M. Jenkins, who points out that 'the perceived inability of African Americans to conform to middle-class understandings of family and appropriate sexual behavior has hardly diminished since its origins during the antebellum period' (2007: 10).
30 See also Jenkins (2007: 23).
31 See McCarthy (1997), Owens (2001), and O'Reilly, Nollen and Foor (1997).
32 Transnational adoption may also be related to inter- or transnational crises and concerns; for instance, Judie Newman examines the political implications of Prager's parental adoption narrative, *Wuhu Diary*, which deals with a visit to China in 1999, together with her adopted Chinese daughter, that 'coincided with the bombing by US planes ... of the Chinese embassy in Belgrade ... which lead to widespread (and orchestrated) anti-American unrest in China' (Newman, 2007: 64).
33 Levander considers the USA to be 'a particularly rich venue for analyzing the child's importance to the racial premises underpinning liberal democracy because the nation emerges out of a series of racial encounters between Mexican, Native American, Anglo, and African peoples' (2006: 4).
34 *Echo of Lions*, quoted in Rushdy (2001: 116–17).
35 This question is the title of Levander's 2013 book as well as of her keynote address at 'Currents and Countercurrents,' the Nordic Association for American Studies conference at Karlstad University, Sweden, 24 May 2013.
36 See Evan B. Donaldson Adoption Institute (2008), V. Carter (2010), McRoy and Griffin (2012), and online reports from Adoption and Foster Care Analysis System (AFCARS) for some of these statistics.

2

From captivity to kinship: Native American orphans and sovereignty

> If our struggle is anything, it is the struggle for sovereignty, and if sovereignty is anything, it is a way of life. (Warrior, 1995: 123)

Multiculturalism fits uneasily with Native America. As we have seen, multiculturalism is at once a descriptive and a normative concept of cultural difference, purporting to account in neutral ways for the actual racial or ethnic diversity of a politically 'unified' American nation, while also affirming cultural distinctiveness in the face of the oppressive forces of assimilation or racism. Native identities and communities, however, are not only cultural, but also political, since tribes are also sovereign nations. This status is fraught, precarious, and often contested, and issues surrounding political sovereignty and land ownership remain urgent, falling outside the realm of the 'merely' cultural. In addition, multiculturalism contains a utopian or idealistic dimension in its insistence upon the possibility of peaceful co-existence and respectful interchange among and between cultural groups, the elimination of racism, sexism, ageism, ableism, and other threats to the potentially harmonious but always heterogeneous social lives of American citizens. Native peoples do not always accept or prioritize the goal of inclusion in the US nation, but perhaps more importantly, the concept of multiculturalism can also be seen to delegitimize Native sovereignty by erasing the historical as well as the contemporary, on-going colonization of Indian lands.[1]

Threats to Native sovereignty abound. Native American Studies scholars David E. Wilkins and K. Tsianina Lomawaima characterize the relationship between American Indian tribes and the US federal government as 'an ongoing contest over sovereignty' with high stakes: 'fundamental questions of identity, jurisdiction, power, and control' (2001: 5).

Shari M. Huhndorf echoes this view of the special character of the relations between indigenous and Euro-American nations: 'Because of the unique histories and legal status of indigenous communities, political sovereignty arguably constitutes the most pressing issue in Native North America. Consequently, to a greater degree than related fields, Native studies remains grounded in questions of nation' (2009: 7). While Huhndorf endorses the anti-colonial ambitions of Native nationalism, she also seriously questions the efficacy of its colonial critique, preferring a transnational approach to indigenous studies. Other scholars, notably Jace Weaver, Craig S. Womack, and Robert Warrior in their influential book *American Indian Literary Nationalism* (2006), argue for the importance of a nationalist paradigm, in spite of the dangers they acknowledge in some forms of nationalist thinking. For these theorists, nationalist or transnationalist, Native sovereignty remains crucial, in politics as well as in literature.

In this chapter, we examine Indian orphans in contemporary literature. While literary representations of indigenous peoples by non-Native writers – common in US literature through the early 1900s – have become uncommon outside of popular genres, Native representations of Indian orphans are common. Writers such as Sherman Alexie, Louise Erdrich, Diane Glancy, Linda Hogan, N. Scott Momaday, and Leslie Marmon Silko all feature orphans prominently in their works. We view this as a literary trend growing out of widespread experiences of the loss of children, and we pose our key questions of four works in which orphan figures appear: Barbara Kingsolver's *The Bean Trees* (1988) and *Pigs in Heaven* (1993), Linda Hogan's *Solar Storms* (1995), and Leslie Marmon Silko's *Gardens in the Dunes* (1999). We ask what 'signifying capabilities' do Indian orphans have? What specific challenges to American and/or Native identity do authors respond to through their use of orphan figures? In what types of narrative or ideological processes are Indian orphans involved? Our analysis suggests that authors use the figure of the orphan to interrogate the possibilities and limitations of American and Native nationhood, particularly in regard to their ability to accommodate, assimilate, or otherwise mediate difference. In the process, writers of fiction establish theoretical alliances or antipathies with multiculturalism as a model for American or Native social and political life.

Indian orphan figures, we suggest, bring unique histories to bear on the multicultural ideal, particularly the history of captivity. Unlike their literary predecessors who, Diana Loercher Pazicky has shown, served as scapegoats and 'cultural orphans' against which an emergent American nationalism could define itself, Indian orphans in fiction today are often a means to critique Euro-American values. In Kingsolver's debut novel and particularly in its sequel, the combination of native orphanhood and feminist and multicultural social critique creates disturbing tensions, and in the works of Hogan and Silko, Indian orphans are used to signify and even to forge an indigenous concept of kinship that may provide an unsettling alternative to the idea of multicultural America.

Our analysis focuses on two dimensions or orientations in which Native orphans have a particularly strong role. First, we make a broad survey of the role of literary and critical representations of Native peoples, particularly in connection with orphanhood and adoption. From the time of Native–European contact, Indians in America have served as 'cultural orphans' in Euro-American discourses. We see this metaphorical orphan status to be strongly connected to the well-documented myth of the vanishing American. While the shape of this myth has altered through history, primarily in response to the needs white cultural producers have had to convert it to new purposes, its broad outlines remain remarkably recognizable, continuing to circulate in a variety of discourses in the USA and abroad. Native writing offers a challenge to this perspective on indigenous peoples, and it often deliberately counters this point of view. Kinship is an indigenous epistemological and social concept that belies disappearance by asserting continuity with a sovereign past and with a sovereign future.

Second, we examine the trope of captivity – a trope that lives in American and in Native American cultural memory and that is deeply rooted in historical practices and in the literary genre of captivity narratives. In pre-contact and in colonial America, Native peoples abducted members of other Indian groups as well as Euro-American colonizers for a variety of reasons and for different purposes. Historian Christina Snyder summarizes that: 'Captivity, which both colonizers and Native people practiced, included a broad range of forms extending from temporary bondage to hereditary slavery. Through sexual relationships, adoption, hard work, military service, or escape, captives could enhance their status or even assume new identities' (Snyder, 2010: 6). Captivity can certainly be viewed as an 'orphaning practice,' for the key feature of captivity is the forcible removal of the captive from his or her immediate or cultural family. Yet, as Snyder also indicates, captivity also makes possible new social and kinship arrangements.

Narratives of captivity from Puritan times to the present typically – but not exclusively – depict 'savage' Indians capturing Euro-Americans. Pauline Turner Strong observes that written accounts by Europeans and Euro-Americans form a 'selective tradition' which dominates cultural understandings of the phenomenon. The captivity narrative, arguably unique to the USA, exhibits a pattern involving first abduction, then trial or ordeal, and finally an outcome ranging from escape to tribal incorporation. The genre has functioned as spiritual allegory, political propaganda, and adventure or sentimental literature, and it lives on in popular film and fiction, including Westerns and stories of alien abduction.[2]

In spite of the dominance of this selective narrative tradition, the capture of Native individuals by Euro-Americans has an equally long and brutal history. Pauline Turner Strong documents how European settlers captured Indians in battle, and how Indian captives were used for purposes of negotiation and hostage exchange. In our view, captivity of Native people by Euro-Americans emerges with even greater clarity in the history of Indian Removal in the 1800s and of Indian Boarding Schools. Both mechanisms featured types of 'orphaning' – tribes 'orphaned' from their ancestral lands, children from their families and kin – as ways of containing, assimilating, or exterminating Native peoples. Indeed Marilyn Irvin Holt traces the origins of modern child removal practices to the nineteenth century and the Creek Wars of 1813–15 (2001: 2).

In the twentieth century, the adoption of Indian children by whites can be seen as a continuation of these practices. In the late 1970s, Native peoples protested the documented loss of their children through removal and adoption, and inquiries led to the passage of the Indian Child Welfare Act. In spite of this landmark legislation, many, perhaps even the majority, of Native families in the USA today have direct or indirect experience of the orphaning practice of child removal through state intervention. Certainly, such practices have loomed large in the imaginations of Native writers.[3] We examine the tradition of Native voices critical of the practices that have involved 'abduction,' 'captivity,' or 'orphaning' and then examine how the writers in our study counter or reverse traditional captivity tales. We find that the trope of captivity is astutely manipulated in *Solar Storms* in order to speak to a tribal consciousness, and to strengthen tribal or Native identity. In Hogan's novel, and in Silko's *Gardens in the Dunes*, a radical reworking of the captivity trope brings into relief a contrast between Indian freedom and sovereignty from Western captivity. Native values, extant, intact, and whole rather than vanishing, fragmented, or in decline, bring clear-sighted criticism of US imperialism, environmental degradation, and social values. Kingsolver's novels mount a similar critique, but its force is undercut by its adherence to, or nostalgia for, American mythologies.

Native Americans have had a constitutive role in discourses about American national identity from the Puritan period onwards. Historical records and literary works indicate that indigenous peoples in North America served as demonized 'others' against which the first settlers defined themselves. Indeed, scholars in American Studies have developed the thesis that Native Americans have figured persistently in discourses about American culture and identity. Richard Slotkin, for example, argues that the early encounters between indigenous people and colonial settlers generated and shaped American national mythology. Representations of Native American savagery in Puritan captivity narratives and in accounts of Indian wars were shaped by the fears, anxieties, and complex desires of colonial settlers, particularly the desire to justify the subjugation, extermination, and later displacement of indigenous peoples. Although Christopher Castiglia has demonstrated that white women captives frequently attempted to maintain positions in between Indian and early American cultures – as echoed in a contemporary context in Kingsolver's *Pigs in Heaven*, as we will see – their tales were framed by editors and others to keep boundaries firmly in place. Nationalist literature, dime novels, and Western movies have subsequently mediated aspects of the captivity narrative and this foundational myth.

Scholars have identified and analyzed the role commonly assigned to indigenous people in most versions of US mythology, specifically in the role of the vanishing American. Louis Owens bluntly attributes the persistence of this image today to the desires of contemporary white readers: 'They want what they have always wanted, from Fenimore Cooper to the present: Indians who are romantic, unthreatening, and self-destructive. Indians who are enacting, in one guise or another, the process of vanishing' (2001: 82). From Cooper's *The Last of the Mohicans* (1826) to Costner's *Dances with Wolves* (1990), the disappearance of Indians from the American scene has been staged and restaged in a reassuring re-enactment of white dominance and Native subjugation. Mainstream critiques of this mythology, such as Kingsolver's or Disney's *Avatar* (2009), seem powerless to avoid indexing and thus in some guise perpetuating this familiar stereotype – a problem common even to revisionary projects.[4] Native writers counter this mythology with what Gerald Vizenor terms a literature of survivance: 'Survivance is an active sense of presence, the continuance of native stories, not a mere reaction, or a survivable name. Native survivance stories are renunciations of dominance, tragedy, and victimry' (1999: vii).[5] Orphans feature prominently in stories of survivance by Hogan and Silko.

The links between Native Americans, American culture and identity, and orphanhood have also developed over time, sometimes in contradiction, sometimes in agreement with verifiable histories of Native American orphanhood. From colonial times to the present day, Native Americans have been figured as cultural orphans who represented difference from the dominant population. Examining early texts by Euro-Americans, Pazicky charts the ways that settlers' fears of orphanhood – of not belonging either to a spurned European or an emergent American family – were displaced onto minority groups: 'As the citizens of the republic struggled to carve out a new identity for themselves as Americans rather than colonial subjects, certain novels of the early nineteenth century expressed the dream life of the republic, transforming the quest for identity into a family drama that used the metaphor of orphanhood to raise the question of what it means to be American' (1998: 86). In other words, in fiction by early American writers such as Cooper and Lydia Maria Child, Indians, sometimes demonized, sometimes romanticized, could be made to serve the dream life of the nation by functioning as cultural orphans or figures of difference. Through them, the sameness and unity of the American nation could be assured.

Despite the fact that during colonization Native peoples were 'orphaned' of family and of culture, the orphan protagonists of early American literature are often white. Indeed, as noted in Chapter 1, the American hero in the form of the 'American Adam' of R.W.B. Lewis is a kind of orphan: 'an individual emancipated from history, happily bereft of ancestry, untouched and undefiled by the usual inheritances of family and race ... an individual standing alone, self-reliant and self-propelling' (Lewis, 1955: 5). White orphans such as Huckleberry Finn could thus become nationalist heroes. This pattern is perpetuated in part in *The Bean Trees* and *Pigs in Heaven* when Kingsolver displaces a metaphorical sense of orphanhood onto her gutsy protagonist, Taylor, the only child of a poor, single mother, sending her west with the silent Native child she 'adopts.' While there are variations among Euro-American renditions of orphanhood, the orphan's status as self-reliant individualist seems almost indispensable.

From a Native perspective, however, an Indian orphan is a contradiction in terms. According to social historian LeRoy Ashby, 'no Indian language includes the words *orphan* or *adoption*' (1997: 143), although the word 'orphan' did make its way into Native vocabularies in the 1900s. Native children have of course lost their birth parents, and forms of adoption have long been practiced among many tribal peoples, but Ashby's point is that kinship is differently conceived. Silko's *Almanac of the Dead* expresses how lack of kinship may be regarded as a kind of psychic, social, and spiritual failing or disease:

> The ancestors had called Europeans 'the orphan people' and had noted that as with orphans taken in by selfish or coldhearted clanspeople, few Europeans had remained whole. They failed to recognize the earth was their mother. Europeans were like their first parents, Adam and Eve, wandering aimlessly because the insane God who had sired them had abandoned them. (1991: 258)

Adoption, moreover, is the practice of making kin, and it has historically been a key way for many Native peoples to relate to strangers or outsiders.

But in Pazicky's analysis of Euro-American discourses on family and nation, Native Americans, as well as African Americans and other immigrant groups, have played key roles at different historical moments in consolidating a sense of American identity. We return to this idea in Chapter 5. The demise of the melting pot ideal and the notion of *e pluribus unum* – where out of many, one America is forged – underwent transformation in the period after World War II. With the new social movements and the political and cultural goals of the 1960s, Euro-American writers and others turned to Native peoples for alternatives to 'traditional' values, finding inspiration in the communal aspects of tribal identity, and in the 1980s and 1990s, Native Americans began to figure in dreams of an alternative, multicultural America. As Huhndorf notes, 'Today, Native cultures and identities comprise objects of desire rather than objects of revulsion' (2001: 167). Yet, scholars have also shown that the investment of symbolic meaning in Indians is too often sentimental or nostalgic, a New Age attempt to 'go Native' by appropriating Native American cultural practices, artifacts, and even identities. Kathryn Shanley, for example, comments incisively on the issue of appropriation:

While American Indians struggle to regain power to determine their cultural identities and futures through economic, governmental, social, educational, and kinship refigurations, the 'Indian' voices most popular in mainstream America are often those of would-be Indians, who reinscribe nineteenth-century, romantic images of 'noble savages.' Playing Indian has become an American pastime. (2001a: 28)

More than a plea for authenticity, Shanley argues that Native American identity, if defined solely in terms of culture, can too easily be appropriated, and its requirements can more easily be assuaged than the real social and economic issues that accrue from a notion of political identity founded on sovereign power. Such tensions, we believe, are at work in Barbara Kingsolver's representation of orphans and Indians.

Native multiculturalism?: Barbara Kingsolver's *The Bean Trees* and *Pigs in Heaven*

Annawake's jaw tenses with this familiar frustration: explaining her culture to someone who believes America is all one country. She thinks about what she wants to say, and sees in her mind *family*, a color, a notion as fluid as *river*. (Kingsolver, 1993: 227)

Barbara Kingsolver is a writer of Euro-American and Native ancestry, whose Cherokee great-grandmother, she relates, 'was quite deliberately left out of the family history for reasons of racism and embarrassment about mixed blood' ('Barbara Kingsolver', 1988: 148). Kingsolver touches upon mixed ancestry in works that include Native American characters. Her first novel, *The Bean Trees*, features Native Americans quite prominently, and its sequel, *Pigs in Heaven*, wrestles explicitly with the challenge of understanding indigenous culture, particularly Cherokee culture, from the outside. Kingsolver is thus unusual as a writer of contemporary fiction where, with the exception of 'Indian romances' and Westerns, few non-Native writers represent Indian characters. As in the works of Linda Hogan (Chickasaw) and Leslie Marmon Silko (Laguna Pueblo), the Indian orphan is an important figure in Kingsolver's vision of identity and dreams of community, particularly in her depiction of American multicultural community. Yet, our analysis will show that orphan figures are deployed in crucially different ways by these writers and with significantly different results. Clearly, such a comparison of the work of Native and non-Native writers runs the risk of setting up a predictable binary opposition between essentialist categories of identity and authenticity. We propose, however, that the different effects of these Indian orphan tales are attributable not only, or primarily, to the authors' ethnicities, but to their modes of engagement with literary genres and with the particularities of history – particularly the history of Indian captivity and adoption.

The core of Kingsolver's bestselling debut novel and its sequel lies in the fraudulent adoption of an orphan Indian child by a westward-journeying young white woman, Taylor Greer. The invocation of the Western motif in *The Bean Trees*, coupled with its (mis)representation of Indian orphans and adoption history, encourages our reading of the text in terms of captivity. Taylor, daughter of a poor but loving mother, Alice, and an unknown father, comes of age in the 1970s in rural Kentucky, where few career options are available for young women. Taylor avoids getting pregnant long enough to graduate from high school and find a job at the local hospital. Before long, however, she is heading west, on the road and on her own, in a dilapidated car. From the start, the mythic pattern of rugged individualism familiar from the road novel and the Western is complicated and attributed with a feminist spin. In a parking lot outside a bar somewhere on Cherokee land on the plains of Oklahoma, a woman gives Taylor a tiny Indian child. Taylor, who has spent the last seven years of her young life avoiding pregnancy, somewhat inexplicably accepts the child, and drives off with her into the night. She soon discovers physical evidence that the child, whom she names Turtle for her strong grip, has been abused. The novel then charts Taylor's and Turtle's journey to Tucson, Arizona, and Taylor's gradual incorporation into an alternative, woman-centered, multiethnic 'family' loosely composed of, among others, two fugitives, Esperanza and Estevan, who have lost their daughter to corrupt Guatemalan authorities. At the end of the novel Taylor formally but fraudulently adopts Turtle with the assistance of Esperanza and Estevan, who impersonate Turtle's Native American parents, renounce their parental rights, and consent to the adoption, because legislation requires the voluntary consent of Native parents. Taylor tells Turtle that the adoption certificate means 'You're my kid ... and I'm your mother, and nobody can say it isn't so. I'll keep that paper for you till you're older, but it's yours. So you'll always know who you are' (Kingsolver, 1988: 232). It is on this off-key note of confidence about identity and belonging – Taylor's and Turtle's – that Kingsolver's first novel closes. *Pigs in Heaven*, by contrast, opens with such confidence explicitly shaken, once Taylor's illegal adoption of Turtle comes to the attention of a tribal lawyer and the Cherokee tribe to which Turtle may be said to belong. In what follows, we discuss first *The Bean Trees* and then *Pigs in Heaven*.

The feminist, revisionary agenda of *The Bean Trees* is crystal clear. Critics have shown how the novel invokes and manipulates the genre conventions of the Western and the road novel to critique the masculine bias of American values of self-reliance and independence.[6] Taylor achieves maturity and freedom within an alternative 'family' built upon voluntary but committed ethical, empathic relations of mutual dependence with others. Motherhood derives from choice and agency and, as Marianne Novy notes, 'adoptive nurturing becomes a natural process' (Novy, 2005: 189). Some critics have therefore focused on how adoption in the novel represents a non-patriarchal form of family that incorporates difference and so may serve as a model for egalitarian community. In a lengthy analysis, Magali Cornier Michael emphasizes that *The Bean Trees* attempts to show that 'an inclusive notion of family allows for diversity and difference, which makes possible the construction of new kinds of families and communities at a time in which the United States is becoming increasingly multiethnic and multiracial' (Michael, 2006: 88). Novy and Michael admit that Kingsolver's narrative appears less progressive in the historical context of non-Native adoption of Indian children, but they emphasize the positive in her project's imagining alternative families and forms of community. Cynthia Callahan considers representations of Indian adoption as rescue or captivity to be 'very much in the eye of the beholder' (Callahan, 2011: 109), and she traces the reception of the novel among critics and writers, including Sherman Alexie (Coeur d'Alene/Spokane) and Silko, both of whom took issue with the way that Kingsolver's feminism and her dream of multicultural America leave in place the stereotypes of Native peoples and replicate a colonial view of Indian adoption.[7] Kathleen Godfrey also shows how Kingsolver commodifies, ritualizes, and idealizes Cherokees, despite a 'politicized sensibility' (Godfrey, 2001: 259), and Kristina Fagan analyzes *Pigs in Heaven* as a nationalist fantasy of racial and cultural reconciliation between settlers and Native Americans that privileges a Euro-American perspective. Fagan points to the deep contradiction between the roles that orphans and orphanhood play in American nationalist mythology and the actual history of Indian adoption, but she does not explore the implications of this contradiction for

Kingsolver's fiction. Kingsolver's engagement with American nationalist mythology combined with her lack of engagement with the history of Native child removal and adoption, we suggest, mars her fiction's new vision of a multicultural America.

The history of Indian child removal runs counter to ideologies of American self-invention and self-reliance. From the early 1800s, US government assimilation policies removed countless Native American children from their families and placed them in boarding schools, making these children de facto orphans. Considerable fiction and non-fiction writing about boarding school experiences has been produced by Native writers and scholars.[8] With the advent of social work and child welfare systems in the twentieth century, the practice of removing Native American children from their families or mothers was supplemented by social workers largely ignorant of Indian cultures and child-raising practices. In indigenous societies, a child 'under an older person's care was not a candidate for investigation and possible removal. Nor were the parents guilty of neglect. Elders had an important, traditionally sacred role,' but this role could be misunderstood by child welfare authorities, as could other practices such as that of Native children 'wandering from house to house, staying with one family after another' (Holt, 2001: 11, 18). Marilyn Irvin Holt, who has observed that placements in on-reservation Indian orphanages kept Native children close to home and thus helped preserve family and tribal ties, argues that particularly in the 1950s there was 'a white, middle-class "interpretive impression" that permeated the social worker mind-set' and caused social workers to pressure especially young, unmarried women into giving up their children for adoption (2001: 5). More reprehensively, the Child Welfare League of America (CWLA) and the Bureau of Indian Affairs collaborated in 1958 on the Indian Adoption Project to facilitate the adoption of Indians by white families who were deemed 'more suitable' to child-rearing.[9]

The removals of Native American children – whether they were due to deliberate policies of assimilation, ethnocentric assessments of Native American family life, racism, or efforts to protect children from abusive home environments – clearly influenced the rates and risks of Indian children in care until the late 1970s. The adoption rate of these children varied state-wise, with some states showing adoption rates for Native children that were up to nineteen times higher than that of non-Native children. Nationally, Indian children constituted and estimated 35–40 per cent of the children available for adoption in the

USA, even though Native Americans accounted for only about 2 per cent of the total population. Nationally, Indian children were twenty times more likely to be placed in foster care than non-Indian children. As many as 35 per cent of all Indian children were placed in foster care or adopted.[10] Native protest against adoption as a form of cultural genocide led to the passing of the Indian Child Welfare Act (ICWA) of 1978, an act which restores tribal jurisdiction over Indian child welfare, and which promotes Native custody and adoption arrangements in the best interests of *both* child and tribe. Today, though fewer Indian children are adopted, and the percentage of them in foster care and in the public adoption pool appears to have stabilized, at least one study suggests that Native Americans remain over-represented in foster care; an evaluation of placements in 2006 concludes that the 'disproportion of American Indian/Alaskan Native children in out-of-home care has persisted almost 30 years after the passage of the Indian Child Welfare Act' (V. Carter, 2009: 840). Moreover, the ICWA is continually threatened by factors such as the perceived need for adoptive children by non-Indian families, the legitimate need to prevent foster-care drift and to promote permanency planning, and to otherwise serve 'the best needs of the child.'[11] Though the Supreme Court has reasoned that the continuity of tribal affiliations is part of any Indian child's 'best interests,'[12] debates continue concerning the importance of ethnic and/or 'racial' identity, difference, and belonging.

The representation of adoption in *The Bean Trees* demonstrates Kingsolver's ignorance of this deplorable history and the Native critique of adoption practices as forms of cultural genocide in the USA. Kingsolver had not known about the Indian Child Welfare Act until after her novel was published (Wagner-Martin, 2003: 89). Uncannily, however, the adoption she envisions replicates aspects of this history. When Taylor is 'given' a child by a Native woman, she thinks only briefly about relatives who might miss the child, and she has no thought of tribal members who might have a legitimate claim to raise her. Instead, her instinctual feeling that the men in the bar are dangerous – 'The way [the Indian woman] looked at them made me feel like if I had better sense I'd be scared' (Kingsolver, 1988: 16) – and that an Indian woman is helpless to protect a child leads Taylor to accept her. Taylor's tacit assumption that she – though a poor, jobless, unmarried young woman in a car that hardly runs – can take better care of the child than the nameless Indian woman or any other Native person coincides with the jaunty confidence readers expect of male literary heroes, but it also resounds with the arrogance, or at best paternalism, behind policies of Indian child removal from at least the days of boarding schools. The narrative corroborates Taylor's assumptions, moreover, when she finds signs of abuse. Most importantly, while Taylor's innocence – measured by her poverty and how far she is removed from patriarchal power and privilege – works to guarantee her lack of complicity with the state power that has dictated the removal and maltreatment of indigenous peoples, her physical removal of Turtle from her tribal lands perpetuates the practice of appropriation and displacement. In our reading of this novel, Taylor can be seen as taking Turtle captive.

Seen in this light, the 'gift' of an Indian orphan to a kind-hearted white woman emerges as a textual fantasy that erases the history of violence and exploitation of Indian removal, captivity, and adoption by whites, just as earlier nationalist orphan tales had done.[13] This textual fantasy is part and parcel of the American mythology Kingsolver attempts to revise, but instead winds up perpetuating. In fact, it is tempting to see Taylor in this scene as a stand-in for the author whose engagement with the myth of America – in spite of the critical mode of that engagement – necessitates the literal and literary appropriation of the Indian orphan and the simultaneous repression of the history of white-Native relations.

The erasure of the historical specificity of white adoption and the captivity of Indians to accommodate American mythology leaves discernible traces in the plot, especially in the incongruity of the gift and of Taylor's equally incongruous acceptance of it. Even Michael, who views Taylor's taking of the child as an 'empathic' act, admits that Taylor's response is 'odd' and may be attributable to 'general American assumptions about bad mothers and more specifically, in this case, bad Native American mothers' (Michael, 2006: 82). Silko protested that the rescue scene serves to 'soothe the collective conscience of white America. The subtext of such stereotypical portrayals is: Take the children, take the land; these Indians are in no condition to have such precious possessions' (quoted in Callahan, 2011: 113). Indeed, Taylor herself comments on the incongruity of her taking the child: 'If I wanted a baby I would have stayed in Kentucky' (Kingsolver, 1988: 18). Moreover, repression of thought and feeling, or selective amnesia, figures in the scene of the handover, which emphasizes Taylor's uncharacteristic lack of clear thinking. She talks back assertively to 'the gray-hat cowboy' at the bar, but the next minute she is somnambulant:

'The air in there was so hot and stale I felt like I had to breathe it twice to get any oxygen out of it. The coffee did nothing to wake me up' (*ibid.*: 16). Even after eating, she reflects, 'I still felt like my head had been stuffed with that fluffy white business they use in life preservers. I imagined myself stepping outside and the wind just scattering me' (*ibid.*: 16–17). When the Indian woman bluntly demands that she take the baby, Taylor 'waited a minute, thinking that soon my mind would clear and I would understand what she was saying. It didn't' (*ibid.*: 17). Taylor makes one effort to insist that someone will miss the baby, but she has 'a foggy understanding' that she 'wasn't arguing the right point,' and when the woman walks away, leaving the child on Taylor's front seat, Taylor is unable to think of what to do before first the woman, and then the men drive away from the bar. The entire scene, in other words, is constructed to emphasize Taylor's passive acceptance of Turtle, a curious lethargy associated with her whiteness, and an uncharacteristic lack of volition and agency.

The incongruities associated with the handover and acceptance of the child both repress and call attention to similarities between adoption and captivity. A link to captivity is further established by Taylor's rambling thoughts as she drives with the silent child wrapped up like a mummy beside her. She wonders whether she may have been given a dead child, and recalls 'a story in Senior English about a woman who slept with her dead husband for forty years. It was basically the same idea as the guy and his mother in *Psycho*, except that Norman Bates in *Psycho* was a taxidermist and knew how to preserve his mother so she wouldn't totally rot out. Indians sometimes knew how to preserve the dead. I had read about Indian mummies out West' (*ibid.*: 20). Taylor's stream-of-consciousness narrative links the situation involving Turtle with cultural representations of perverse captivity and preservation. Faulkner's Emily in 'A Rose for Emily' (1930) and Hitchcock's Norman Bates in *Psycho* (1960), the film based on Robert Bloch's 1959 novel, are not like the Indian woman who relinquishes Turtle; instead, they offer a disturbing, unwitting commentary on the person Taylor risks becoming in this book and its sequel as she struggles to preserve her relationship with her illegally adopted daughter. In a similar manner, the way that Esperanza and Estevan have been forced into exile and into relinquishing their child for 'adoption' by the Guatemalan government cannot fail to remind readers that adoption can function as a euphemism for captivity. Adoptions can be coerced, and governments have historically played dubious roles in adoption practices. As one critic provocatively puts it, 'Adoption is still captivity, though in a milder form, for the basic elements of captivity are present. The adopted person surrenders his or her identity, accepting a new identity and a new name, a new language, new clothes, new duties, a new life' (Griffin, 1986: 46).

Indeed, even traditional accounts of Euro-American captivity identify similarities between captivity and adoption. Early narratives display an 'archetypal' pattern involving 'Separation (isolation from one's culture and symbolic death), Transformation (a series of excruciating ordeals in passing from ignorance to knowledge and maturity, accompanied by ritualized adoption into a new culture), and Return (symbolic rebirth with a sense of moral or spiritual gain)' (VanDerBeets, 1984: x).[14] In the latter part of the eighteenth century, when narratives became more literary, 'the Indian's symbolic function was heightened and altered ... The captivity experience itself became an experience of adoption or initiation [of white captives] into the Indian's world' (Slotkin, 1973: 247). Female captives may have held a special appreciation for Native societies which in some cases offered less restrictive social roles to women, a point of importance to Kingsolver's sequel.[15]

To read *The Bean Trees* in terms of captivity, however, is to read the novel against the 'selective tradition' of captivity that erases the fact that Native Americans were taken captive by whites, arguably on a far more extensive scale than whites were captured by Indians, that Europeans 'used captivity as a strategy of colonial domination' (Strong, 1999: 7), and that Indian captivity of settlers was a practice that was in part shaped by contact with *European* practices of captivity, and vice-versa. Strong's scholarship departs from the simple but profound observation that Indian captives such as Tisquantum (Squanto) or Matoaka (Pocahontas) are not usually understood as captives, but as 'personifications of the noble but vanishing Indian' (ibid.: 19), their nobility measured in relation to their willingness to aid the endeavors of early settlers. Indians were taken captive in battle, and for a host of purposes. Holt suggests that the first recorded instance of white removal of an Indian child may have occurred in the Creek Wars of 1813–15, when Andrew Jackson took an Indian child whose parents were killed (Holt, 2001: 2). Similar 'adoptions' occurred through the nineteenth century, like that of Lost Bird of Wounded Knee.[16] Andrew Jackson's military removal of indigenous peoples from their homelands to the confines of Indian territory may also be considered a form of captivity, as may the incarceration of Natives in reservations and in boarding schools.

Just as a Native presence helps to consolidate an emergent US national identity in the hegemonic tradition of white captivity, so Kingsolver's endeavors to imagine a feminist and multicultural America are assisted by a Native figure. The young, silent, dependent, and traumatized but slowly healing Turtle offers Taylor – and the narrative – an opportunity to suggest that young, single women can successfully raise children, including adopted children of color. Turtle's primary narrative function is to highlight Taylor's resourcefulness, her patience, toleration of difference, and independence – all American virtues, and all-American virtues. Taylor narrates *The Bean Trees* in a distinctive voice much praised by readers and critics.[17] Her voice, though, defines itself against Turtle's silence, her maturity against Turtle's status as a child, her agency in all but the handover scene against Turtle's passive victimhood. Kingsolver's progressive vision of American multiculturalism, as well as her dream of female agency and independence, relies on the deployment of an Indian orphan figure, but it neglects the historical role that white adoption of Native children has played in cultural assimilation or eradication. In sum, the trope of adoption as captivity in this novel undermines Kingsolver's feminist and multicultural agenda.

Belatedly recognizing problems of representation in her first novel, Kingsolver wrote *Pigs in Heaven* to compensate for her earlier portrayal of Indian adoption. As noted, Kingsolver did not learn about the 1978 Indian Child Welfare Act until 'long after *The Bean Trees* had been published; once she became informed, however, she saw a way to make amends for Taylor's duplicity in her adoption of Turtle' (Wagner-Martin, 2003: 89). Kingsolver put it this way: 'I had the option and the *obligation* to deal with the issue [of white adoption of Native American children] because the moral question was completely ignored in the first book' (quoted in Novy, 2005: 187). Although Kingsolver understood that her readers sympathized with Taylor and Turtle and the strong bond between them, she asserted that 'there was another view, and I wanted to bring readers to sympathize with the tribe, too' (quoted in Murrey, 1994: 160). In this way, Kingsolver made a deliberate attempt to represent a Native American viewpoint, specifically a Cherokee one, approaching her subject in the spirit of 'recognition and apology' that Shanley suggests may enable 'a new kind of hearing,' a different attentiveness to Native voices (Shanley,

2001b: 225, 226). Such self-conscious listening, it seems, might grow out of attentiveness to the specificities of Native histories and cultures, especially those at odds with American nationalist mythology. Yet, in spite of her careful attention to the histories of adoption and captivity, Kingsolver's sequel does not wholly succeed in the task it set for itself.

In the sequel, the Cherokee tribe disputes Taylor's adoption of Turtle. The efforts of a tribal lawyer, Annawake Fourkiller, to discuss Turtle's and the tribe's best interests send Taylor and Turtle underground. Taylor cuts herself and Turtle off from friends and family, moving repeatedly to prevent Turtle's 'capture' by the Cherokees. These desperate actions jeopardize Turtle's health and well-being. At the same time, Taylor's mother Alice finds kin among the eastern band of Cherokee in Heaven, Oklahoma, and is drawn into the wide embrace of the Native community. The novel ends with Taylor losing legal guardianship to Cash, Turtle's grandfather, but gaining a fair division of child custody that will strengthen Turtle's Native identity and the tribe while also affirming the strong bond between Turtle and Taylor: Turtle will spend summers with her grandfather Cash on the reservation, but there she will also be with her grandmother, Alice, who has discovered meaning in her Cherokee blood, is accepted into the tribe, and agrees to marry Cash.

Some critics have praised Kingsolver's efforts to re-examine the ethical dimensions of Taylor's adoption of Turtle. Novy insists that the novel 'helps its readers see the complexity of transracial adoption and the tragedies of Native American history' (2005: 110). Michael's focus on 'new visions of community' leads her to view Kingsolver's 'idealization or romanticization' of Cherokees as an inevitable result of her political and utopian agenda.[18] Others remain critical of the results. Fagan finds that Kingsolver presents both the claims of adoptive parents and the claims of Indian tribes sympathetically, but that, as previously noted, the narrative – especially its contrived ending – must be viewed as a nationalist fantasy of 'racial and cultural reconciliation in the United States' (2001: 251). In our view, this fantasy governs Kingsolver's earlier novel as well, and it is articulated most clearly in its evocation and disavowal of the history of orphanhood, captivity, and adoption.

Pigs in Heaven's overt concern with historical accuracy and cultural sensitivity about the ICWA, however, either generates, or is powerless to offset, a new set of problems. The tropes of orphanhood and captivity are not replicated but displaced in this novel. In this second novel, it is Taylor who – in spite of her self-reliance, hard work, and thrift, and in spite of her loving mother's support – experiences upheaval, homelessness, powerlessness, and poverty, and who, in short, becomes figuratively 'orphaned.' The critique of the American dream of self-reliance and upward mobility is unmistakeable; the rags-to-riches tales of Horatio Alger tales are referred to as 'compost' (Kingsolver, 1993: 246), for example, and Taylor's stubborn insistence on going it alone is shown to jeopardize Turtle's health. The car, a symbol of mobility and freedom hijacked for feminist purposes in *The Bean Trees*, becomes an unhealthy alternative to decent housing in *Pigs in Heaven*, when bad weather holds them 'hostage' in the car, and when Turtle is forced to stay alone in the car so Taylor can work (*ibid.*: 286, 290). Thus, Taylor's economic entrapment and social vulnerability curiously make *her* the cultural orphan in this drama. She is explicitly compared to another resourceful orphan, Dorothy from Kansas (*ibid.*: 245) in *The Wizard of Oz* (1900), and the scenes of captivity described above are related in a chapter appropriately titled 'Surrender Dorothy.' As Taylor finds it increasingly difficult to care for Turtle while on the run, her boyfriend Jax and the thought of marriage begin to suggest the 'home' there is 'no place like.' Yet, it is the Cherokee nation with its strong communal cohesion which becomes the family, and the nation, outside of which Taylor remains. While Alice joins a stomp dance and 'feels completely included' (*ibid.*: 271) for the first time in her life, Taylor must confess that she is without family, and that a mother-daughter dyad is not enough to make 'a whole family' (*ibid.*: 291). She tells Annawake, 'We don't have any backup. I don't want to go through with this thing anymore, hiding out and keeping [Turtle] away from people. It's hurting her' (*ibid.*: 320–1). Taylor's experience of the isolation that results from poverty contrasts starkly with Alice's experiences of place-based community that remains intact in spite of material deprivation.

In the narrative logic of *Pigs in Heaven*, we argue, Taylor becomes orphaned and displaced, as does the American dream of self-reliance. Indeed, Taylor's voice – so distinctive, humorous, and spunky in *The Bean Trees* – is muted and diffused in the third-person narrative of *Pigs in Heaven*. In comparison with Kingsolver's first novel, the narrative almost abandons Taylor, focalizing events through the viewpoints of many other characters. The multiple narrative perspectives, notably those of Annawake Fourkiller and Alice, de-privilege and de-center Taylor's point of view. Their conversations about the plight of Taylor and Turtle – instructive and staged to enlighten the reader about the history of Native–white contacts and the rationale for the ICWA – shed a different light on Taylor's adoption of Turtle, and may well lead readers to 'sympathize with the tribe, too,' as Kingsolver wished. Nevertheless, *Pigs in Heaven* remains very much Taylor's story. Because Kingsolver presents Taylor and her love for Turtle sympathetically, and because Taylor's loss of voice and autonomy is so marked in relation to the first novel, the text's explicit debunking of the myth of American individualism, coupled with a prosaic relation of historical facts about the ICWA, the Trail of Tears, and other attempts at genocide, indirectly affirms the value of individualism through sentimental nostalgia. Taylor becomes what Pazicky calls 'a mock orphan' (*ibid.*: 109) and, by appropriating the outsider status more commonly assigned to indigenous peoples, she gains the strongest sympathy from readers. Kingsolver's sequel shares strategies with James Fenimore Cooper's *The Prairie* (1824), in which, Pazicky argues, Cooper 'appropriates the values of Indian civilization … and then subsumes them to a national ideology …' (Pazicky, 1998: 110). While Cooper can be seen to subsume a spiritual and respectful attitude to the land to the ideology of Manifest Destiny, Kingsolver can be seen as uncomfortably or incompletely subsuming Native values of inclusive community to the American ideology of multiculturalism.

At the end of the novel, having lost sole custody of Turtle, Taylor remains disconcertingly detached from mainstream society and only tenuously linked to the Cherokee nation through an as-yet-unclaimed birthright, through her mother's coming marriage to Cash, and through her shared custody of Turtle. The thought of heading west with Turtle once again occurs to her, but she realizes she is 'connected to' Turtle's relations '[f]rom now until the end of time' (Kingsolver, 1993: 341). This modestly conceived and carefully articulated connection – one that resists both appropriation and easy integration into a Native family – does not satisfy Taylor's longing for home. Modifying the feminist spirit of the previous novel, Taylor looks forward to marrying her boyfriend and imagines him as Turtle's 'official daddy' (*ibid.*: 341). As unsettling as this modification of the novel's feminist vision may be, more unsettling is what is implied by Alice's fate. Once Cash silences his TV, Alice, too, celebrates a more perfect union, as the 'family of women' can 'open its doors to men. Men, children, cowboys, and Indians' (*ibid.*: 343).

Towards the end of the novel, Alice has begun to reclaim her Cherokee identity and has been accepted by the Cherokee community, but this acceptance comes very easily. Being Cherokee is described loosely as 'more or less a mind-set' (*ibid*.: 275), and tribal enrolment, for which Alice is eligible by birth, is based partly on descent and partly on living 'our way of life' (*ibid*.: 279). Acceptance may come too easily, even though the Native adoption of outsiders – captives, explorers, anthropologists, and others – is a well-known historical practice. As one scholar puts it, 'Kinship ... has always been the central idiom of social relations in Native American societies' (Kan, 2001: 3). Relations of kinship are key to tribal society and identity, as Kingsolver, but also Hogan, and Silko show in different ways, but as in Kingsolver's first novel, where the voluntary 'gift' of Turtle both erases and reinstates tropes of captivity, so here Alice's voluntary claim to a Cherokee or mixed-blood identity, and the ease with which she is 'adopted' by the community, gloss over the difficulties of transracial adoption and, by extension in our reading, of issues around multiculturalism in the USA at the time of publication.[19]

The contrived utopian ending of *Pigs in Heaven* has been read as a dream of easy racial harmony.[20] In our view, both of Kingsolver's novels struggle, first inadvertently, then deliberately, to impart a progressive and strongly egalitarian vision of family and nation. The failure of that struggle is most obviously marked by the contrived endings and, we believe, these arise from Kingsolver's seemingly unintentional invocation of captivity tropes. In a different but not unrelated context, Rachel Blau DuPlessis analyzes narrative endings, observing that 'a disjunction between narrative discourses and resolutions ... may be felt as the "patness" of a resolution, or as the ironic comment of an author at closure. There may also be a sense of contradiction between the plot and the character' (1985: 7), deriving from the conflict between an author's desire or imagination and the constraints of the narrative, informed as it is by ideological structures and social scripts. Literary critics such as Slotkin, Castiglia, Strong, Vizenor, and Owens have made us aware of the structures and scripts that govern tales of captivity and histories of adoption, and DuPlessis discusses how, 'when that closure is investigated, the repressed element is present in shadowy form' (*ibid*.: 7). If the repressed element in Kingsolver's first novel is Turtle's voice and a history of cultural genocide with adoption functioning as a strategic practice in that history, the repressed element in *Pigs in Heaven* is Taylor's voice, the discourse of the white American child hero, scripted by frontier ideology and the American dream. Taylor's loss of voice and agency in moving from the first to the second novel, does not afford more agency to Turtle. Her point of view is rendered in little more than a single page, the disconnected language and disturbing images of the passage conveying a vulnerable and reactive child, whose traumatic memories are all too easily triggered, as when Taylor bursts into tears over her inability to feed her daughter properly.[21] Here Turtle's orphan status is overshadowed by Taylor's maternal guilt, her anguish eliciting strong sympathy for her plight. In other words, the neat resolution of Kingsolver's novel supplied by the intercultural marriage, shared child custody, and the promise of a multicultural and feminist community is troubled by nostalgia for an independent, American voice – the voice of Taylor, silenced, at least temporarily, as she stands on the verge of a multicultural future.

The orphan's return: Linda Hogan's *Solar Storms*

> Sovereignty ... argues for maintaining an entire cultural entity. It involves aspects of social, political, and tribal life. It includes the right to one's children, as well as jurisdictional control over decisions affecting children's lives. (Holt, 2001: 6)

In the prologue to Linda Hogan's *Solar Storms*, the protagonist and primary narrator of the story, Indian orphan Angel Wing, is explicitly compared to 'all the children lost to us, taken away' (Hogan, 1995b: 17). In this way, Hogan introduces into her work the trope of captivity and the history of Indian child removal, and she signals their continued resonance. Her writing, however, has a different orientation than Kingsolver's, which was directed primarily toward feminist explorations of American identity and multiculturalism. Hogan's novel, like Silko's *Gardens in the Dunes* which we later discuss, employs the motif of the orphan's return from 'captivity' in non-Indian territory in order to explore Native sovereignty as well as Native thought and culture in critical relation to Euro-American social and environmental practices. Representations of orphanhood, we propose, have particularly strong resonance for societies devastated by the loss of children, societies in which the various forms of child removal – capture, boarding- or mission-school placement, adoption, and foster care

– have historically served as tools for assimilation or, indeed, cultural genocide. The disproportionate number of Native children that were made available for adoption or placed in foster care before the passage of the ICWA, and their continued overrepresentation in foster care clearly implies that a significant part of the Native American population has directly or indirectly experienced separation from family, culture, and birthplace or tribal locations. Indian orphans in Hogan's work specifically, and in that of Native writers more broadly, embody this history. Simultaneously, they encourage imaginative performances of other forms of kinship which offer viable alternatives to dominant systems of Euro-American life. In contrast to the myth of 'regeneration through violence' that Slotkin saw as 'the structuring metaphor of the American experience' (2000: 5) as portrayed in American literature, Hogan and Silko present what we would like to call 'regeneration through kinship,' and they use orphan figures to do so. Taking our cue from Daniel Heath Justice's ideas about 'kinship criticism,' in which community and kinship function as 'interpretive concepts' in literary and cultural analysis, we examine how Hogan's novel envisions indigenous kinship as the basis of regeneration for the modern world.

Hogan's work also chimes with recent theoretical accounts of developments in Native fiction. While Native literature and literary criticism have worked with unflagging persistence to resist stereotypes about vanishing American Indians and to reclaim, recover, or reconstitute indigenous identities, some criticism suggests a marked change of emphasis. From roughly the 1990s, Native literature and theory have built on the success of previous projects of cultural affirmation such as N. Scott Momaday's *House Made of Dawn* (1966) and Silko's *Ceremony* (1977), works in which 'mixed blood' orphans struggle, in different ways, to overcome their alienation from modern and tribal societies, articulating in the process revitalized Native identities, at once new and yet rooted in tradition. Increasingly, Native writers begin, rather than end, with the integrity of indigenous identity. Moreover, they use this situated perspective to interrogate the value of Euro-American thought and practices.[22] Native American criticism has also arrived at a point where Native perspectives can confidently be turned on Native cultures, and also more critically on the literatures and theories generated alongside or outside indigenous paradigms. While such critical observations have a history as long as Indian–white contact, the ways in which Native artists and intellectuals have influenced theoretical developments in literature and the history of ideas have, Craig S. Womack affirms, reached a 'historical threshold,' a 'turning point' (2008: 95).[23] In what follows, we look at how this critical turn plays out in Hogan's novel, and how the literary orphan is used both to embody a history of dispossession and to call into imaginative being other forms of kinship and community.

Solar Storms features multiple female orphan figures – orphaned in the literal sense of having lost one or both birth parents, and in the metaphorical sense of being neglected, cast off, destitute. Indeed, readers learn that the very first women at Adam's Rib, the community on the boundary waters between the USA and Canada to which Angel Wing returns, called themselves 'the Abandoned Ones' (Hogan, 1995b: 28). The novel centers, however, on Angel, the most prominent orphan in a legacy of abducted, abused, and abandoned females of fictional tribal affiliations. The series of orphan figures – Angel's grandmother, Loretta; Loretta's daughter, Hannah Wing; Hannah's daughter, the protagonist Angel; and Angel's mixed-blood half-sister, Aurora, whom Angel discovers late in the novel when she finally meets her mother – together chart a history of transformation in forms of kinship and the bounds of community, to which Angel's three surrogate grandmothers – Bush, Agnes, and Dora-Rouge – also contribute.

In many indigenous societies, parentless children have been viewed and treated differently than in dominant culture, and Native child-raising practices tend to involve extensive family and kinship networks, with the mother or maternal relatives carrying much of the responsibility for child-raising (Agtuca, 2008: 17). Holt observes that because 'it was common for a family group or a designated relative, such as a grandmother, to take in a child who had lost one or both parents, it was almost impossible for a child to be left totally alone and vulnerable' (2001: 23). Angel, however, is a modern-day captive of the social welfare system. The authorities take Angel from her abusive birth mother, and, unable to recognize the kinship care provided by her grandfather's wife, Bush, send her to a series of foster homes from which she habitually runs away, until she finally returns to her relatives in a search for knowledge and understanding of her past and her people. With a narrative present of 1972–73, the novel also encompasses the factual Inuit and Cree resistance to the Hydro-Quebec power project, a damming and river-diversion project that resulted in significant social and environmental destruction, but that also generated political protest and alliances.[24] The story of Angel's return to family and place, then, becomes intimately intertwined with a story of Native resistance on the US/Canadian border. These parallel stories signify upon captivity narratives in order to counter stereotypes and the myth of the vanishing race, and above all to reconstitute indigenous kinship and the sovereign status that implies. That Hogan's novel does this so successfully is due in large part, we suggest, to her deliberate manipulation of the tropes of orphanhood and captivity.

Edward M. Griffin speculated in 1986 that '[p]erhaps the first captives in American history are Native Americans who are captured by white slave traders and taken from their homeland' (1986: 48). In work focusing on Native captivity and slave-holding practices, Christina Snyder also observes that indigenous peoples participated in captivity 'as both victims and masters' and that 'Indians were among the first slaves owned by Virgina and Carolina planters' (2010: 8–9). Strong's scholarship on captivity narratives, as touched on earlier, demonstrates that the 'selective tradition' of captivity narratives emphasizes Native people as captors, rather than captives, even though 'in numerical terms the captivity of English colonists among Indians pales in comparison to the abduction, imprisonment, and enslavement of Indians by the English' (1999: 13). The work of these scholars complements that of literary critics who have examined how fictional and non-fictional accounts of Indian displacement or reverse captivity signify on the traditional, Eurocentric captivity narrative.[25] Literary works that rewrite captivity narratives from an indigenous perspective contribute to the project of literary sovereignty. By countering mythologizing plots and characterization with historical specificity and cultural critique, *Solar Storms* may be read as contributing to this project.

Solar Storms represents significant reversals of the traditional plot of captivity. With roughly a three-part structure, the novel begins where these narratives typically end, with the return and reincorporation of the captive into his or her birth community, and it ends where traditional captivity narratives begin, with battle. The return in *Solar Storms*, though, is a return to Indian country, and the battle involves Native resistance to non-Native dominance. This form of reversal, together with the re-orientation of the central part of the novel involving transformation, constitutes a counter-narrative. The many images of captivity and captivity tales embedded in the novel also thematize captivity and its constitutive opposites – sovereignty, agency, and, we suggest, kinship – because from a Native perspective, 'the opposite of slavery was not freedom: the opposite of slavery was kinship' (Snyder, 2010: 5). Hogan's work suggests that kinship, rather than individualism, is the key to full humanity as well as social inclusion.

The prologue to Hogan's complexly narrated novel provides an indirect but unambiguous reference to the loss of Indian children. It recounts the ceremony Bush invents to honor and grieve the loss of the infant Angel, taken from her by social workers. The long history of Indian child removal – acts in which the state can be said to have orphaned children and culturally orphaned their relations – is subtly but powerfully reversed by the ceremony of loss, which paradoxically takes the form of a feast and results in the people of Adam's Rib incorporating both Bush, an outsider, and the lost Angel into their lives. The symbolic death of Angel, brought about by her removal, is transformed into a symbolic adoption, as everyone in the community leaves the feast willingly sharing the burden of Bush's sorrow: 'It was small now, and child-sized, and it slid its hand inside theirs and walked away with them. We all had it, after that. It became our own' (Hogan, 1995b: 18). In symbolically adopting the orphaned Angel, the people claim her, transforming her absence into a kind of presence, her loss into a reclamation that serves to bind the community. Thus, Bush's invented ceremony counters the danger of social and cultural dissolution that is historically so strongly linked to Indian communities' loss of children. The prologue invokes but simultaneously resists captivity and orphanhood.[26]

The abundant tropes of captivity in *Solar Storms* link captivity to orphanhood, but also to land dispossession and, ultimately, to cultural dispossession and genocide. Pazicky, writing about the legal construction of Native Americans as wards (i.e. orphaned children) of the state in the 1830s, notes that Indians gave their land the attributes of parents, and that dispossession 'mirrored their treatment as real and cultural orphans' (1998: 104). For Hogan, the disruption of kinship parallels the disruption of ties to the environment, and she persistently associates the dissolution or perversion of maternal bonds to the conquest and exploitation of the land. Through flashbacks, readers learn that Loretta, Angel's grandmother, 'the one who hurt others,' abuses her child, Hannah, because she has witnessed 'the desperate people of her tribe' die of starvation or poison from eating poisoned deer meat used by settlers to bait wolves (Hogan, 1995b: 39). The abused and abandoned

Hannah, whom Bush finds in ice-cold water, horribly scarred and near death, is a tormented child. She is represented as incapable of rest, pacing through the night, 'the way an animal or man might sound in a room, closed in, in a jail' (*ibid.*: 101), and when she disappears from her community, she lives with a man who keeps caged animals that 'would cry at night like humans' (*ibid.*: 77). Returning to Adam's Rib to give birth to Angel, she perpetuates the familial pattern by abusing and disfiguring her infant, leaving Angel out in the snow to die. Hannah is 'more ruined than the land' (*ibid.*: 231), and as Angel learns about this history, she reflects: 'We were shaped out of this land by the hands of gods. Or maybe it was that we embodied the land. And in some way I could not yet comprehend, it also embodied my mother, both of them stripped and torn' (*ibid.*: 228). Through Loretta and particularly through Hannah, Hogan compares the abuse of Native women to the exploitation of the land.

Ultimately, Hannah is represented as possessed – another form of captivity. Suffering from loss of soul, Hannah is a *windigo* figure, a demon-like figure from Cree and Ojibwe mythology which is strongly associated (as is Loretta) with gnawing cold, starvation, and cannibalism.[27] Simultaneously, she is the embodiment of the horrors of colonial history, which the novel figures in terms of scars.[28] When, shortly after finding the ten-year-old child, Bush insists on bathing her, she finds that: 'Beneath all the layers of clothes, [Hannah's] skin was a garment of scars. There were burns and incisions. Like someone had written on her. The signatures of torturers ...' (*ibid.*: 99). Hogan describes this macabre personal history and the obvious, irredeemable damage it causes Hannah as 'memory,' but also as a place, a house, a crossroad, 'where time and history and genocide gather' (*ibid.*: 101). In this and other ways, Hannah's loss of soul, her 'bad spirit' and 'heart of ice' (*ibid.*: 98), is connected to Native myth and also 'explained' in terms of the larger history of conquest, in which the devouring greed of the colonizers devastates the land and the Native peoples who live there. Moreover, Hogan's linking of practices of scarring and writing provides a horrendous twist to the Lockean notion of children as *tabula rasa*. If Hannah's child's body is a blank slate, *Solar Storms* figures its 'blankness' as the vulnerability of Native peoples to sadistic exercises of imperialist power, and its social formation as a deformation through the historical evils of conquest.[29] To the extent that Hannah represents the history of North American indigenous peoples, her Indian childhood is not empty but full; she embodies trauma and its silent yet graphic history. Hannah's scarred body, claimed and 'signed by torturers,' records a legacy of colonial abuse of indigenous women.

Rendered incapable of forming bonds of kinship, Hannah remains enthralled to this historical trauma and first repudiates, then bites, tortures, and scars her infant daughter, Angel. When Angel is removed from Bush's care by white social workers, she repeatedly runs away from the series of foster homes in which she is placed. In her representation of these escapes, Hogan references but reverses the power relations in traditional tales of captivity by stressing Angel's status first as victim but then as an agent who effects her own escape, return, and empowerment through the reclamation of kinship.

Angel returns to her birth community as a teenager, searching for her origins, for beginnings, for the inauguration of her personal history. Her great-grandmother Agnes struggles to account for this, linking personal history, particularly maternal history, to the history of indigenous people in North America: 'I don't know where the beginning was, your story, ours. Maybe it came down in the milk of the mothers. Old man said it was in the train tracks ... It might have started when the crying children were taken away from their mothers or when the logging camps started and cities were built from our woods ...' (ibid.: 40). Angel's well-being will finally depend upon her ability to reclaim kinship with the land and with her mother. Angel comes to understand that, 'My beginning was Hannah's beginning, one of broken lives, gone animals, trees felled and kindled. Our beginnings were intricately bound up in the history of the land' (ibid.: 96). It is this understanding which empowers Angel. She is presented as a turning point in a long history of environmental exploitation, sexual victimization, and internalized self-hatred which Hogan attributes primarily to the violence of colonialism in its historical and current forms. Angel's story becomes one of survivance: 'Like me, it was native land and it had survived' (ibid.: 224).

Angel is called 'the girl who would return' (ibid.: 31), and indeed, as we have seen, *Solar Storms* reverses the traditional opening of a captivity narrative by beginning with the escaped captive coming home to Adam's Rib. There, Angel learns about an earlier return. Set out in the snow by her mother to die, Angel is found by Bush, who puts the freezing infant under her shirt. Bush tells Angel, '*You searched out warmth. You wanted to live. You were tiny, you were cold, and you wanted to live*' (ibid.: 113, original emphasis). In *Solar Storms* the desire to live and the will to act are strong forces, and Hogan's novel invests Angel with an agency far greater than that routinely attributed to the role of captive victim or of vanishing American.[30] Her return is an effort to 'remake' herself (ibid.: 106), for, as she puts it, 'I was at the end of my life in one America, and ... this end was also a beginning' (ibid.: 26). Again, Hogan reworks the captivity pattern, as Angel foresees her rebirth into Indian ways. Rejecting her condition as a captive of foster care, Angel takes on a new identity as the girl who comes back home. She increasingly defines herself by way of her kinship relations as well as her own gifts and actions.

Agency is represented not only in Angel's actions, but also through her narrative voice. Unlike Kingsolver's Turtle, Hogan's orphan is old enough to tell her own story. Most of the novel is Angel's first-person narration, emphasizing her agency, but she surrenders narration at significant junctures. Angel opens the prologue, for instance, but quickly gives voice to her grandmother Agnes's first-person account. In this way, the prologue signifies on traditional captivity tales, which were often prefaced by editors who sought to frame the captive's experiences. Such editorializing sought to discipline both captives and readers, in part by ascribing the status of victim to women narrators. The prologue to *Solar Storms*, then, conjures up the preface to the captivity narrative but substitutes an editorial voice with an indigenous one. Angel's words open the preface, 'Sometimes now I hear the voice of my great-grandmother, Agnes. It floats toward me like a soft breeze through an open window' (ibid.: 11), but the narrator then yields respectfully to another teller, giving presence to, rather than silencing or appropriating, the voice of a loved and respected elder, Agnes.

Captivity narratives in the 'selective tradition' sometimes emphasize the hardships that captives undergo in their transformative acculturation: 'This process of transformation in the captivity experience involves first a ritual initiatory ordeal, followed by a gradual accommodation of Indian modes and customs ...' (VanDerBeets, 1984: 43). The transformative experience narrated in the second part of *Solar Storms* provides an ironic twist to this pattern of acculturation. Angel, Bush, Dora-Rouge, and Agnes travel by canoe through the endangered boundary waters to ancestral lands, each in pursuit of a private, but shared, meaning. The journey that the four women undertake reverses colonial settlement: 'we were undoing the routes of explorers, taking apart the advance of commerce, narrowing down and distilling the truth out of history' (Hogan, 1995b: 176). This journey becomes a vision quest with profoundly transformational effects, for the women all recover the spiritually informed indigenous knowledge of the living world that is otherwise under siege by Euro-American 'civilization' as exemplified in the novel by the dam project. Yet, because the women are 'already' Indian, the transformation becomes instead a reclamation of Native kinship and indigenous ways of life, and a performance of Native sovereignty.

In most indigenous frameworks, kinship is not only a term for human relations to other humans, but it also refers to human relations to the non-human world. Individual, communal, and world health involves attentive maintenance of these relations. Broken relations are healed by way of story and ceremony. In an essay describing a sweat lodge ceremony, Hogan explains: 'It is part of a healing and restoration ... The participants in a ceremony say the words "All my relations" before and after we pray; those words create a relationship with other people, with animals, with the land. To have health it is necessary to keep all these relations in mind' (1995a: 40). Similarly, in *Solar Storms*, the journey through the boundary waters becomes a ceremony of healing and restoration for Angel because it is during this journey that she affirms kinship with her grandmothers and with creation beyond the boundaries of family, nation, or tribe.[31] Angel reflects that after a time 'our arms were strong and we were articulate in the languages of land, water, animal, even in the harder languages of one another. I'd entered waters and swamps, been changed by them. I'd dreamed medicines' (Hogan, 1995b: 193). Though Angel cannot gather those medicines in time to save Agnes, who becomes gravely ill during their journey, the novel presents her death as part of the cycle of rebirth and continuation that the women come to understand.[32]

The last section of the novel stages an ironic disruption of captivity patterns, as Angel participates in the struggle to protect the boundary waters and the ways of life connected with them. While the boundary waters lie on the border between two nations, Canada and the USA, they are depicted as obscuring that border. Poring over maps with Bush, Angel notes that 'land refused to be shaped by the makers of maps,' and beavers are 'true makers of land' who create geographies through their dam building (*ibid.*: 123). When government and corporate interests unite to build a dam for a new hydroelectric plant, however, massive flooding occurs, displacing people and their villages, radically altering the landscape, and destroying wildlife. Ironically, attempts to regulate water inadvertently create a new, frontier-like space and transform the area to a state of continental wilderness.[33]

Traditional captivity narratives are also set on the frontier, but a frontier typically conceptualized by Euro-American writers in the binary terms of civilized and uncivilized space. Though scholars have shown that the western frontier was in fact a highly ambiguous territory of multicultural encounter and exchange, captivity narratives tend to demarcate and uphold a geographical but also highly symbolic boundary between civilization and savagery, self and other. Peter Alan Froehlich and Joy Harris Philpott summarize that 'In reinforcing colonial America's resistance to diversity, in defining violence as the only acceptable means of acculturation ... and in establishing a hostile relationship to the environment ... , the captivity narrative contributes to the frontier's legacy of individualism, isolationism, racism, and environmental degradation ...' (Froehlich and Philpott, 2001: 100). Dora-Rouge describes the legacy of Europeans in related terms, as 'the removal of spirit from everything' (Hogan, 1995b: 180). In the final section of the novel, the flooded waters and new-formed land become a different kind of frontier for a different kind of 'Indian War' – one waged to prevent the destruction of the environment and Native ways of life. In this way *Solar Storms* ends where traditional captivity narratives begin: with battle and Native resistance to non-Native dominance. In this implicitly ironic fiction, however, the battle ends not in individual captivity but in group survivance, in regeneration through kinship and acts of Native resistance.

In face of the threat of corporate and government plans for hydro-electric power, Dora-Rouge wonders: 'how do conquered people get back their lives?' Connecting survivance and sovereignty to kinship and resistance, she knows that 'protest against the dams and river diversions was their only hope. Those who protested were the ones who could still believe they might survive as a people' (*ibid*.: 226). Indigenous notions of kinship and relatedness provide a conceptual framework for understanding the failures of Euro-American power; Angel understands, for instance, that 'when the officials and attorneys spoke, their language didn't hold a thought for the life of water, or a regard for the land that sustained people from the beginning of time. They didn't remember the sacred treaties between humans and animals' (*ibid*.: 279). Though the novel dramatizes internal dissension and debates over the best methods of resistance, the exercise of individual and group agency is shown to be crucial to the spirit that animates a Native presence. Angel, who gains in confidence as she works to enhance group agency and survival, explains: 'For my people, the problem has always been this: that the only possibility of survival has been resistance. Not to strike back has meant certain loss and death. To strike back has also meant loss and death, only with a fighting chance. To fight has meant that we can respect ourselves ...' (*ibid.*: 325). Although *Solar Storms* ultimately renounces violence, it emphasizes through the wisdom of tribal elder Tulik that resistance is indeed essential to maintaining a Native identity: 'he knew that this fight would be forever, that it would never end, but he knew, also, that he was in it and would always be' (*ibid.*: 328). The unusual syntax of this sentence (as opposed to the usual phrasing, 'and always would be') suggests in microcosm, as Hogan's novel does overall, that not only Native sovereignty but also the process of being is located in and dependent upon resistance to exploitation and subjugation.

Hogan's strategic reversal of the narrative structure of the captivity genre emphasizes Native survivance, particularly through the agency of the orphan who returns to claim kinship and make home. Agency is highlighted in each part of the novel – in Angel's return to her birth community, in the voyage of four generations of women, and in the stand they take as a community to protect the land from 'civilization' and 'progress.' By the end of the narrative Angel can state, 'I've shaped my own life, after all. Like a deer curled into grasses, or the place a moose slept' (*ibid.*: 346). The imagery is striking because it suggests human will and action in harmony with and sheltered by the natural world. The images are peaceful, evoking deep quiet. Unlike the aggressive, power-wielding actions of the dam builders, Angel's actions are respectful of the environment, demonstrating that kinship with creation 'isn't a static thing; it's dynamic, ever in motion. It requires attentiveness ...' (Justice, 2008: 150). Hogan's images emphasize that kinship can best be achieved in a non-intrusive exercise of agency, and it does not require the subjugation of others in order to function.

Solar Storms's representation of Native agency counters stereotypical representations of Native Americans as a vanishing race, tied hopelessly to the past, and doomed to extinction. Angel puts it thus:

> To others, we were such insignificant people. In their minds we were only a remnant of a past. They romanticized this past in fantasy, sometimes even wanted to bring it back for themselves, but they despised our real

human presence. Their men, even their children, had entered forests, pretended to be us, imagined our lives, but now we were present, alive, a force to be reckoned with. (Hogan, 1995b: 343)

In particular, Hogan's representation of Indian orphans allows her to represent what Justice calls 'the decolonization imperative,' a demonstration of continuity from the past into the present, extending into a Native future (Justice, 2008: 150). This extension into the future is represented by the novel's final orphan, Angel's half-sister, Aurora. Angel rescues her when she finally finds her mother Hannah who, though already near death, has set the infant outside to die, just as she once had tried to kill Angel. But unlike Angel, who is taken by social workers from Bush and her birth community as an infant, Aurora is restored to a Native community and grows into a happy baby, 'the child of many parents' (Hogan, 1995b: 264) who the people refer to as 'Our Future' (ibid.: 318). The fictional tribe sees in her their ancestors, so she is called 'grandfather' and is respected as an elder (ibid.: 258). Thus, Aurora, like other children in literature, functions as a symbol of regeneration. The novel ends, countering captivity, in a ritualized performance of regeneration through kinship, with Angel and her boyfriend Tommy in a marriage dance, holding Aurora high and showing her off, thereby incorporating her into an indigenous community.

The Indian orphan is central to Hogan's radical reworking of the traditional American captivity narrative. *Solar Storms* replaces the orphan as a figure for historical trauma and victimization with a new figure of survivance and hope. In short, the narrative thrust of *Solar Storms* describes a movement from woundedness to health, from victimhood to agency, from captivity to kinship. As Bush tells Angel, 'Some people see scars and it is wounding they remember. To me they are proof of the fact that there is healing' (ibid.: 125). Regeneration, Hogan posits in this novel, requires the active reclamation of kinship. While Hogan anchors kinship in indigenous thought, she also explores kinship as an epistemological condition. Understanding connection, relation, and reciprocity is something that is socially transmitted, learned, and adopted in the novel. Angel learns to claim her difficult past and even to feel compassion for the mother who abuses her.[34] Throughout the novel, kinship with the natural world is envisioned as a deeply ethical relation, performed through solidarity, and proposed as a viable alternative to capitalist land exploitation.

This kinship community and the sovereign future are finally represented by the traditionally enacted marriage of one orphan, Angel, and the communal adoption of another, Aurora.

Crossing borders: Leslie Marmon Silko's *Gardens in the Dunes*

> Like the slaughter of the buffalo, the removal of Native American children to boarding schools was a calculated act of cultural genocide. ... But the calculations failed. (Silko, 1996: 179)

In Kingsolver's and Hogan's works, Indian orphans are key to their authors' explorations of the present and the future, of multicultural America and Native sovereignty, today and tomorrow. Leslie Marmon Silko's *Gardens in the Dunes* focuses instead upon the past, though like much historical fiction, as we explore in Chapter 5, the past illuminates important aspects of the present. This novel uses the orphan figure to rewrite histories of captivity and to reimagine kinship in a transracial and transnational perspective.[35]

Like Hogan, Silko uses orphan figures to conceptualize kinship, to advance a critique of Euro-American social practices, and to affirm indigenous lifestyles. The novel, set in the 1890s, is narrated in the third person, focalized through several characters, but most prominently through Indigo, the child of the fictitious Sand Lizard tribe in the American south-west. At the beginning of the novel, Indigo is 'orphaned' by war, first when her mother goes missing after an army raid on a Ghost Dance gathering, and later, after her grandmother dies, when she and her Sister Salt are forcibly taken from their desert lands and sent to Indian boarding school. Indigo escapes from the school, and is taken in by a newly married, highly educated white woman, Hattie, and her overbearing botanist husband, Edward. These three characters travel eastward through the USA and then Europe.[36] During their journey, the marriage undergoes a series of crises from which neither spouse can recover. Throughout, however, Indigo's sense of indigenous selfhood remains unshaken by the potentially assimilative pressures of boarding school, extensive travel in the US and Europe, and close interactions with white society.[37]

Critics have commented, though only in passing, on Silko's focus in *Gardens in the Dunes* on the child Indigo. The child's perspective has been said to 'endow the world with strangeness and newness' (Murray, 2007: 124), to foreground 'the visionary and prophetic aspects' of the Ghost Dance (*ibid*.: 129), to animate the novel with 'a fundamental optimism' (Moore, 2007: 95), and to raise the question of the suffering of the innocent – both children and Indians – because 'Indigo, though a child, stands in for a Native voice' (*ibid*.: 105). Indeed, in spite of the obvious hazards of equating a child's perspective with a Native perspective, this is what Silko does in her novel. It is, moreover, through the figure of the orphan child that Silko brings a Native perspective to bear on Euro-American ideas of patriarchy and imperialism of the late nineteenth century, launching a critique of the cultural eradication of indigenous peoples, as well as the values that result in the subjugation of women and exploitation of the environment. The novel posits that it is the colonial world of global capitalism represented by Edward's and others' schemes for botanical theft, profit, and environmental destruction that is truly a wasteland, a world in need of regeneration.[38] The child's innocent view elicits a critical perspective among readers more knowledgeable than the character Indigo of the histories of Indian–white relations in the late 1800s.

Indigo's orphan status provides special opportunities for Silko to rework these deplorable histories, for the novel quickly and effectively alludes to historical disruptions of indigenous kinship through Indian removal policies, boarding-school practices, religious persecution, and outright murder. Silko refuses to grant these traumatic histories decisive power over indigenous identity and thought. Early in the novel, for instance, the abduction of Indigo and Sister Salt by Indian agents is presented as a dehumanizing outrage: though she fights 'with all her strength' (Silko, 1999: 62) to resist being captured and sent to boarding school, Indigo is tied up in the same way as the mules are hobbled. With understated irony, the narrative reports that the Indian policemen 'knew from experience how fast these wild Indians could escape' (*ibid*.: 62), thus necessitating the bondage of a young girl. Such understated irony pays tribute to the resistance of Native peoples, even children, to assimilation and containment. The Apache scout talks of 'the Mojave and Chemehuevi children who ran away the instant he untied them' (*ibid*.: 63), and warns the sisters not to throw themselves from the wagon, because a previous captive child has been killed in that manner. Indigo knows, as does the scout, that 'the boy preferred death' to captivity in a boarding school (*ibid*.: 63). In this and other ways, Silko's narrative stresses a history of indomitable will and resistance: as David Moore puts it, *Gardens in the Dunes* 'retells the story of victimhood in ways that can envision surviving desperate changes' (2007: 109). It retells captivity in terms of escape.

In her reversals of captivity tales, Silko also affirms the solidarity between the two sisters, who immediately devise escape plans and do their utmost to stay together. However, they are separated when Sister Salt is thought to be beyond redemption, incorrigible: 'There was hope the little ones might be educated away from their blankets. But this one? Chances were she'd be a troublemaker and might urge the younger students to attempt escape' (Silko, 1999: 67). This is precisely what Sister Salt does, before the two are separated early in the novel.

Silko de-emphasizes Indigo's position as a victim and emphasizes her courage and her ability to deal with her situation at the boarding school. Sent to the Sherman Institute in Riverside, California, Indigo refuses to cry, she does not 'mind' the darkness of the closet in which she is locked, and she escapes from the school as quickly as possible, finding temporary shelter in Edward's and Hattie's garden. The notion of containing the 'wild Indian' recurs when Edward, holding a rope, approaches the child and his pet monkey, Linnaeus. His wife Hattie, who is suprprised to learn that the rope is for the child rather than for the monkey. Hattie dissuades Edward from taking Indigo captive, though he assures her that the rope is 'only a precaution – for the child's own good,' so that she does not run and lose herself in the desert, and he is assured in his confidence that 'Hattie had no experience with Indians – certainly not these wild Indians' (*ibid.*: 106). Edward's superior paternalism in this scene is matched only by his ignorance; though he identifies Indigo as 'one of those renegade bands of desert Indians,' 'a wild one' (*ibid.*: 107), Indigo tells Edward that she is able to speak English, 'way better than you talk Indian' (*ibid.*: 108) and, of course, as an inhabitant of the desert she hardly needs to be protected from it. Exercising as much rational thought and agency as she can, Indigo soon *chooses* to accompany Hattie and Edward east, considering it the best strategy for finding her lost mother and abducted sister, and for seeing the Messiah. Though Indigo's actions are externally circumscribed, her integrity remains intact and her determination grows in the course of her travels and her eventual return to her desert homeland.

Indigo's position as an outsider strongly rooted and secure in her indigenous identity affords her a critical perspective on the Euro-American practices she encounters. For example, the difference between the subsistence farming of the Sand Lizard tribe and the elaborate landscaping of New England estates emerges as stark. Indigo's openness to the world, her knowledge of plant life, and her desire to learn, prevent her from being judgmental about what she sees, yet her observations and experiences open a vantage point for readers to regard different ways of relating to the natural environment. Her perspective provides a location from which the novel explores a capitalist system of class privilege that drives consumption, exotic acquisition, and colonial appropriation. As one critic observes, 'Silko reverses the ethnographic gaze and produces an ethnography (or ethnoarchaeology) of "white" gardens that explores similarities and differences' (Isernhagen, 2003: 129).[39] Indeed, Silko uses Indian orphan figures – Indigo and to some degree Sister Salt – and a figure that embodies cultural orphanhood – Hattie – as the primary instruments of this reversal. At the end of the novel the fragile eco-system in the dunes has quietly regained its equilibrium, in spite of the deliberate destruction wrought by marauders and in spite of the addition of 'exotic' species; Grandma Fleet's apricot trees are sprouting anew, and Indigo's gladiolus corms provide nourishment as well as beauty in their new environment.

Gardens in the Dunes is full of unexpected reversals, and the turn involving Hattie is of great significance. While Indigo and her Sister Salt have been read as twin protagonists (Isernhagen, 2003), we consider it equally fruitful to consider how Silko pairs Indigo and Hattie to effect her imaginary border crossings and to explore an alternative to multiculturalism. Although Hattie ostensibly educates Indigo by teaching her to read and write, the novel is as much about the education of Hattie by Indigo. For example, when Hattie and Indigo are detained by Italian authorities because Edward has smuggled plant material, it is the child – simultaneously innocent and savvy – who assures a shocked Hattie that such ordeals can and will be survived: 'she told Hattie the stories about the times Grandma Fleet was caught by soldiers or by the Indian police, only to escape later; Mama even escaped Fort Yuma. ... Hattie mustn't be sad – at home people got arrested for no reason all the time. There was nothing to be ashamed of; this wasn't bad at all' (Silko, 1999: 322). This shift in perspective brings into relief the unjust treatment of Native Americans under US law, the genuine culpability of Edward and his boundless sense of entitlement, and also Hattie's vulnerability as a woman in a patriarchal system.

The steadfast certainty of Indigo is contrasted with the uncertainty of Hattie's position as she becomes figuratively orphaned. Sexually harassed and expelled from Harvard, exploited, betrayed, and bankrupted by Edward, Hattie becomes farther and farther removed from the values of her own community. When she finally returns Indigo to her sister Salt, helping to transform a tale of child removal into a tale of homecoming and liberation, she is overcome by 'a dreadful sense of how alone she was' (ibid.: 410), until she realizes that 'oddly enough, she was the one who no longer had a life to return to' (ibid.: 439). The phrase 'oddly enough' brings history to bear on the relationship between two 'orphans,' Indigo and Hattie, for it secures indigenous survivance against great odds. In addition, because of her association and solidarity with Indigo, she is seen by white settlers as a 'white squaw' (ibid.: 413). Without the protection of a husband, her travels on the American frontier become precarious, and she is raped, beaten, and left for dead. This also reverses patterns of Native barbarity and abduction, for although the townspeople blame the rape on Indians, Hattie's attacker is a white man, the 'sullen' driver of her wagon. Indians, by contrast, are her 'rescuers' (ibid.: 458), who 'dropped their rakes and hoes to run to help her' (ibid.: 457) when they see her walking naked and bloody along the road. After the rape, even her parents betray her in a tragic re-enactment of captivity. When they come to collect her after Edward has died and left her destitute, Hattie's parents find her in Native garb, believing in the Messiah of the Ghost Dance, and unwilling to return to white, middle-class society. She struggles with her parents, now her 'captors' who attempt to 'subdue her,' pretends to collapse, and then attempts 'to make a run for it' (ibid.: 471). Silko describes how 'the excitement of the escape gave her strength' (ibid.: 472), and Hattie burns down the town of Needles, which has conspired to protect her attacker, and runs away. Hattie leaves the USA for Europe because 'she could never return to her former life among the lies' (ibid.: 459), and from this distance she attempts to maintain her relationship with Indigo, who has at last made home with her sister and her sister's baby in their ancestral gardens. Hattie's experience of 'going native,' in other words, brings with it dire consequences, but also the recognition of her own culture as seriously flawed.

As in Hogan's work, it is a second child, Sister Salt's fatherless baby, who represents the continuity of indigenous life at the end of the novel. The infant, though 'racially' mixed, is unambiguously referred to as a Sand Lizard baby, suggesting that racial descent need not determine tribal belonging. In the womb, he speaks the Sand Lizard language and angrily repudiates the noise and greed of the camps. Born under inauspicious circumstances, the weak, tiny baby is nevertheless 'a tough customer who wouldn't die anytime soon' (*ibid.*: 342). Moreover, 'He was a serious baby who didn't smile often but who cried only when he was angry; wet or hungry, he remained silent because he was a grandfather and not someone new' (*ibid.*: 432). Thus, the infant referred to as 'the little black grandfather' symbolizes a delicate yet durable link between past, present, and future. By using this figure, and Indigo, to project the precarious continuation of the Sand Lizard tribe into the future, but equally important, by using Hattie to suggest the possibility of respectful exchange and reciprocal obligations, *Gardens in the Dunes* affirms the adaptive, performative, and inclusive aspects of indigenous kinship, which are so at odds with Euro-American values and practices in the novel. Recalling Silko's words from *Almanac of the Dead*, Euro-Americans might be considered 'orphan people' who have failed to remain whole because of their failure to recognize and honor various forms of kinship relation. Hattie is indeed *of* 'the orphan people,' but she paradoxically and painfully orphans herself from her society in pursuit of a life that is informed by values of indigenous kinship.

Silko's orphan tale, like that of Hogan, and in part those of Kingsolver, represents indigenous kinship as a dynamic process and an active practice. As Justice puts it, 'kinship is best thought of as a verb rather than a noun, because kinship, in most indigenous contexts, is something that's *done* more than something that simply is' (2008: 150). Hogan and Silko underscore the adaptive, performative, and potentially inclusive character of indigenous kinship through their creation of orphans like Angel and Indigo who make home as much as they find home, as well as through their creation of fictional tribes. In our view, the invention of the Fat Eater and the Sand Lizard tribes allows the authors not only to side-step the fraught issue of authenticity and to stymie artifactual readings of the novels, but also to suggest in indirect but important ways the possibilities that indigenous conceptions of kinship offer for both Native survivance and for the modern world.

Solar Storms and *Gardens in the Dunes* mobilize this concept of kinship through their use of orphan figures, which open up affirmative perspectives on Native knowledge and spirituality, and represent them as viable alternatives to other kinds of relations to the natural and social world. The dreams embodied in Angel and Indigo, and in Aurora and 'the little black grandfather' are dreams of participatory kinship. In the works of both writers, regeneration privileges indigenous identity and community first and foremost. Importantly, though, the regeneration through kinship that the novels envision is imagined and performative, unrestricted by tribal affiliations and at least theoretically open to others who are willing to join the 'fragile web of rights and responsibilities' (*ibid.*: 154) accruing to ethical relationships with all kin.

The figure of the child helps generate 'alternative national narratives' in fictions that enable, even as they threaten to rupture, 'the 'official story of America' (Levander, 2006: 53). To recast this story as a colonialist one, and to return indigenous peoples to its center, complicates the familiar narrative of multicultural America. This is what Moore means when he claims, 'Writing the Indian back into history is to interrupt America dreaming of itself' (2007: 102). As children, the Indian orphan figures bring an uncorrupted perspective to bear on the communities around them; like another literary orphan, Huckleberry Finn, they serve as a lens through which to critique aspects of Euro-American societies. As children, Indian orphans have a regenerative function. Again like Huck, they leave behind the corruption of mainstream America for an alternative, but unlike Twain's character, the wilderness they encounter is, in fact, home – the 'civilized' space of kinship relations, including ethical relations with the non-human environment.

Hogan's novel ends by affirming a vision of a future for Native peoples in North America: 'we'd thrown an anchor into the future and followed the rope to the end of it, to where we would dream new dreams, new medicines, and one day, once again, remember the sacredness of every living thing' (Hogan, 1995b: 344). The indigenous future imagined in *Gardens in the Dunes* evolves through transnational contact and exchange, but remains grounded in place and in indigenous kinship. Both Hogan and Silko signify on captivity and orphanhood, changing and enlivening each with imagery of Native survivance. Kingsolver, on the other hand, remains closely aligned with the frontier mythology. Although *The Bean Trees* struggles to affirm a multicultural America, and to some extent succeeds in doing so, traces of captivity and conventionalized representations of Indians seriously undermine that struggle. Her displacement of 'cultural orphanhood' onto Taylor in *Pigs in Heaven* mourns the loss of a 'place' for Taylor's distinctly American individualism and self-reliance. Silko might be said to make of Hattie a 'cultural orphan' as well, but Hattie's position outside Euro-American capitalism and patriarchy and in contact with Native America, contains no nostalgia. Thus, although an Indian orphan is present in, even crucial to, each of these three authors' dreams of community, their dreams are not equally compelling. Turtle's captivity, Taylor's loss of voice, and the contrived ending of *Pigs in Heaven* suggest an anxious uncertainty about white encounters with others in a multicultural America, while Angel's and Indigo's resistance to captivity, and the narrative reversal of the captivity narrative and its tropes, allow *Solar Storms* and *Gardens in the Dunes* to explore indigenous relations anew, extending them into a shared human future.

Notes

1 We use the terms 'Native,' 'indigenous,' and 'Indian' interchangeably. Though 'Indian' is clearly a white construct, and none of the terms conveys the diversity of Native identities, these terms mark positions and perspectives in the margins. 'Euro-American' and 'white' have similar drawbacks, but also advantages.
2 See Troy (2010b: 1116–18).
3 It has also had an impact on Native filmmakers. See, for instance, Georgina Lightning's film *Older than America* (2008), re-released as *American Evil* (2012), on the boarding-school legacy.
4 See Kathryn Shanley's comments on the reinforcement of 'the idea of an inevitable dominance by nonindigenous people' (2012: 82) in *Avatar* and Native fiction.
5 We use Vizenor's term throughout the text to indicate survival coupled with resistant endurance.
6 Women, lacking mobility, independence, and freedom outside the home, have long been marginalized in these genres. See Fagan (2001), Himmelwright (2007), and Michael (2006).
7 Callahan also compares the interracial adoptions in Kingsolver and Silko (Callahan, 2011: 110–21).
8 See Adams (1995), Child (2000), Lomawaima (1994), Skolnick and Skolnick (1997), and Zitkala-Sa (1921). Margaret D. Jacobs (2006) compares the USA and Australia, arguing that indigenous child removal, 1880–1940, was deliberately genocidal.
9 See Holt (2001). See also V. Carter (2009) on the CWLA's official apology for this policy in 1999.

10 See Ashby (1997: 143). Figures vary; Holt writes that in South Dakota in 1960, half of all children in foster care were Indian and, nationally, one out of every four Indian children was separated from family in the mid-1970s (Holt, 2001: 5). See also Briggs (2012: 79).

11 The Multi-Ethnic Placement Act of 1994 amended by the Removal of Barriers to Interethnic Adoption Provisions (IEP) of 1996 prohibits racial and ethnic 'matching' in placement decisions; the Indian Child Welfare Act is explicitly exempted from the provisions of this controversial act. Briggs (2012: 121–5) argues that the ICWA asserts political autonomy, not racial difference.

12 In reviewing the *Mississippi Band of Choctaw Indians vs Holyfield* in 1989, the Supreme Court affirmed the core of the ICWA (Duthu, 2008: 150–5).

13 See, for example, Pazicky's discussions of Crèvecoeur (1998: 76–80) and James Fenimore Cooper (*ibid.*: 99–109) for nationalist anxieties and fantasies played out in early American writings.

14 Castiglia discusses the borders of the genre as imposed by ministers and editors; he finds greater variation in narrative structure than definitions by Roy Harvey Pearce, Richard VanDerBeets, and Slotkin suggest. See Castiglia (1996: 19–33).

15 The foreword to Castiglia's study (1996) reports that about 60 of 723 known female captives chose to stay with their Native captors. See Seaver's *A Narrative of the Life of Mrs. Mary Jemison* (1823) for one such account.

16 The story of Lost Bird, infant survivor of Wounded Knee (1890) taken captive/adopted by General Colby and his suffragist wife Clara, is recounted by Flood (1998).

17 See Jack Butler's review (Butler, 1988) and Wagner-Martin (2003).

18 It is fascinating that Michael explicitly excludes *Solar Storms* from her analysis of new visions of community on the grounds that it asserts nationalistic concepts such as sovereignty (2006: 75–6).

19 See Godfrey (2001) on the ways Kingsolver idealizes and essentializes Native American community.

20 See Fagan (2001) and Novy (2001), who disagree slightly on the ending. For Novy, it encourages readers to consider issues of adoption and to imagine a functioning multicultural society. Fagan finds Kingsolver misrepresenting issues of non-Native adoption of Indians and issues of multiculturalism in the USA, and she notes that the conflict is resolved on an individual basis, despite an emphasis on community (2001: 260). Callahan identifies an irony in adoption being the novel's 'central conflict and its ideal solution' (2011: 118).

21 Claudia Castañeda, whose analysis of how the race and the history of the child figure are evacuated in transnational adoption practices was discussed in Chapter 1, argues that 'When global relatedness is envisioned

through the child, this vision should also be accountable to the child and to the history of the adult uses of the child' (2002: 295).
22 See Krupat on the turn towards cosmopolitanism (2003: 91), Huhndorf (2001) on the shift towards the transnational, and Weaver, Womack, and Warrior (2005) on literary nationalism.
23 The volume of Native criticism *Reasoning Together* (Womack, Justice, and Teuton, 2008) builds upon and extends Warrior's influential notion of intellectual sovereignty.
24 Jim Tarter (2000) examines Hogan's novel in light of the (semi-) successful resistance to the James Bay Hydro-Quebec project. Barbara Cook comments on Hogan's use of a setting that is 'both Quebec and the Boundary Waters and at the same time neither' (2003: 43).
25 See, for example, Adamcyk (2001) on Lost Bird, or Froehlich and Philpott (2001) on Silko's *Ceremony*.
26 Tales of captivity embedded in Hogan's novel reverse the conventional position of civilized and savage. Dora-Rouge's tale of Indian boarding schools illustrates the idea that such schools did indeed provide, as historian David Wallace Adams (1995) describes, an 'education for extinction.' Moreover, embedded stories of animal captivity in *Solar Storms* (as in all of Hogan's work) draw parallels to human captivity, and they establish a commonality between native humans and animals.
27 Laura Castor discusses Hogan's use of this figure to create a site of healing for Angel, but also for 'global manifestations of *windigo*' (2006: 173). Fisher-Wirth observes that Hannah is modeled on one of Hogan's adopted daughters, Marie (2003: 61). Hogan's painful account of adoption appears in *The Woman Who Watches Over the World* (2001).
28 See Arnold (2007) for a discussion of how Hogan uses the imagery of scars and mirrors to revise Lacanian theory.
29 Karen Sánchez-Eppler (2005) has shown how different conceptions of childhood co-existed in nineteenth-century America, including the Calvinist idea of children as sinful, the Lockean idea of children as blank slates, and the romantic notion of children as natural, innocent beings. Claudia Nelson (2003) characterizes childhood in modernity as gaining in emotional value to adults. In Hogan and Silko children are portrayed both as individuals *and* as re-incarnations of ancestors.
30 Griffin writes that 'the fundamental lesson of captivity [is that] the captive is utterly dependent upon the sovereign will of her captor; she has no volition of her own' (1986: 44). Castiglia (1996), Strong (1999), and Snyder (2010) emphasize how Euro-American captives sought to negotiate their positions.
31 Hogan's novel, *Power* (1998), involves a similar ritual journey. In both novels, the protagonists take on positions outside of mainstream society,

but *Power* involves a greater, uncompromising distance from non-Native culture.

32 Agency is also asserted in death, as characters like Agnes and Dora Rouge embrace their own deaths in harmony with Native tradition (Hogan, 1995b: 188; 348–9).

33 Another irony is that the changed landscape sparks a return to indigenous epistemology, a central preoccupation of Hogan's work, seen also in how Agnes's lover, John Husk, and Bush, syncretize Native and Western sciences.

34 Other figures in the novel learn and practice ethical relations: LaRue, for instance, whose name suggests regret, gives up the practice of taxidermy and learns instead to value living creation, and Bush, who assembles bones of animals, describes her work as a practice of respect.

35 Huhndorf identifies a shift towards the transnational which she exemplifies with the 'different emphases' (2009: 15) of Silko's early *Ceremony*, which 'puts the community at the center of indigenous resistance,' and later *Almanac of the Dead*, which 'finds revolutionary possibilities in transnational alliances ... ' (*ibid.*: 15). Arnold Krupat considers *Gardens* to be informed by a syncretic, cosmopolitan worldview, and Hogan's work to be more in line with an 'indigenous' perspective (2003).

36 See A. LaVonne Brown Ruoff (2007) and A.M. Regier on Salt as intertextual or intercultural reference. Regier views Hattie as a character inspired by Margaret Fuller and Alice James (2005: 144, 146).

37 Indigo and Sister Salt are forcibly 'orphaned' by removal from tribe and family, but they are still 'entirely secure in their Indian identities' (Krupat, 2002: 113). David Murray also situates Silko's novel in a general move toward 'hybridity and transnationalism' (2007: 119).

38 Commentary on Silko's novel has examined representations of gardening practices and her understanding of hybridity. See Terre Ryan on Silko's contrast between settler and indigenous land practices, the latter reaffirming 'the authority of Native lifeways ...' (T. Ryan, 2007: 116).

39 See Regier on ghost dancing and transculturation; she argues that Silko rewrites previous anthropological accounts of the prophet Wovoka, the Messiah, and thus transforms the 'intellectual capture' (2005: 137) of the prophet into the revolutionary capability of transcultural encounters.

3

Literary kinships: Euro-American orphans, gender, genre, and cultural memory

> The writers I most consciously respond to are the nineteenth-century American writers like Melville, Dickinson, Poe, and Twain. (Robinson, 1992: 157)

Though literary orphanhood has carried different meanings in different historical periods, it has often worked as a prism, refracting and reflecting ideas about national identity and belonging. The canonization of orphan tales and the popularity of genres featuring literal or metaphorical orphans, particularly in the nineteenth century, along with the later invention of an American literary tradition departing from such works, have made literary orphans integral to US cultural memory. Literary criticism and literature are sites of memory construction and memory maintenance that contribute to a collective memory in the USA, and to constructing the nation as a 'mnemonic community' (Misztal, 2003: 15). Literary kinship and continuity, in other words, tend to support collective ideas about what it means to be 'American'.

The intimate links between literature, literary criticism, and national identity explain the impassioned and sometimes embittered controversies concerning American literature during the so-called 'culture wars' of the 1990s. As Gregory S. Jay points out in his historicizing analysis of struggles for representation, multiculturalism, and curricular innovation, 'the institutional history of American literary studies is closely tied to the history of American nationalism' (1997: 177). But literary canons have always been shaped and reformed by competing forces and ideologies, and such struggles for representation – which literary texts stage or bear traces of – generate changes in the curricular and cultural ground. Fiction has come to have important functions in the recovery work undertaken by feminist literary critics, and in the memory work of ethnic minorities whose histories include being treated as cultural orphans in the USA, as explored in Chapter 2 on Native American orphans. Many writers and critics have turned to literary texts outside the established canon as archives of counter-memories, generating in the process new critical perspectives on literary and social values, including changing ideas about writing in the USA and about the borders or legitimacy of American Studies. Writers and critics have also revisited earlier genres and works to explore these changing ideas.

The contemporary novels featuring white orphans that we examine in this chapter engage intertextually with the Euro-American canon, claiming a type of literary kinship, at the same time as they draw upon a feminist counter-tradition as a form of recovered cultural memory. In this chapter, we investigate Marilynne Robinson's *Housekeeping* (1981), a novel that features two white female orphans and that is steeped in allusions to canonical literature and critical traditions. We also analyze Michael Cunningham's *Specimen Days* (2005) and Jonathan Safran Foer's *Extremely Loud and Incredibly Close* (2005), two novels that have been termed 'post-9/11 narratives.' In Cunningham's novel, Walt Whitman figures prominently in the past, present, and future, while Foer's novel, we argue, revisits the nineteenth-century sentimental novel. These novels engage aesthetically and ideologically with genres,[1] critical traditions, and particular canonical texts as cultural memory by using the orphan figure. We investigate how these contemporary orphan tales activate connections between national identity and the traditions of literary history and criticism, and how they challenge biases of gender, class, and to some extent race, even as they also partly re-inscribe them. *Housekeeping*, *Specimen Days*, and *Extremely Loud and Incredibly Close* critique the nuclear family ideal and respond to the ostensible dissolution of the American literary canon – the result of, among other things, feminism and multiculturalism – and the representational crisis many US critics have claimed was triggered by 9/11.[2] We explore how these novels negotiate Euro-American literary history, both in their employment of genres and their representations of orphans.

The capacity of the orphan character to represent various ideological concerns is demonstrated by the differences between earlier and current uses of this figure. Therefore, we provide a brief overview of the diverse functions of white orphans across American literature, specifically in the texts to which the Euro-American orphans in contemporary novels relate in various ways, focusing particularly on issues of gender and class privilege. Against the relatively solid gender entrenchment of analyses of girl and boy orphans in US literary history, we foreground how dichotomous gendered trajectories have been problematized by feminist scholars, especially since the 1980s. We trace Euro-American girl and boy orphans in genres that have been dominant forms for telling orphan stories: the *bildungsroman*, the domestic or sentimental novel, and the picaresque narrative. As in the case of the Indian captivity narrative, genres constitute a particular kind of cultural memory that has ideological as well as narrative implications. The *bildungsroman* and the sentimental novel are imbued with white bourgeois values, whereas the picaresque is often a reaction against these values, even as it registers them through the picaro's interaction with different social classes. A prominent literary motif in American literary traditions is the quest, whether social, material, emotional, or spiritual. Traditionally based on a strictly male and patriarchal pattern (Heller, 1990: 3–4, 11), the quest motif is reworked in different ways in the contemporary novels we investigate in this chapter.

In the nineteenth century, orphan stories proliferated across literary genres. The white orphan boy, embodied in characters ranging from Tom Sawyer to Horatio Alger's Ragged Dick, has often been interpreted as a reinforcement of ideas about a specifically American masculinity, marked by individualism and a resistance to family and domesticity. White orphan girls, such as Ellen in Susan Warner's *The Wide, Wide World* (1850) and Gerty in Maria Cummins's *The Lamplighter* (1854), are just as common as orphan boys in nineteenth-century American literature, yet have not figured as prominently in literary history. This is partly because they have typically appeared in genres like the domestic novel that were devalued until the last decades of the twentieth century.[3] By the same token, sentimentality has been regarded as a strictly gendered mode by literary critics, linked above all to femininity and the 'popular,' and thus different from purportedly serious literature.[4] This critical convention is based on an 'aesthetic of restraint' (Shamir and Travis, 2002: 15) that persists in spite of studies in past decades that have investigated links between masculinity, emotion, and sentimentality, and in spite of feminist attempts at 'rehabilitating the sentimental.'[5]

Both girl and boy orphan stories can be read as countering anxieties in the nineteenth century concerning the role of children in US society, and exploring the ideological struggle between social constraint and personal freedom. Diana Loercher Pazicky, for example, observes that

> the fictional orphan can be viewed as a reaction to middle-class anxiety about change, loss, and poverty; in short, about the precariousness of social identity in a rapidly changing world. Within this context, the formula of loss and recovery represents a symbolic effort to allay anxiety, and the orphan serves as a representative of the status quo insofar as the novels, in repeating the same formula, reiterate the fantasy of middle-class stability. (Pazicky, 1998: 150)

It is the nineteenth-century Euro-American tales of orphan girls that have typically been thought to bolster white middle-class values, even though classic stories of orphan boys also contribute to upholding socially accepted middle-class values such as individual industry and self-reliance. In a similar manner, classic boy orphans have more affinity with ideas about family and domesticity than might be expected. Contemporary novelists, we show, appropriate the white orphan figure in literary history to (re)negotiate gendered boundaries of adventure, quest, domesticity, and sentimentality. These novels relate to discourses – in fiction as well as in literary criticism – on earlier girl and boy orphans, and they also claim kinship with specific literary genres in which orphans have typically appeared.

A major genre for earlier orphan stories – and one we return to in Chapter 4 – is the *bildungsroman*. Definitions of this genre have traditionally built on novels about a white male protagonist's education and experience from boyhood to his coming of age. In the 1980s, however, nineteenth-century and early twentieth-century American orphan fictions with female protagonists figured in feminist critical reconsiderations of the *bildungsroman* that foregrounded the significance of gender difference.[6] In a 1984 article, Beverly R. Voloshin highlights the tension in nineteenth-century novels between independence and self-reliance, on the one hand, and the ideology of domesticity, on the other. Voloshin argues that the girl orphan is 'an extreme version of the American individual,' who 'generally internalize[s], at least for a time, the values of self-reliance, of liberal individualism, which the dominant culture valued in men' (1984: 298). However, the ending of the female *bildungsroman* usually mutes or contains the conflict between these values and those of the ideology of domesticity by reintegrating the girl orphan into society, typically through marriage, thus confirming a class bias and idealizing domesticity in a socially conservative manner (*ibid*.: 299).

In 1987 Eve Kornfeld and Susan Jackson arrived at a slightly different conclusion about the female *bildungsroman* as a sub-category of the domestic novel. They argue that traditional masculine qualities are not valued in what they call 'these matriarchal utopias,' where male characters are frequently feminized.[7] Spinsters are often put in a positive light, while marriage is not. In spite of these subversive elements, however, the heroines are still 'precluded from entering [a] male world fully and finally' (Kornfeld and Jackson, 1987: 74). Although attentive to the limits of subversion and gender transgression, feminist criticism in the 1980s began to undo the formerly strict dichotomization of the trajectories of male and female orphans in literary criticism, and to problematize generic conventions in American literature.

In addition to being located in the catch-all category of the 'female *bildungsroman*,' novels about female orphans have been variously termed 'domestic fictions' and 'sentimental novels.' Although there is no absolute consensus about the boundaries between these genres, it might be said that the domestic setting defines the former, whereas the emphasis on sentiment or affect defines the latter (Howard, 2001: 231). The orphan tale provides 'the dominant plot formula in women's sentimental fiction during the 1850s,' writes Pazicky, and it 'enacts a middle-class fantasy of loss and recovery in fictional form' (Pazicky, 1998: xvi). Poverty is often a factor for female orphans in nineteenth-century sentimental novels, but only temporarily, for they eventually find the 'right family' and wealth, too, in the end. In treating poverty as 'a temporary obstacle rather than an ineluctable condition,' mid-nineteenth-century sentimental fiction betrays that it is firmly grounded in capitalist ideology (*ibid*.: 150).

Unlike the critically marginalized sentimental novel, the picaresque, typically featuring a male protagonist, is a popular 'orphan genre' that has been regarded as central to the development of American literature. Indeed, although often figuring in discussions of the American *bildungsroman*, *Adventures of Huckleberry Finn* more closely resembles a textbook example of the picaresque. One group of critics enumerates seven 'chief qualities' of this genre, and most, if not all, are evident in Twain's novel: it is told in the first person; the 'chief figure is drawn from a low social level'; the novel is episodic rather than tightly plotted; there is little or no character development; the style of the story is realistic; satire is an important element of the picaresque and the *picaro* meets people from every social class; the hero is a rascal but 'usually stops just short of being an actual criminal' (Thrall, Hibbard and Holman, 1960: 352–3). Twain's novel represents a protagonist who is an innocent, who journeys between social strata, takes on different roles in relation to different 'masters,' and whose trajectory is circular rather than linear (Guillen, 1971: 81–5).

Deeply connected to the picaresque as well as to the *bildungsroman* is the figure of the American Adam, the male orphan who escapes from family and hence from history, that has been so central to understandings of American fiction since the 1950s. For example, Kenneth Millard links R.W.B. Lewis's idea of the American Adam to the *bildungsroman* form to suggest that this genre has enjoyed 'a unique position in terms of national identity because of the ways that it appropriates and refurbishes that mythology for its own contemporary purposes' (2007: 6). We maintain, though, that contemporary orphan novels draw on a number of different literary genres in order to question the viability of the American Adam, even as they endow this figure with new meanings.

In the following sections, we examine *Housekeeping*, *Specimen Days*, and *Extremely Loud and Incredibly Close* and the particular processes that white orphan characters are involved in: processes of inclusion, exclusion, recentering, and critique. We argue that contemporary orphan stories renegotiate conventional gender divides in the American quest or picaresque, the *bildungsroman*, and domestic or sentimental fiction, for in these novels the trajectories of boy and girl orphans entail a repositioning in terms of gender and genre. In claiming literary kinship with earlier genres, they draw on cultural memory but also challenge central American myths.

Girl orphans with and against traditions: Marilynne Robinson's *Housekeeping*

> Whereas the dominant tradition portrays the male individualist in flight from society, the women writers did not visualize a world without society. Thus, while the dominant masculine tradition focused on the insularity of the individual, the women writers portrayed characters that were enmeshed in a community of interpersonal relationships.
> (Warren, 1993: 11)

Marilynne Robinson's novels are all concerned with family and domestic situations, as signaled by the titles of her first and third novels: *Housekeeping* (1981)[8] and *Home* (2008). The novels are set in the 1950s, and complicate the image of the nuclear family in different and very precise ways. Her second novel, *Gilead* (2004), details an aged father's letter to his very young son that he hopes the son will read in the future. Age and age differences – between husband and wife, father and son – cause this fatherly narrator to express a number of anxieties about family as an institution and a responsibility. *Home* returns to the setting and characters of *Gilead*, but focuses on a neighboring family with another aging father who is also a widower. This novel goes further in its exploration of family; it can be seen as elaborating on the definition of family that Robinson posits in her 1998 essay titled 'Family':

> one's family are those toward whom one feels loyalty and obligation, and/or from whom one derives identity, and/or to whom one gives identity, and/or with whom one shares habits, tastes, stories, customs, memories. This definition allows for families of circumstance and affinity as well as kinship, and it allows also for the existence of people who are incapable of family, though they may have parents and siblings and spouses and children. (Robinson, 2005: 87)

Glory, one of two returning middle-aged children in *Home*, and the focalizing character, highlights the strains and costs of this type of loyalty and obligation, whereas her brother Jack – though a son, brother, husband, and father – appears to be 'incapable of family.' From childhood he experiences a strong sense of orphanhood and alienation even with family and home. Both *Gilead* and *Home* also criticize the limitations of the American family in the 1950s, specifically in terms of race relations, as Jack feels unable to start a new life with his African American wife and their son in the small town of Gilead, despite its Abolitionist history.

Orphanhood and its dynamic relation to family are also central to *Housekeeping*. The narrator Ruth and her sister Lucille have never known their father, and their mother commits suicide while they are still young children.[9] They spend five years with their grandmother until she dies, after which they are cared for by their deceased grandfather's two sisters for a brief interlude. This short period lasts until Ruth and Lucille's transient aunt Sylvie, their mother's sister, arrives at their grandparents' house and inaugurates an unorthodox style of housekeeping. As a transient, Sylvie belongs to a group of people who are socially orphaned and live on the margins of US society. Ruth eventually chooses a life as a drifter together with Sylvie, while Lucille opts for a more conventional life when, as a teenager, she moves in with her Home Economics teacher, Miss Royce, who adopts her.

Memory is essential to *Housekeeping*, with Ruth (re)creating her relationships to her relatives and in the intertextual cultural memory work the novel performs via allusions to genres in which white orphanhood has been prominent and to critical traditions featuring the American Adam and the white female orphans of what Nina Baym calls 'woman's fiction.' As the epigraph to this chapter illustrates, Robinson has always been open about her close literary relationship to canonical nineteenth-century writers. She also often mentions eighteenth-century Calvinist minister and theologian Jonathan Edwards as an important influence on her writing, and this influence can be traced in *Housekeeping*'s resonances with Puritan narratives.[10]

The mother figure is much more important in Robinson's first novel than mothers are in *Gilead* and *Home*, even though Ruth and Lucille's situation before their mother commits suicide is far from ideal. Living in two rooms in a tall apartment building in Seattle, Helen is a single working mother, 'selling cosmetics in a drugstore, and Bernice [an elderly neighbor] looked after us while she was at work, though Bernice herself worked all night as a cashier in a truck stop. She looked after us by trying to sleep lightly enough to be awakened by the first sounds of fist fights, of the destruction of furniture, of the throes of household poisoning' (Robinson, 1981: 22). To Ruth, their 'putative father' is just a name – Reginald Stone – and an unopened letter (*ibid.*: 13, 52). Searching for the father is, however, not part of the plot of *Housekeeping*. Instead, as Martha Ravits summarizes, 'Ruth as a bereaved quester asserts the primacy of the relation to the mother as none of the male orphans so prevalent in American literary history before have done' (1989: 648). The loss of her mother haunts Ruth throughout the novel and is a strong force behind her attempts to conjure presence out of absence.

Housekeeping opens with Ruth introducing herself as narrator and protagonist and claiming family connections in a manner that resonates with Poe's Arthur Gordon Pym, Melville's Ishmael, and the Bible's genealogical lists:

Literary kinships

> My name is Ruth. I grew up with my younger sister, Lucille, under the care of my grandmother, Mrs. Sylvia Foster, and when she died, of her sisters-in-law, Misses Lily and Nona Foster, and when they fled, of her daughter, Mrs. Sylvia Fisher. Through all these generations of elders we lived in one house, my grandmother's house, built for her by her husband Edmund Foster, an employee of the railroad, who escaped this world years before I entered it. (Robinson, 1981: 3)[11]

The women Ruth mentions are those who take care of her and Lucille after Helen leaves them outside her mother's house and drives off a cliff to disappear into Lake Fingerbone. It is clear that the reason Ruth grows up in this house is not generational continuity, but rather rupture and loss.

In Ruth's story, Helen's suicide echoes her father's death years earlier in a train accident, in which the train derailed on the bridge over the same lake. Ruth's imagining of the aftermath of this disaster, and of her grandparents' lives before it occurred, constructs a backdrop against which her own and Lucille's life choices accrue meaning. She associates her grandfather Edmund Foster with a linear, masculine stance, and contrasts it with the cyclical, domestic sense of time that she imagines her grandmother and her daughters experience after his demise. His investment in the American dream of public advancement and success is closely connected to an upward mobility that rests on a Protestant work ethic: 'he was a dutiful and industrious worker, and bound to rise. In no more than a decade he was supervising the loading and unloading of livestock and freight, and in another six years he was assistant to the stationmaster' (*ibid.*: 5). Nevertheless, it is in his westward move, and as an artist and an eccentric though self-sufficient house builder, that Edmund Foster most clearly embodies American ideologies recognized in and supported by the cultural memory of literary and critical traditions.[12]

Hence, in Ruth's story the grandfather emerges as an example of the American Adam, that archetypal white male orphan figure of American literary criticism, but he is reimagined through the eyes of his orphaned granddaughter, who one critic, Maureen Ryan, goes so far as to call the 'New American Eve.' Indeed, Ruth's relationship to her grandfather could be seen as a parallel to Robinson's relation to American cultural memory in the form of a white male critical tradition: while Ruth envisions her grandfather as the American Adam but also renegotiates this figure, Robinson's *Housekeeping* with

Ruth as the central questing subject is an intervention in and negotiation of the Adamic critical tradition.[13] In Ruth's account, her grandfather is conspicuously alone in a sod house in the Midwest with only his travel literature for company before he leaves it to go further west, which underscores the masculine individualism of his story. Only later does the reader discover that his sisters Lily and Nona were also there, taking care of their mother until she died.

When Ruth assumes her grandmother's perspective on Edmund Foster, she struggles with traditional American gender roles and behavior. For instance, when the grandmother thinks about being reunited with her husband in death, 'She hoped that he would somehow have acquired a little more stability and common sense ... The bitter thing about his death, since she had a house and a pension and the children were almost grown, was that it seemed to her a kind of defection, not altogether unanticipated' (*ibid*.: 10). Here the white American woman stands for domesticity and stable civilization, from which the white American man traditionally flees at all costs, an archetypal scenario in, for example, R.W.B. Lewis's male-centered account of American literary history and Leslie Fiedler's critique of such accounts (Fiedler, 1962).

There is a subtle criticism of such gender dichotomies from the grandmother's perspective as well. At one point in *Housekeeping*, the grandmother's memories of her husband, as reimagined by Ruth, appear to be a riff on Fiedler's discussion of Thoreau in *The Return of the Vanishing American* (1968), where Fiedler sees Thoreau's relationship in his texts to the American Indian as illustrating 'the wild man that lives next to the mild husband at the heart of all American males' (Fiedler, 1972: 104). In *Housekeeping*, Ruth's grandmother remembers a spring when her husband

> wore a necktie and suspenders even to hunt wildflowers ... and ... put out his elbow to help her over the steep and stony places, with a wordless and impersonal courtesy she did not resent because *she had never really wished to feel married to anyone*. She sometimes imagined a rather dark man with crude stripes painted on his face and sunken belly, and a hide fastened around his loins, and bones dangling from his ears, and clay and claws and fangs and bones and feathers and sinews and hide ornamenting his arms and waist and throat and ankles, his whole body a boast that he was more alarming than all the death whose trophies he wore. *Edmund was like that, a little*. (Robinson, 1981: 17, emphasis added)

In this season, Edmund Foster – like Thoreau, the naturalist – is absolutely intent on what he finds in nature: 'eggshells, a bird's wing, a jawbone, the ashy fragment of a wasp's nest ... He would peer at them as if he could read them, and pocket them as if he could own them' (*ibid.*: 17). Even though his interest in nature makes him forgetful of his suspenders and of Methodism, as well as of his wife, it is still depicted as appropriative; in this scene Edmund Foster resembles Hattie's husband Edward in Leslie Marmon Silko's *Gardens in the Dunes* (1999).

The dichotomy in US literature that Fiedler establishes between the interests of the white man, at ease in the wilderness, and the white woman, who upholds civilization's and society's strictures, is also challenged in the novel when the grandmother accompanies her husband on his excursions, and in the statement that she 'had never really wished to feel married to anyone.' Moreover, although the combination of 'the mild husband' and 'the wild man' is beautifully visualized in the passage about Edmund Foster that ends with the comment 'Edmund was like that, a little,' this scene is imagined from a Euro-American woman's point of view (the grandmother's, Ruth's, indeed Robinson's); and the juxtaposition of the two in this depiction of the white American man is exposed as slightly absurd, as underlined by the qualifying comment: 'a little.'

Thus, Ruth's story or meditation[14] reflects on and wrestles with national ideologies or myths from the perspective of a white female orphan. *Housekeeping* also engages intertextually with genres that have featured orphans as protagonists: the picaresque with Ruth as a female Huck Finn or Western hero; the *bildungsroman* or coming-of-age narrative and the domestic novel through Lucille's development. As indicated, Ruth's first-person narration situates *Housekeeping* in a long tradition by referring back to Puritan writings as well as to works by canonical nineteenth-century Euro-American writers, many of whom also drew on that Puritan heritage.

The way Ruth expresses her sense of orphanhood resonates with the strong sense of cultural and spiritual orphanhood in the writings of the Pilgrims and Puritans. As Eileen Simpson points out, the opening pages of William Bradford's seventeenth-century *History of Plymouth Plantation* in which he relates the settling of Pilgrims in the New World, 'read like a fairy tale about the ordeal of children without parents in search of a home' (1988: 221). The American Puritans can also be read as cultural orphans; Pazicky posits that they saw themselves 'metaphorically as children separated from their "mother," who variously represented England and the Anglican church, and their "father," who variously represented God and the king,' and that they 'strove to mitigate the trauma and assuage their guilt by rationalizing that as God's children, they were joining a spiritually superior family' (Pazicky, 1998: 6). Despite attempts to see themselves as belonging to 'God's family,' they could not entirely avoid the 'uncomfortable suspicion that by abandoning their "father" and "mother," they had turned themselves into orphans' (*ibid.*). Pazicky assesses the difference between the Puritans' and the Pilgrims' identification as homeless orphans and as God's adopted children, suggesting that the latter 'expressed their feelings of desolation more openly,' and she quotes Robert Cushman's 'Reasons and Considerations Touching the Lawfulness of Removing out of England into the Parts of America' (1622):

> But now we are all in all places strangers and pilgrims, travellers and sojourners, most properly, having no dwelling but in this earthen tabernacle; our dwelling is but a wandering, and our abiding but as a fleeting, and in a word our home is nowhere, but in the heavens in that house not made with hands, whose maker and builder is God ... (quoted in Pazicky, 1998: 12)

At the very moment when Ruth's sense of orphanhood is most acute, when she is at an abandoned homestead in the woods, she expresses a similar idea, and in language that approaches that of the white settlers of the seventeenth century: 'Let them [the ghost children who haunt this place] come unhouse me of this flesh, and pry this house apart. It was no shelter now, it only kept me here alone, and I would rather be with them, if only to see them, even if they turned away from me. If I could see my mother, it would not have to be her eyes, her hair. ... The lake had taken that, I knew' (Robinson, 1981: 159). Ruth literally becomes the homeless wanderer, the image of the Pilgrim's spiritual condition, reflected in the move to the New World. When Ruth observes on the last page of *Housekeeping* that 'the perimeters of our wandering are nowhere' (*ibid.*: 219), she echoes Cushman's 'our home is nowhere,' although, like the Pilgrims, she is not alone in her wandering: it is shared with Sylvie.

Travelling with Sylvie, Ruth encounters the first of two Native Americans, representatives of the ever-vanishing American, who appear in the novel. In Fiedler's terms, encounters with Native

Americans, however brief, may have generic consequences for *Housekeeping*; they make it a kind of Western: 'The heart of the Western is ... the encounter with the Indian, that utter stranger for whom our New World is an Old Home ...' (1972: 19). The first Native American is a woman who Ruth and Sylvie meet in a boxcar when they return by freight train from the abandoned homestead in the woods, where Ruth has become initiated into Sylvie's way of life: 'There was an old Indian woman sitting in the corner with her knees drawn up and her arms between her knees. Her skin was very dark except for an albino patch on her forehead that gave her a tuft of colorless hair and one white brow' (Robinson, 1981: 171–2). There is a short familial interchange between this woman and Sylvie about Ruth, the function of which seems to be to confirm the existence of a community of female transients, and to include Ruth in this community (*ibid.*: 173).[15]

In this brief encounter, Robinson rewrites Fiedler's West(ern),[16] where men alone live, and where men live alone, having escaped society by forming a relationship with the Native man. Examining Sylvie and Ruth as a two-person community of Western travelers that 'overturns a sense of hierarchy,' Sheila Ruzycki O'Brien observes that in 'traditional Western narratives, cross-racial bonds between travelers are common but unbalanced and cross-gender bonds less common but also unbalanced. These tales elevate the handsome, powerful, mobile white male hero' (1993: 224). The interaction between Sylvie, Ruth, and the Indian woman obviously supports O'Brien's observation on *Housekeeping*'s revision of the traditional Euro-American Western tale, but this encounter is too brief to give serious weight to the Native American character.

Only a few pages after the encounter with the Indian woman, Ruth mentions the old chief of the fictional Fingerbone tribe when she describes the sheriff, who 'regularly led the Fourth of July parade, dressed in buckskins and tooled-leather boots,' carrying 'an oversized flag ... followed by the frail old chief of the Fingerbone tribe, and his half-Irish stepdaughter, and the oldest children of her first marriage' (Robinson, 1981: 176). Submerged in this parade, which celebrates the United States as a nation and commemorates its beginnings, and overshadowed by an oversized flag, this Native American appears to be frail indeed, but also a necessary figure together with the leather-clad sheriff in order to perpetuate a Euro-American history and mythology. The parade and the flag are signs of an ideology that supports national collective memory. However, the mention of the chief's half-Irish stepdaughter and her children gestures towards family relations outside the nuclear birth family.

In her facility for making home outside of blood relations, as well as in her relation to Ruth as a sister, Lucille is a significant orphan figure. In *Orphans: Real and Imaginary*, Simpson points out that '[t]o be reasonably lucky, an orphan should have a brother or a sister close in age, a modest inheritance (large ones cause trouble), and hospitable relatives' (1988: 135). Ruth and Lucille fit the description of the 'reasonably lucky' orphan in that they are close in age, inherit their grandmother's house, and are cared for by a succession of relatives: their grandmother, their grandfather's sisters, and – more problematically for Lucille and the townspeople of Fingerbone – their aunt Sylvie. That sisterhood is of utmost importance to Ruth is made clear throughout her story, but especially after Lucille has left her and Sylvie to move in with her Home Economics teacher, Miss Royce, a single woman and a professional housekeeper: 'Miss Royce gave her the spare room. In effect, she adopted her, and I had no sister after that night' (Robinson, 1981: 140). Right after Lucille's flight from what she sees as Sylvie's inadequate housekeeping and Ruth's unwillingness to improve herself by adapting to societal conventions, Ruth finds herself alone at the abandoned homestead, haunted by lonely, orphaned ghost children. She muses: 'Having a sister or a friend is like sitting at night in a lighted house. Those outside can watch you if they want, but you need not see them ... Anyone with one solid human bond is that smug, and it is the smugness as much as the comfort and safety that lonely people covet and admire' (ibid.: 154). Ruth only expresses this definitive sense of loneliness – '[l]oneliness [as] an absolute discovery' (ibid.: 157) – as an orphan and outsider after she has lost her sister and apparently also been abandoned by Sylvie.

As orphaned sisters, Ruth and Lucille share a common history, particularly of anxieties: 'We had spent our lives watching and listening with the constant sharp attention of children lost in the dark. It seemed that we were bewilderingly lost in a landscape that, with any light at all, would be wholly familiar' (ibid.: 130). One such cause of anxiety is a story Sylvie tells them about children being made wards of court (ibid.: 67): 'That was the first Lucille or I had heard of the interest of the state in the well-being of children, and we were alarmed' (ibid.: 68). The threat that Ruth will become a ward of the state and that Sylvie will lose custody of her increases after Lucille has left the house to live with Miss Royce and Ruth and Sylvie are seen returning on a freight train in the morning after their night on the lake. Sylvie tries to avert this threat by engaging in a spectacular house-cleaning frenzy to demonstrate that she is a responsible guardian, but Ruth's being out in the garden at night when the sheriff comes by seals their fate. In order to stay together they must leave the house: 'It is a terrible thing to break up a family ... The sheriff knew it as well as anyone, and his face was slack with regret. "There'll be a hearing Mrs. Fisher," he said wearily, because whatever Sylvie might say, he could make no other reply' (*ibid.*: 190). In Ruth's mind fear of separation from Sylvie produces a multi-layered image built on fragments of different stories of child removal and abduction: 'If a judge were to appear and whisk me under his black robes like a hobo in our grandmother's cautionary tales, and carry me off to the rumored farm, a shock would roll through the house, and rattle the plates, and totter the cups, and ring in the glasses for days, perhaps ...' (*ibid.*: 190). The judge replaces the hobo as a threat, as Ruth is now ready to leave the house with Sylvie and join the community of drifters. 'In renouncing the shelter of the familial home, being "put out of house," as Ruth expresses it, the protagonist chooses the unfettered freedom that in American fiction has been reserved for males' (Ravits, 1989: 662). This final abandonment of the house, and their attempt to burn it down, constitutes at least an equivalent shock to domesticity to the one Ruth imagines would be caused by her forced removal.

Lucille, in contrast, eagerly and energetically endeavors to learn socially condoned feminine virtues. In this way *Housekeeping* connects to the nineteenth-century literary tradition featuring a white female orphan, and to the discourse of domesticity. Like Gerty in Maria Cummins's *The Lamplighter*, Lucille works very hard to improve herself in the eyes of socially established female role models and manages to find a home with one of them. Miss Royce can profitably be read as a descendant of one of the master architects of the cult of domesticity: Catharine Beecher, who published *Treatise on Domestic Economy* (1841). Despite the gendered ideology she promoted, Beecher was an unmarried public intellectual and teacher. Some of Lucille's strategies to improve herself also recall two male 'self-orphaned' and self-made figures from American history and literature: Benjamin Franklin and F. Scott Fitzgerald's Jay Gatsby. In this too, she resembles Gerty and other nineteenth-century orphan heroines who temporarily internalize characteristics that American culture valued in Euro-American men, such as self-reliance and liberal individualism (Voloshin, 1984: 298).

Thus, we suggest that it is through Lucille's development, in social and biological terms, from an orphan girl to a 'little woman' that *Housekeeping* can be said to participate in the surge of interest in the female *bildungsroman* evident in the 1980s. Ruth's story, on the other hand, does not really have that much in common with different permutations of the *bildungsroman*, male or female. Rather, her story represents a rejection of middle-class values and comforts, and a turning away from American materialism as well as from American individualism. In contrast to Ruth, Lucille actively chooses to embrace norms that have served to restrict the development, or block the participation, of women in a number of different arenas, in order to be socially integrated and to avoid the social orphanhood that Sylvie's way of life stands for. However, although she severs ties to her sister and aunt and opts for a more conventional female life, she ends up in the company of another female figure without a husband, Miss Royce, which strengthens the novel's focus on matrilinearity.

This resolution to Lucille's story may have satisfied readers who saw an orphaned child's material well-being as a first priority, but from a late twentieth-century feminist perspective, Lucille's trajectory and ultimate integration into society are a disappointingly conservative alternative for a white girl in a contemporary female *bildungsroman*. In the 1980s, feminist critics were looking for feminist role models,[17] evidence of sisterhood, and of radical departures from gender norms, and some found them in Ruth and Sylvie.[18] Since its publication, the critical responses to *Housekeeping* have steadily increased in number and they explore a wide range of different aesthetic and ideological issues and concerns.

Although we certainly agree with those critics who see Ruth's loss of her mother and yearning for her as absolutely central to the novel, we would argue that Ruth's intense desire to merge with others – often expressed in the grammatical shift from 'I' to 'we' but also in her assuming the perspectives of others – can also be related to what Elizabeth Aldrich sees as 'a paradox intrinsic to Puritan personal narrative itself' (1988: 22). This paradox is 'its *resistance to individuation* of parent from offspring, of self from community, of personal history from that cosmic historical unfolding which ... is God's plan for his Chosen in the New World' (*ibid.*: 22, original emphasis). Ruth is severed from most of her relatives and she is repeatedly orphaned, but she (re)creates ties to her family throughout her narrative: to her grandfather (whom she has never met), her mother, her grandmother, and her sister Lucille. She is never really an integral part of the community of Fingerbone, but she becomes part of Sylvie's 'we,' the fluid community of transients.

Housekeeping can thus be said to offer a critique of the figure of the American Adam, individualism, and materialism. It re-genders the orphan figure in the travel narrative and the Western, and the orphaned narrator's quest is for the missing mother, not the father. The novel revisits and remembers domestic fiction and the nineteenth-century female *bildungsroman*, in a 1950s setting and a 1980s context, through Lucille's development. Ruth's trajectory, in contrast, stands for a rejection of the *bildungsroman* with its material, bourgeois connotations in favor of a kind of spiritual autobiography that harks back to the Pilgrims and Puritans, to whom the writers of the American Renaissance also looked back. Through its two orphan girls, then, *Housekeeping* remembers Euro-American literary traditions through revisions of genre and family.

Not 'one story': American Adams in Michael Cunningham's *Specimen Days*

> Most terrorists are children [who have] been told one story and embrace it with childlike certainty. (Cunningham, 2006: 4)

Michael Cunningham has stated that he is obsessed with the 'postnuclear' queer family, and his novels, although featuring characters haunted by the nuclear family ideal, typically center on non-normative family constellations (Coffey, 1998: 54). His novels often have orphan boys as central characters. In *The Hours* (1998), Richard is the celebrated but unhappy American author whose mother abandoned him when he was a child, a traumatic event that shapes his life and authorship. Bobby, one of the protagonists in the breakthrough novel *A Home at the End of the World* (1990), has a mother who commits suicide, and a father who dies a few years later, making the boy an orphan who continually tries to establish new forms of family. In both novels, Cunningham employs orphan boys to explore and critique different kinds of American middle-class families. Similarly, Cunningham uses the notion of family and the figure of the orphan in *Specimen Days* to scrutinize meanings of 'America' in a specifically post-9/11 context. Here the orphan carries ambiguous meanings; orphans are uncanny, representing that which cannot be included in the American family, but they are also poor, vulnerable, and in need of inclusion.

As in earlier novels, Cunningham uses canonical literature as intertexts to build his narrative in *Specimen Days*, and the novel weaves its critique of the American family into a claim for a position within US literary history.[19] The title signals its link to Walt Whitman's *Specimen Days in America* (1887), a collection of short texts, notes, and letters, many of which were written during the Civil War. This intertext suggests that the present is not singularly traumatic, and that the USA can instead be understood as being in a continuous state of 'post-disaster.' Whitman's collection dwells on the horrors of war and the suffering and deaths of young soldiers, and is marked by a tone of doubt and negativity that is very different from the hopeful, celebratory tone of 'Song of Myself.' Despite its title, however, Cunningham's novel is only implicitly linked to Whitman's late work, whereas it overtly references the far more canonical 'Song of Myself,' which, like the bard himself, appears explicitly in the narrative. To further complicate the ways that the novel works intertextually with the American canon, the American Adam is implicitly evoked throughout the narrative, a figure that in R.W.B. Lewis's view was emblematic of Whitman's writing. Hence, as the following analysis will demonstrate, Cunningham's novel not only critically engages with Whitman, but also with the literary perpetuation of the Adamic myth as elucidated by Lewis. It explores this figure's possible re-formulation, finally effecting a splitting and a reconceptualization of the Adamic self.

Structurally, *Specimen Days* is a triptych consisting of three separate but interlinked tales: 'In the Machine,' 'The Children's Crusade,' and 'Like Beauty.'[20] All three stories are set in New York City, but at different moments in history separated by 150-year intervals: the first in the late nineteenth century, the middle story in a post-9/11 'present,' and the final story in the future of the twenty-second century. Each story features a white, male American orphan as a central figure, and these orphans are physically marked as unusual, either because they are physically malformed, or because they are non-human – the orphan in the final story is an android. Thus orphans in the novel are clearly envisioned as American others. Each of these orphans is also linked to a central female character placed in what can be termed a maternal position, and all the stories deal with the death of parents, especially fathers. Although narrated from an omniscient perspective, the first and last tales are focalized through the orphan himself, and the middle tale is focalized through the maternal figure. These differences stress that the shifting meanings of the orphan figure depend in part on whether they are situated as children perceived by adults, or situated as subjects with self-perception, self-awareness, and, ultimately, agency.

The first story, 'In the Machine,' is an eerie tale set in the late nineteenth century. The central character and focalizer is Lucas, a poor, physically deformed twelve-year-old boy who has lost his elder brother Simon in an accident at a metal-works factory. Lucas takes his brother's place at the machine that makes housings out of sheets of metal. Gradually, he distances himself – orphans himself – from his poor, ill parents who soon starve to death in their apartment, and attaches himself to his dead brother's fiancée Catherine. Eventually, he is injured at the factory and dies. 'Like Beauty,' the third story, is a science fiction tale set more than a century into the future, when Nadians, humanoid lizards from the planet Northea, have migrated to Earth. New York City has been turned into a theme park called 'Old New York,' where androids work tricks on human tourists looking for a fake fright in Central Park. One of the androids, or simulos, is Simon, the orphan protagonist and focalizer of the tale. Simon meets Catareen, a female Nadian who works for a white family in what resembles domestic slavery. Together, they escape New York to go to Denver, where she dies and he, literally, meets his maker. On the westward journey, they pick up an orphan boy named Luke, and together the three of them form a temporary, provisional family.

The middle story, 'The Children's Crusade,' is set in the 'present' of a post-9/11 US.[21] It introduces Cat, an African American forensic psychologist whose work is to take phone calls from potential terrorists and to detect the tone and wording of the authentic threat, of 'true intent.' However, she fails to catch the authenticity of a call from a young white boy, who then wires himself to a bomb and kills a white businessman by embracing him 'right by Ground Zero' (Cunningham, 2005: 98), and soon, there is a second attack, in which a black boy kills a black working-class man. Shortly thereafter there is a report of yet another similar attack in Chicago, and the police realize that the attacks may pose a national threat. As the story unfolds, Cat learns that the killers are orphans. When the last of the boys appears on her doorstep, she sees that he is a deformed child, 'just over three feet tall. A midget child' (*ibid.*: 177), with a small body and an oversized head, who evokes her pity and compassion. Cat, whose three-year-old son died ten years earlier, decides to rescue the boy instead of turning him in, and together they escape the city on a southbound train.

Whereas the second tale most explicitly brings the figure of the orphan boy into our own time, all three stories – despite their shifting temporal settings and their suggested linearity – clearly reflect contemporary anxieties about childhood, orphanhood, family, and national identity. As Pazicky points out, 'orphan imagery [tends] to erupt at times of [national] challenge and crisis,' which 'supports its grounding in specific historical events and its connection to identity issues' (1998: xiii). Cunningham's three tales also indicate historical differences in the significance of orphanhood, and emphasize shifts in social anxieties about children and families in the USA. The late nineteenth century, the setting of the first tale, was a time when orphans were becoming an inner city problem and a central target for charity work, and when orphans began to figure prominently in both sentimental fiction and rags-to-riches narratives.[22] Additionally, this story highlights the interrelatedness of class and race in the figure of Lucas, a poor Irish immigrant boy in New York at a time when not all European immigrants were considered equally 'white.'[23] However, the child labor described in the story, while certainly alluding to historical realities during industrialization, also displaces current anxieties about child labor and the 'death of childhood' onto a temporally distant setting.[24] Interestingly, in this tale, the burning twin towers of 9/11 are also temporally displaced onto the event – based on a historical incident[25] – of a fire in the Triangle shirtwaist factory, during which burning women fall or jump out of the burning building. Notably these women also re-gender and displace the image of the 'falling man' in the twin tower attack. Similarly, although set in the future, by introducing androids and creatures who are both 'lizards' and 'people' (Cunningham, 2005: 244) in familial contexts, the third tale activates anxieties about alternative families, genetic engineering and biotechnology, as well as about migrant and racial minority women as surrogate parents.[26] In other words, into these three stories Cunningham writes historical specificities as well as contemporary social developments and long-standing national anxieties in the USA.

The temporal setting of 'The Children's Crusade' brings the orphan child into our own times, introducing a situation where the formative national disaster has already occurred. In the US media coverage of the events of September 11, 2001, the deaths of men or fathers were given much space, and were typically linked to hero status, whereas women or mothers typically figured as the bereaved.[27] Throughout his novel, Cunningham focuses on the figure of the bereaved woman, thereby drawing on imagery from media, and he privileges the boy child as the embodiment of parental loss. Partly, this is consistent with his *oeuvre* in general, but this gendering of the disaster orphan also foregrounds the vulnerability of boys in a way that counters the representations of independent and industrious boy heroes in American canonical and popular fiction. As several commentators have pointed out, children orphaned by the deaths of a parent in the 9/11 attacks have been especially important figures for imagining the nation, and the Twin Towers Orphan Fund (TTOF), which was set up to support these children on the day after the attacks, illustrates that orphanhood in post-9/11 US culture may be connected to special status and national recognition.[28]

Quite unlike the TTOF orphans, the lethal orphans in 'The Children's Crusade' are represented as underprivileged to the point of being 'nobody' and 'already dead' (*ibid.*: 102). They are expendable children in Cunningham's dystopian envisioning of the USA as a nation where babies are abandoned, sold, and abused. An elderly woman who calls herself 'Walt Whitman' has saved them, but has also trained them as assassins for an underground organization called 'The Family.' She explains to Cat that the boys 'were dead anyway' because '[n]o one wanted them. One was left in an alley in Buffalo. He weighed just under three pounds. Another one was purchased from a prostitute in Newark for two hundred dollars. The middle boy had been a sex slave to a particularly unpleasant person in Asbury Park' (*ibid.*: 169). In stark contrast to popularized media narratives of male heroism and rescue, female maternal instincts, and nationally significant orphans,[29] Cunningham represents orphan boys who have no fathers and have been abandoned or sold by their birth mothers. His central characters, in other words, exist on the margins in each of the three historical US contexts envisioned.

These, then, are children whose position is located outside of any idea of a normative American family. Familial otherness is a quality that the terrorist orphan boys share with the main characters in the other two stories, but the ways in which they become orphans differ. In the first tale, Lucas in effect starves his parents by eating their food, even taking the food from his mother's mouth, and kills his father by removing his 'breathing apparatus,' thereby orphaning himself in an uncanny and not clearly deliberate way. Simon the android – a young male in his twenties, yet really only five years old – is an orphan and an outlaw since he has 'stolen himself' from the company that produced him. He tells Catareen: 'as stolen property, we're inherently illegal. We break the law by continuing to own ourselves' (ibid.: 245).[30] Late in the narrative he renounces his father/inventor, telling him: 'I am not your son' (ibid.: 281). Although the acts performed by Lucas and Simon are dissimilar, they both activate the idea of the self-orphaning hero in classic American novels by, for instance, Twain, Salinger, and Kerouac.[31] Instead of representing orphanhood as a matter of choice, however, Cunningham complicates matters by using the confused child's perspective in the first tale to suggest Lucas's inability to anticipate the consequences of his actions, or to read the reactions of those around him, and Simon's nonhuman perspective in the final tale to suggest that his actions may not be the result of personal choice but of the way he is 'programmed.' The notion of orphanhood is further problematized by Cunningham's casting even more characters as orphans: the unborn baby as well as Catharine in the first tale, Cat in the second, and the abandoned young boy Luke in the last one. Orphans, then, are everywhere, which certainly speaks against the idea of the nation as one tightly knit nuclear family, suggesting instead the idea of Americans being 'orphans, each and all' as in Toni Morrison's *A Mercy* (2008).

The otherness of the main orphan characters is compounded by their being linked to forms of violence and suffering, phenomena that run counter to dominant ideas of the child as happy and innocent.[32] The tension between violence and innocence in the boy orphans takes different shapes in the three stories, however. In the first tale Lucas is victimized by poverty and hardship; he is harmed in the factory and dies because of his injuries. But he also creates unease in those around him, who are upset by the eccentricity of his behavior, speech patterns, and appearance. Also, of course, he causes the death of his parents. In the second tale, the child terrorist 'Luke' and his brothers kill others, trained to do so by an adult in the name of the organization called 'the Family,' but they have also been violated or abandoned by biological and/or adoptive parents. In the third tale, Simon's job is to harm those who want it and pay for it, but he short-circuits if he tries to harm anyone else, which makes undesired violence impossible. Nevertheless, in renouncing his creator he may also be read as symbolically killing the father. In various ways and to various degrees, then, the orphans in the three stories – while they also find families – cause the death of adults, and provoke unease, fear, even terror, which serves to strengthen their positions as others.

The otherness of these boy orphans calls to mind the paradoxical significance of the child in US history. The meaning of childhood has shifted over time.[33] In the late nineteenth century, James Kincaid explains, '[t]hinking of "the child" as complex and independent, as a *species* ... made it a distant and exotic being, which heightened its attractiveness, but at some cost: the cost of remoteness. ... The child we have inherited from the Victorians is both inside us and distant from us, a repository of nostalgia and a hope for the future, weak and powerful, alluring and revolting' (1998: 67–8). This doubleness, he further notes, is mirrored in the highly diversified status of 'adored' literary children and real children: 'the chimney sweeps dying of cancer of the scrotum, the factory children being mutilated, cast-off kids being left to wander the streets and peddle their bodies' (*ibid.*: 54). Such discrepancies, he observes, should come as no surprise, however, since the twenty-first century is marked by 'similar contrasts between tender protestations and brutal actuality' (*ibid.*). Indeed, such contrasts are evident everywhere, not least in the context of orphans in post-9/11 America.

The idea that children are innocent *and* other, and the consequent fluctuation between adoration and neglect in attitudes towards the child, is a powerful one in Cunningham's novel. In 'The Children's Crusade' there is a continuous process of naming the orphan boys, and this process also has Cat and her colleagues oscillating between seemingly irreconcilable opposites; the orphan terrorist is, on the one hand, just a '[l]ittle boy' (Cunningham, 2005: 144, 163, 184, 195); and, on the other hand, he is a 'freak ... [o]r maybe a savant' (*ibid.*: 143); he is a 'little fucker' (*ibid.*: 151), as well as 'a ghostly creature ... [a] Gollum, a changeling ... a convincing member of the dead' (*ibid.*: 153). The 'brothers' are called 'crazy little boys' (*ibid.*: 154), 'deranged boys' (*ibid.*: 156), and 'little killers' (*ibid.*: 174), and looking at the boy asleep Cat thinks, with irony: 'Here was the devil – a malformed child ...' (*ibid.*: 186). Upon first seeing him, Cat is 'seized by a spasm of *dreadful compassion*. Here was a monster; here was a frightened child. Here was a tortured little boy who could at any moment blow them both away' (*ibid.*: 179, emphasis added). Once she decides to rescue the last of the boys, her heart softens when she thinks: 'Please be okay, little killer' (*ibid.*: 187), a phrase that oddly defuses 'killer' and makes it almost cute by the addition of the epithet 'little.' As they begin their journey she also sees him as an innocent: 'just a little boy, happy for the first time in his life' (*ibid.*: 195). By placing these alternatives in the minds of adult characters, the novel foregrounds the extent to which the orphan child is an adult invention. The orphan boys as terrorists are ultimately the outcome of the actions of their biological, adoptive, and potential new surrogate parents, far from the self-made men and boys of classic American literature.

The ways that orphan boys in *Specimen Days* desire and discover families – across generations and even across species – also set them apart from their literary predecessors. Ever since the American Renaissance, fictional orphan boys have been positioned in opposition to family as well as 'sivilization,' and their trajectories have not necessarily led to the 'right' family, as is typically the case for fictional orphan girls. Instead, the male orphan in American literature, in his escape from family and hence from history, is firmly linked to the idea of the American Adam, formulated by Lewis as 'an individual emancipated from history, happily bereft of ancestry, untouched and undefiled by the usual inheritances of family and race' (*ibid.*: 5), as a man directed only towards the future, and 'happily' so.[34] Lewis advances Walt Whitman as the epitome of the Adamic mode, observing that *Leaves of Grass* contains 'no complaint about the weight or intrusion of the past' (Lewis, 1955: 44).[35] In a sense countering Lewis's claim, Cunningham places Whitman and his poetry centrally in his stories about boy orphans, while also clearly complicating the 'happiness' of historylessness.

The orphan killers in 'The Children's Crusade' are linked explicitly to Whitman's 'Song of Myself.' They have lived in an apartment where they have literally been surrounded by the poem: 'It might have been the low-budget version of an army barracks or an orphanage. Except of course for the fact that everything – the kitchen cabinets, the windows – was plastered over with pages' (Cunningham, 2005: 174). As the epigraph to this section indicates, Cunningham relates terrorism to children being told one story. Here, the poem – the 'one story' that the boys have been told – that covers every surface in their home has been used by the boys' adoptive mother as a rationale for killing people. At one point, one of the boys misquotes a line from the poem to explain the act of killing and suicide: 'Every atom of mine belongs to you, too' (*ibid.*: 123). Another boy writes 'TO DIE IS

DIFFERENT FROM WHAT ANYONE SUPPOSES, AND LUCKIER' as graffiti on the wall outside Cat's apartment (*ibid.*: 130).

While in 'The Children's Crusade,' Whitman's poem is the orphan boys' 'one story' and a rationale for murder, it figures differently in the other two tales. In the first one, Lucas has memorized 'Song of Myself,' and quotes lines from it at odd moments, finding strength in it for himself, but upsetting those around him who find his behavior disturbing. At a late point in the story he actually meets the bard, and is overwhelmed: 'He looked up and beheld Walt's face. Here was the gray-white cascade of beard, here his broad-brimmed hat and the kerchief knotted at his neck ... His eyes were bright as silver nails ... His voice was clear and deep, penetrating; it was not loud, but it was everywhere' (*ibid.*: 66). Although the poet does not seem to understand Lucas's predicament, the boy still trusts 'the book,' believing that it will provide him with what he understands as 'soul': 'a vigor ... a defiant, uncrushable aliveness' (*ibid.*: 12). For Lucas, the poet's voice seems to be 'everywhere,' the same is true for the killer orphans in the middle story, although the text – now imbued with other meanings – is no longer voiced by the bard himself but by the murderous members of 'The Family.' Like Lucas, Simon the android in the final story speaks lines from the poem in ways that are not deliberate. He has a poetry chip implanted in his circuitry, because his inventor thought it would help him develop emotions and free will. Towards the end of the narrative this proves to have been correct, for Simon rejects his inventor/father Emory Lowell and decides to stay on Earth while Lowell's small colony of humans and Nadians travel into space to find a new planetary home. Hence, the use of 'Song of Myself' in the three stories underscores the significance of canonical texts as cultural memory, highlighting how they function in the formation of individual and group identities. However, Cunningham's novel also suggests the shifting status of literary texts, and hence the way that a literary text is never just 'one story': while the poem is new and radically different in the first tale, and a canonical text in the second one, in the final story – although still important for the identity formation of the main character – it is a quirk, a remnant from a forgotten past.

Specimen Days also revises the Adamic myth in significant ways. While there are numerous references to rebirth and historylessness in the novel, not least in 'The Children's Crusade,' their link to optimism is less than certain. At one point, Cat reflects that she 'liked the fact that all over the city, people were having their coffee and showers, deciding on their clothes. This was as close as it got to collective innocence, this mass transition from sleep (however troubled) to wakefulness (however tormented) ... Here we are, all of us, *going through this daily miniature rebirth*, and doing it together' (*ibid.*: 114, emphasis added). The passage locates rebirth and innocence in the realms of everyday practice and collectivity, but also in the realm of the unachievable, the impossible, 'as close' as it gets, but not quite the real thing. The American Adam is thus not only revised, but also re-located onto an African American woman, a move that serves to disrupt implied whiteness, and 'de-masculinizes' the Adamic self.[36] In another passage, Cat fantasizes that 'she could slip out of her life altogether, could be just anyone anywhere ... a woman with a job and a child and the regular array of difficulties, the questions of rent and groceries. It seemed ... an unimaginable happiness' (*ibid.*: 187). This 'rebirth,' too, is firmly placed in the realm of fantasy, or even beyond fantasy. It thus seems that even while reiterating the attraction of Adamic self-/regeneration the narrative repeatedly underscores its unreality, particularly for an African American woman like Cat, but also in more general terms, since characters in the novel, far from escaping their past histories, always carry the past with them in the present.

Another means by which Cunningham revises the Adamic myth is by 'familiarization'; that is, rather than existing separately from family, his Adamic characters are parts of non-normative familial constellations that, although ambiguously charged, nevertheless serve to sustain them. While we are told that Cat and her colleagues never 'spun out over the collapse of the family, or of civilization at large' because such practices belong to 'the callers' realm' (*ibid.*: 119), they live alone or have what is conventionally termed 'broken' families. Nevertheless, throughout the story the idea of family is pervasive. For example, Cat frames not only her private relationships, but also her working relationships, in familial terms. Pete is Cat's 'Brother' at work, while she is 'Mama' to her white lover Simon, and 'Momma' waiting for callers. Finally, Cat informally becomes the adoptive mother to the surviving orphan boy. Notably, while it may echo earlier fictional representations of black adults caring for white children, the representation of black adoptive mother and the white, deformed orphan or adoptive child is also a reformulation of family that seriously questions American familial and national histories, for in social reality this form of transracial adoption is hardly visible.[37] As Cat notes, they are too strange not to be noticed, even shunned, by others, who are unlikely to perceive them as 'family.'

Finally, instead of privileging historylessness and anonymity, *Specimen Days* presents such qualities as suspect and even murderous. To save the last of the orphan boys (as well as herself), Cat decides they must leave New York, and they get on a train heading south. While she temporarily forgets that the members of 'The Family' have renounced their given names as 'false' and taken on new identities, the orphan boy alerts her to the implications of her own attempt to become somebody new, when he says, 'Now you're in the family, too' (*ibid*.: 196). Cat reflects, 'He had ended her life and taken her into this new one, this crazy rebirth, hurtling forward on a train into the vast confusion of the world, its simultaneous and never-ending collapse and regeneration ...' (*ibid*.: 196). This, then, is a 'crazy rebirth' – regeneration through violence – not into independent self-definition, but into the destructive terrorist network of 'The Family.' Assuming a new identity and attempting to escape one's past history is a practice that is marked as impossible, criminal, and mad.

Whereas the ending of 'The Children's Crusade' is both sinister and open, it is not the end of Cunningham's novel, which continues with 'Like Beauty,' a story set in the future that is at least mildly hopeful, and that clearly suggests that 'The Family' in the preceding story did not, after all, bring about the end of the world. In this final story, family encompasses cross-species relationships between humans and Nadians. It is this kind of cross-species family that ultimately presents a hope for human survival, and that also harbors the Luke of that story, another deformed boy abandoned by his mother. The android Simon remains outside of this family formation and stays on Earth to care for Catareen, who is dying. Previously, however, he has experienced familial 'recall' with Luke and Catareen: 'Simon had seen a vid once, ancient footage of a family engaged like this. The father was cooking meat on a fire as his wife and child waited for it to be done' (*ibid*.: 259). Whether his reactions are spontaneous or based on programmed images remains open, but the connections he makes between himself and that other family – by way of movie imagery – contribute to his process of 'humanization.' Simon is also Americanized, for the novel ends with him riding off towards the western horizon. At this point, he is perhaps the last living man on Earth – yet not a man at all.

Clearly, then, Cunningham's novel engages intertextually with canonical US literature and criticism, both drawing upon and refuting the notion of a literary work as 'one story.' Reading the orphan boys in the novel against Lewis's work on the American Adam serves to problematize this mythical figure, and the ways that Walt Whitman figures in the three stories offer commentary on the many uses – and possible fate – of canonical texts. Both Whitman's literary works and Lewis's criticism exemplify particularized forms of cultural memory. While Cunningham's intertextual play with Whitman may serve to inscribe his own work into American literary history, and to demonstrate 'loyalty to a common repertoire' (Keunen, 2000: 27), the novel also clearly offers new meanings to themes central to Whitman, notably death and rebirth. Moreover, it inserts the orphan trope and the idea of the Adamic self into specifically familial settings in revisionist ways. If Lewis's Adam is historyless and 'happily bereft of ancestry,' Cunningham's revisions of this figure are clearly embedded in social history in ways that inflect meanings of family as well as familylessness. History becomes something that the orphans in all three tales embody and carry with them, the past something that cannot be escaped, but that has set the conditions for the present, and for the (lack of a) future. In 'The Children's Crusade' especially, history is also strongly present in the envisioning of post-9/11 national fears, and the links between such fear and the evocation of national 'family values.'

As Laura Peters observes in her study of Victorian novels in the UK, 'the orphan's very presence is both vital to and a disruption of notions of being – particularly home, nation, discourse and writing. The orphan performs a paradoxical function: he or she is both redemptive and a threat' (2000: 28). *Specimen Days* uses the orphan trope in such ambiguous ways. The novel operates in a web of contemporary American discourses that in various ways define the nation. Bringing the trope of the orphan into settings marked by current conflicts about American identity, the novel 'familiarizes' the American Adam even while it complicates the notion of family; by breaking with normative ideas of family, it worries the idea(l) of American nation-as-family. While the TTOF orphans function as important symbols of hope for the future, the orphan boys in *Specimen Days* stand for both violence and vulnerability. They are un-heroic and neglected, paradoxically positioned both outside and inside the American family.

In the literary criticism of the past few years on writing about 9/11 and on the effects of 9/11 on writing, Cunningham's novel has received little attention. One of the novels that has received the most scholarly attention is Jonathan Safran Foer's *Extremely Loud and Incredibly Close*. Like Cunningham, Foer chooses to envision the aftermath of 9/11 through the trajectory of an orphan boy who is quite different from his literary predecessors in classic American literature, but his novel is much more explicit in addressing the attacks. It may also have attracted scholarly attention because of its experimental style and visually compelling design. However, we would suggest that a major difference between Cunningham's and Foer's novels that may also inform their different cultural status is their treatment of the orphan child as a signifier of national crisis. Orphan boys in the former novel are uncanny, unreliable, and remain outside the family, resisting social inclusion, whereas Foer's orphan protagonist travels via quest and estrangement toward social inclusion, and apparently offers consolation to many readers.

Sentimentality and the boy orphan: 'feeling right' in Jonathan Safran Foer's *Extremely Loud and Incredibly Close*

Although sentimental novels longingly look back to a time when families were understood as consanguineous units, novel after novel is engaged in ridding itself of the paternalism of consanguinity by replacing it with a family that is based on affection ... (Weinstein, 2004: 9)

In a study of sentimental novels in the nineteenth century, Weinstein observes that '"[f]eeling right" informs virtually all sentimental fiction, regardless of political intentions. Novel after novel tells the story of children learning how to feel right about their families, selves, nation, and God in the face of great pain, which almost always takes the form of parental loss' (*ibid.*: 1). Although it is not apparent from the quoted passage, Weinstein focuses on female children; it is girls who learn how to 'feel right' in the nineteenth-century American novel.[38]

In Foer's *Extremely Loud and Incredibly Close*, the white boy Oskar becomes an orphan when his father is killed in the twin tower attack. The emphasis on emotions in the characterization of this orphan suggests that while much has changed since the nineteenth century

Extremely Loud and Incredibly Close is indeed a novel about learning to feel right about family, self, and nation.[39] If to Weinstein, 'feeling right' indicates the emotional/ideological work done by children in fiction to align the family and the nation, Foer's novel is an exploration of right feeling in this sense, but it is also linked to understandings in eighteenth-century moral philosophy of 'sentiment' as a capacity for 'right' feelings of compassion, and having a solid moral compass (Howard, 2001: 223–8). Throughout Oskar's trajectory, the novel investigates meanings of sentiment and sentimentality; meanings that are linked not only to gender, but also to class.

Oskar Schell is a nine-year-old boy with signs of Aspberger's syndrome, a collector, an inventor, an eccentric, 'nerdy' boy with a sophisticated understanding of language and science. Sent home early from school on what he calls 'the worst day' (Foer, 2005: 11), he hears his father's messages from the World Trade Center restaurant Window on the World on the answering machine, but fails to pick up the receiver when the father makes a final call home. He hides the answering machine in his wardrobe, and occasionally listens to the recordings of his father's voice. Although Oskar feels tremendously guilty about hiding his father's calls, he is unable to tell his mother about them, because 'protecting her is one of [his] most important *raisons d'être*' (ibid.: 68). A year after the attacks, Oskar finds a vase in his father's closet, in the vase an envelope with the word 'Black' written on it, and inside the envelope a small key. At first, finding the right lock for the key seems an impossible mission, given the fact that there are, as Oskar estimates, '162 million locks' in New York City (ibid.: 41). Deducing that Black is a name, however, narrows the mission down to visiting 216 addresses listed in the phone book. In the quest that ensues, Oskar turns to these 216 Blacks in the city to try and find his way home. The home he seeks is initially envisioned as paternal, since the search for the owner of the key is an effort to stay close to the father. Oskar reflects: 'Every time I left our apartment to go searching for the lock, I became a little lighter, because I was getting closer to Dad. But I also became a little heavier, because I was getting farther from Mom' (ibid.: 52). At the end of the novel, about two years have passed and Oskar is eleven years old. After some months of searching, he has found the owner of the key, but has also come to the realization that he can never recover his dead father.

According to Foer, Oskar is modeled in part on Oskar Matzerath in Gunther Grass's *The Tin Drum* (1979), a character who refuses to grow after age three, but who has unusual intellectual powers. But Oskar also references characters in American literary history. Like many earlier white American boy orphans, Oskar is undertaking a quest, but in terms of class he is different from Huck Finn as well as other questing orphan boys in New York City, like Ragged Dick. Oskar's habitual white clothing is primarily a sign of class privilege. Furthermore, while his New York quest can be seen as aligning him with the pluck and industry of his boy orphan predecessors, and certainly with their physical freedom to move outside the home, other aspects, such as his liking things that are 'soft and pink' (*ibid.*: 316), do not, nor does his quest *for family*, which instead connects him to the search for the right kind of kinship that Weinstein finds typical of the girl orphan of the sentimental novel. Hence, in Oskar's 'picaresque journey toward healing' (Saal, 2011: 457), emotional work and the domestic orientation of the novel are interwoven with its quest motif, pulling his narrative in two directions that in American literary history have been gendered feminine and masculine, respectively.

Via Oskar, Foer represents the emotions involved in grieving and loss: primarily loneliness, depression, and anxiety, evidenced, for example, in Oskar's recurrent imagined inventions that would keep everyone safe. Oskar attaches easily to strangers but often fails to empathize with his mother and grandmother, and this emotional detachment, or lack of right feeling, balances the overtly emotional aspects – sadness, loss, and fear – of the character. Oskar's narrative often foregrounds intellectual reflection before emotional response, and juxtaposes the violent reactions he would like to have with the mild or neutral ones he actually shows to others. Thus, it comes as a surprise when, in response to his ironically named therapist Dr. Fein's question 'What do you think is going on?' Oskar answers, 'I feel too much. That's what's going on.' When Dr Fein asks, 'Do you think one can feel too much? Or just feel in the wrong ways?' (Foer, 2005: 201), the suggestion is not only that it is possible to feel in 'wrong ways' but also, by implication, in 'right ways.' The therapist subsequently voices the suggestion that something 'good' can come from Oskar's father's death, a notion that Oskar rejects. Nevertheless, this negative experience is also a step in the boy's trajectory toward 'right feeling' at the end of the novel.

Reviewers' reactions to Foer's novel suggest that Oskar's emotional working-through of 9/11 can serve to comfort American readers,[40] for they have asserted that the novel is 'the 9/11 story we needed, whether we knew it or not,' (Jain, 2005), one that is 'everlastingly moving' (Kephart, 2005) yet 'remarkably consoling' (Jain, 2005) – assessments that stress the positive emotional effects of reading and the positive cultural value attached to emotions. However, these reviews also separate emotions from sentimentality. Although disagreeing about whether the novel is sentimental, reviewers who have addressed the element of sentimentality in Foer's novel clearly regard sentimentality as such as undesirable. In one instance sentimentality is labeled a critical 'accusation' and a 'risk' (Ingersoll, 2009: 66); in another the novel is 'sentimentally watery' (Updike, 2005), whereas yet another review lauds the novel because it treats 9/11 'without a hint of sentimentality' (Apte, 2010). Sentimentality, as Milette Shamir and Jennifer Travis observe, can be understood as the foregrounding of sympathy and compassion, an understanding grounded in moral philosophy on 'sentiment' since the eighteenth century. More often, however, sentimentality is understood as excessive or false emotion, as the opposite of authentic feeling. As we have indicated, sentiment/ality has typically figured as a strictly gendered concept in literary criticism,[41] linked above all to femininity and the 'popular,' and thus in opposition to 'serious' literature. Arguably, Foer's representation of Oskar as a cerebral and emotionally detached child serves to balance the sentiment/ality in the narrative to avoid his protagonist's feminization.

Sentimentality operates in Foer's novel on several levels. The narrative explores the link between sentiment – understood simply as emotion – and identification, most strongly perhaps in the meeting between Oskar and William Black, a surrogate father figure. But it also activates the de-essentialized, performative meaning of sentimentality. As June Howard puts it, 'Sentiment and its derivatives indicate a moment when emotion is recognized as socially constructed' (2001: 219), that is, emotion is not natural or authentic. In Foer's novel, sentimentality is also present in this sense, especially in Oskar, whose narrative foregrounds the difference between his actual emotions and the ones he allows others to see, and who moreover undergoes an emotional education in relationship to other people throughout the book, a training that, if emotions were natural, would hardly be needed. Additionally, *Extremely Loud and Incredibly Close* activates sentimentality in terms of generic conventions, since it is a novel that speaks with earlier American orphan stories in the so-called sentimental tradition.

In these earlier orphan fictions, critics including Claudia Nelson have observed, the function of the orphan – typically a girl – is to perform emotional work, and above all to make adults happy.[42] Reading Oskar through this lens underscores the work he does to heal adults: he gives Old Mr Black the gift of hearing, and he also seems to offer some consolation and comfort to Abby Black and her ex-husband William Black, in an extension of the *raison d'être* he states is making his mother happy (Foer, 2005: 7). Oskar is, then, a mourning child who heals adults, who in turn help him to heal. In this way, sentiment and its potential for creating community center on the child figure and Oskar may be read as a reverse Pollyanna. Eleanor Porter's 1913 novel *Pollyanna* represents a sunny and busy orphan girl who offers all she meets the 'glad game' to make life seem brighter.[43] Instead of Pollyanna's 'glad game' Oskar plays a 'sad game.' He walks around with 'heavy boots' and feels that his sadness is a 'big black hole' into which everything happy falls. Oskar is sad about 'everything' (*ibid.*: 42–3), and he has a moment of realization that 'everything was actually horrible' (*ibid.*: 68). Traumatized by the loss of his father, he shares this profound sadness with the people he encounters, and towards the end of the novel it allows him to cry with them. Hence, although lacking the sunny aspect of Pollyanna's game, Oskar's emotions do help to establish community and propel him onward.

Noting the centrality of this emotional work in the novel, Earl G. Ingersoll argues that it is 'Oskar's grandmother and mother who point the way toward healing by bringing together what has been divided and separate, by celebrating the love – even at the risk of "sentimentality" – that passes understanding' (*ibid.*: 66). However, this claim is based on a conventionally gendered division between feeling and reason that causes critical blindness to links between masculinity and sentiment.[44] The female characters are indeed important: Oskar's mother who remains unnamed throughout the novel, but whose power is revealed at the end of it, and the grandmother who tells Oskar that he had better be outspoken about his love for others. However, it is also the emotional work of several male characters that leads to Oskar's realization that rightness of feeling is just as valuable as reason, if not more so; they too guide him towards eventual emotional release, 'feeling right,' and (re)establishing kinship in the last part of the book.

Especially in the last few chapters of the novel, male characters offer a number of moral and emotional lessons, thereby contesting conventional conceptions of the 'affective economy' of US culture wherein 'masculine emotion is "scarce" and feminine emotion is "excessive"' (Shamir and Travis, 2002: 2). One example is the limousine driver Gerald, whom Oskar has befriended. When Oskar asks whether Gerald's two daughters are 'objectively' special the man asks, 'What's that?' Oskar explains: 'Like, factually. Truthfully.' Gerald responds, 'The truth is, I'm their pop' (Foer, 2005: 317), thereby privileging subjectivity and emotion, and rejecting as irrelevant 'objective truth' concerning family relations. Another example is William Black, the owner of the mysterious key, who met Oskar's father briefly and sold him the blue vase. This is as close as Oskar comes to recovering his own father, but at this point Oskar feels that he is 'getting confused about who "he" was' (*ibid.*: 292). Perhaps because of this confusion, he tells William Black the guilty secret about the answering machine, and asks for forgiveness, which he receives. However, this surrogate father figure also offers Oskar a lesson: 'It's easy to be emotional. You can always make a scene ... Highs and lows make you feel that things matter, but they're nothing.' Oskar asks, 'So what's something?' 'Being reliable is something. Being good' is William Black's response (*ibid.*: 297). Yet, he also tells Oskar the story of his own father's death from illness, and they cry together in mourning for their respective paternal losses, thereby demonstrating the futility of trying to reason away emotions. This meeting moreover points to an understanding of sentimentality not only as a genre or a rhetorical mode, but as 'practical consciousness' (Chapman and Hendler, 1999: 6).[45] These and other passages in the novel emphasize the persistent presence of emotion.[46]

Throughout most of the novel, Oskar accuses his mother of unsuitable emotions; he perceives her as being inappropriately happy, and even tells her he wishes she had died instead of the father. Whereas he remembers his father as 'the best person' (Foer, 2005: 256), the mother is not so upheld.[47] Resenting her friendship with a man, Ron, Oskar keeps his eyes on 'her hand with the ring on it' (*ibid.*: 35), obviously concerned that she is not mourning properly, as he sees it. In the final chapter, however, Oskar has realized that his mother knows about his visits to the Blacks. He turns to her, wanting to reveal the secret of the father's phone calls. Instead, she reveals that his father also called her cell phone from the burning tower, and told her he would be all right. In the ensuing exchange between Oskar and his mother, the father is depicted as a man who knew he would not survive, but who wanted to offer his wife some comfort, although 'he knew [she] knew' (*ibid.*: 324). In this exchange, Oskar and his mother envision the father, in a shared moment of remembering 'the worst day,' as a good, caring, and responsible man. During this reconciliatory passage Oskar cries 'so much that everything blurred into everything else' (*ibid.*: 324), and falls asleep in his mother's arms:

> At some point she was carrying me to my room. Then I was in bed. She was looking over me. I don't believe in God, but I believe that things are extremely complicated, and her looking over me was as complicated as anything ever could be. But it was also incredibly simple. In my only life, she was my mom, and I was her son.
> I told her, 'It's OK if you fall in love again.'
> She said, 'I won't fall in love again.'
> I told her 'I want you to.'
> She kissed me and said, 'I'll never fall in love again.'
> I told her, 'You don't have to make it up so I won't worry.'
> She said, 'I love you.'
> I rolled onto my side and listened to her walk back to the sofa. I heard her crying. I imagined her wet sleeves. Her tired eyes. (*ibid.*: 324–5)

At this point, Oskar has arrived at 'feeling right' – in terms of having compassion and being able to make morally right choices (Howard, 2001: 227) – both about his father and his mother. Instead of his mind immediately wandering to other matters when she leaves him, as it does earlier in the narrative, his thoughts stay with the mother in a mode that suggests sympathy and that the mother now, in his eyes, is a full human being. In this way, although Oskar's narrative focuses on his quest to come close to his lost father, the story finally emphasizes the mother–son relationship.[48]

Oskar is a questing boy troubled by too much emotion, a boy who does not escape from family but seems to melt into it by the end of the novel, and who by turning from his dead father to his living mother breaks with the trajectories of boy orphans in literary history. In a sense, he can also be seen to question 'critical master narratives' that 'have masked the continued presence of sentimental men in American culture and letters' (Chapman and Hendler, 1999: 4). While one critic, Ilka Saal, sees the ending of the novel as a 'reconsolidation of the nuclear family' (Saal, 2011: 470), we think the final emphasis on the mother–son dyad suggests a move away from the nuclear family, although it certainly reinscribes the importance of blood kin, and stresses the reintegration of the white orphan boy into a middle-class domestic context.

Although the 'domesticity' of the novel has been read by some as a negation of the 'political,' we would argue, following John Duvall and Robert P. Marzec, that 'the deployment of a domestic situation is not a retreat from but rather a covert engagement with the political' (2011: 386).[49] Oskar's development mixes the conventions of the quest or the picaresque novel with those of sentimental novels, which, again, raises the question of the 'signifying responsibilities' of the figure of the orphan child.[50] Foer's employment of a white child to represent the process of grieving a national trauma is reminiscent of Caroline Levander's observation that American popular novels 'feature children as stand-ins for complicated sets of anxieties about national unity' (2006: 25), and to some degree, Oskar also embodies 'feeling right' in the sense explored by Weinstein since he represents a link between personal and national trauma and healing. However, at least from our European perspective, when juxtaposed with his still-suffering elderly grandparents who experienced the fire-bombing of Dresden during World War II, Oskar's ability to work through his loss in two years serves to temper the exceptionalism and assumed impact of 9/11 as a national trauma by placing it in a larger historical framework.[51]

Especially in the ways they involve questions about the gender, class, and social integration of white orphans, *Extremely Loud and Incredibly Close*, *Specimen Days*, and *Housekeeping* problematize the idea of family as nation and nation as family, as well as the notion of American individualism, and they partly do so by re-activating the literary canon and critical traditions as cultural memory. Indeed, they challenge some central myths in these traditions. Robinson's novel critiques conventional domesticity as the only or preferred choice for girl orphans, while Foer's questions the purported femininity of domesticity and sentimentality. Sentiment and sentimentality operate both generically and rhetorically in Foer's fiction, but Oskar's narrative also highlights sentimentality as indicating the social construction of emotion and its function in building relations with others. We read this as a critique of the conventionally gendered dichotomy of sentiment and reason, but we remain wary of exaggerating the political potentialities of this masculinization of white middle-class emotion.[52]

Both *Housekeeping* and *Specimen Days* engage with and revise the American Adam, that mythic national figure who stands for masculinity, mobility and in particular westward movement, individualism, and historylessness. In Robinson's novel, Ruth's grandfather is an example of this figure, but he is framed and subtly decentered by Ruth's narration. *Specimen Days* de-masculinizes the American Adam in its use of malformed orphan boys as protagonists, and by positioning mother figures as Adams in the stories; these 'mothers' express both the attraction and the ultimate impossibility of this mythical selfhood. In Cunningham's novel the American Adam is embodied by more than one character in each tale: the orphan Lucas and the poet Walt Whitman in the first tale; Cat, the boy terrorist and 'Walt Whitman' in the second; the android Simon, the Nadian Catareen, and the orphan boy Luke in the last one. The novel envisions orphans positioned between a dream of beginnings and a threat of apocalyptic endings, and explores cultural memory in ways that negotiate these two extremes.

All three novels negotiate Euro-American literary traditions in their employment of particular genres and in their representations of orphan characters. *Specimen Days* plays with the conventions of orphan boys, but also represents the orphan boy as an uncanny, unfamiliar presence; here the orphan boys' poverty and marginalization remain unresolved and most often lead to death instead of to riches or unrestrained freedom. In Foer's novel, Oskar's geographical movement, his quest, and his developmental trajectory clearly resonate with those of other orphan boys in literary history. At the same time, Oskar is represented as a child who struggles with emotions in a way that draws upon but revises elements from the reputedly 'feminine' sentimental novel. Moreover, the novel ends with Oskar's domestic integration into a female-headed home. *Extremely Loud and Incredibly Close* thus works intertextually not only with novels by male writers in the canonical tradition but also with tales of orphan girls told by women writers in the sentimental and domestic tradition. In *Housekeeping*, it is Lucille's development that constitutes the intertextual connection to this tradition. She is easily recognized as a latter-day descendant of the heroine of the nineteenth-century American female *bildungsroman*. The first-person narrator, Ruth, cannot be placed easily within these traditions, which have served to allay middle-class anxieties about broken families and homelessness. Her quest for and mourning of her dead mother sets her outside American middle-class materialism and domesticity; her language and sense of orphanhood echo the earliest Euro-American writings of the Pilgrims and Puritans. Like Huck Finn, she eschews society for a transient life, but unlike him she also rejects the individualist mobility of the hero in American literary history: she travels with Sylvie and joins a community of transients. The trajectories of the Euro-American boy and girl orphans in these novels partly entail a repositioning in terms of gender and genre. In Chapter 4, we focus on three contemporary novels that feature Euro-American orphan protagonists and which negotiate gender and genre as well as race and family, particularly in relation to the genre of the *bildungsroman*.

Notes

1. The authors do not necessarily have to be aware of specific genre conventions. See Bakhtin on genre memory in *Problems of Dostoevsky's Poetics* (1984: 121).
2. See for instance Versluys (2009), or Duvall and Marzec (2011) for discussions of the effects on representational practices of the attacks in 2001.
3. For an excellent in-depth discussion of girl orphans in sentimental novels see Cindy Weinstein (2004).
4. Leslie Fiedler, for instance, seems annoyed to discover that there are similarities between Huck Finn and female white orphans in nineteenth-century American novels: 'in *Huckleberry Finn* ... Huck has been permitted occasionally to *gush* over the loneliness of life on the Mississippi in a *schoolgirl style*, which betrays his *unsuspected affiliation* to the female orphans of Susan Warner and Maria Cummins' (1962: 567, emphasis added).
5. The expression comes from Eve Sedgwick (quoted in Chapman and Hendler, 1999: 4); for explorations of masculinity and sentimentality see for example, *ibid.*, or Shamir and Travis (2002).
6. 'Discussions of the female *bildungsroman* began to appear in the critical literature in the early 1970s, when critics recognized its rise as a reflection of the contemporary feminist movement' (Fuderer, 1990: 2), but many of the most important critical discussions of this genre were published during the 1980s. See Elizabeth Abel, Marianne Hirsch and Elizabeth Langland's *The Voyage In* (1983). See also Sondra O'Neale (1982) and Bonnie Hoover Braendlin (1983) on *bildung* in ethnic and African American women's writing.
7. Kornfeld and Jackson's selected novels are Louisa May Alcott's *Little Women* series (1868–86), Margaret Sidney's *Five Little Peppers* books (1881–1916), Kate Douglass Wiggin's *Rebecca of Sunnybrook Farm* (1903), and Lucy Maud Montgomery's *Anne of Green Gables* series (1908–39) (Kornfeld and Jackson, 1987).

8   Critics have addressed domesticity in *Housekeeping*. For instance, Paula E. Geyh (1993) links the house and domesticity to two models of feminine subjectivity: the settled (tied to housekeeping) and the transient (tied to unhousing). She also brings up the connections between the house of the father, house as family, and the house of the nation. For other discussions of domesticity in *Housekeeping*, see Jacqui Smyth (1999) and Christine Wilson (2008).

9   In an article on horizons of grace that emphasizes Helen's suicide in *Housekeeping*, Katy Ryan observes, 'Structurally, the function of the mother's suicide seems obvious. Helen's death creates two orphans – that preferred status in literature that frees characters up for adventure and self-discovery' (2005: 349).

10 'Asked about influences on *Housekeeping* in a 1989 radio interview, Robinson cited the coming together of the physical and spiritual in such nineteenth-century writers as Herman Melville, Emily Dickinson, and Jonathan Edwards [sic]' (Gernes, 1991: 156). For a discussion of Robinson's novel in connection with Jonathan Edwards and Puritan spiritual autobiography, see Troy (1999: 46–50).

11 Poe's novel *The Narrative of Arthur Gordon Pym* (1838) begins 'My name is Arthur Gordon Pym' and then lists male relatives and their professions. Ravits and others have noted *Housekeeping*'s relationship to the 'great texts of the American tradition' as well as its revision of the Bible's patrilinear and patriarchal tendencies (1989: 644–45). Kristin King argues that Robinson's novel, 'with all its resonances of American male voices, does not dismantle a tradition but demands a voice in it' (1996: 575). In an early 1990s interview conducted by Thomas Schaub, Robinson says that the book that she admires 'most in the world is *Moby-Dick*, after the Bible of course,' despite there being no significant women characters in Melville's novel, and she continues: 'I thought if I could write a book in which there are no male characters that men could read – comfortably – then I get *Moby-Dick*' (1994: 234–5). Already at the time of this interview, Robinson remarked that she had 'some claim on *Moby-Dick* ... because men have been very receptive readers of *Housekeeping*' (ibid.: 235), with its focus on female rather than male characters.

12 Sheila Ruzycki O'Brien highlights the 'centrality of the grandfather Edmund as a solitary ancestral quester' and argues that 'Edmund looms as a mythic Westerner in the novel ...' (1993: 218). Millard comments on the novel's linking of mobility and creativity as 'quintessentially western and American' (2007: 133).

13 Maureen Ryan asserts, 'In *Housekeeping*, Marilynne Robinson revises the traditional American myth of freedom and transience, endorsing not independence over commitment, autonomy over family, but both; affirming, finally, female difference' (1991: 86).

14 Millard asserts that Ruth *writes* the narrative of *Housekeeping* (2007: 137), but there is no textual evidence that she does.
15 In a discussion of the female American hobo, where she examines *Little Orphan Annie* (1924–64) and *Housekeeping*, Joanne Hall declares that 'The female hobo defies categorisation: she becomes the "othered" other occupying the margins of a marginalised subculture' (2006: 48).
16 In 'My Western Roots,' Robinson states, 'I feel I have found a place in the West for my West, and the legitimation of a lifelong intuition of mine that the spirit of this place is, as spirits go, mysterious, aloof, and rapturously gentle. It is, historically, among other things, the orphan child of a brilliant century' (1993b: 171–2).
17 In 1982, in conversation with Katrina E. Bachinger, Robinson defined the 'ultimate feminism' as being '[w]hen you can actually put aside that category and write about women, but not as if you were writing about people who are some minor or special strain in the species rather than being simply human, human in the sense that everyone is human' (Bachinger, 1986: 14).
18 In the 1980s, Thomas Foster, Phyllis Lassner, Anne-Marie Mallon, and Roberta Rubenstein read *Housekeeping* as a feminist novel. Siân Mile (1990) however takes issue with this view. In the 1990s, Karen Kaivola (1993: 688) and Christine Caver (1996: 113) address *Housekeeping*'s appeal for feminists, but question the validity of feminist readings.
19 In contrast to the positive critical response to Cunningham's novel *The Hours*, which draws intertextually on Virginia Woolf's life and writing, reviewers were generally not impressed by the references to Whitman in *Specimen Days*: Michiko Kakutani considered Walt Whitman and *Leaves of Grass* 'afterthoughts grafted onto the tales in *Specimen Days* in an effort to lend them extra philosophical weight' and Cunningham's use of the poem 'gratuitous and pretentious blather' (2005: 2); Caleb Cain was disappointed because '[i]t isn't clear that Cunningham likes Whitman' (2005: 1).
20 In this it resembles Cunningham's *The Hours* (1998), which similarly interweaves three different narrative strands and also works explicitly intertextually with another text, Virginia Woolf's *Mrs. Dalloway* (1925).
21 The title echoes that of Kurt Vonnegut's modern classic *Slaughterhouse Five or The Children's Crusade, a Duty-dance with Death* (1969), and like Billy Pilgrim, the central characters in Cunningham's novel become 'unstuck in time.' Historically, 'The Children's Crusade' refers to different historical events that involved children and activism. In 1212 several thousand 'wandering poor' marched through parts of Europe, hoping to peacefully convert Muslims in the Holy Land but instead typically ended up being sold as slaves. In the subsequent narrativization the march was represented as undertaken by poor children. The phrase also denotes

two events in the USA, a 1903 march to protest against child labor in Northern mills and mines, and a Southern march during the civil rights movements in 1963.
22 For orphans in American society in the nineteenth century see Pazicky (1998). See also Lori Askeland (2006) and Claudia Nelson (2003).
23 For discussions of shifts in meanings of whiteness in the USA, see Matthew Frye Jacobson (1999); see also Robert Duggan (2010: 384).
24 On cultural anxieties and public debates about child welfare and child safety in the USA between the 1950s and 1990s see Leroy Ashby (1997).
25 The fire in the Triangle shirtwaist factory in Manhattan occurred in 1911. Accordingly, Walter Kalaidjian places the action of 'In the Machine' in that year (2007: 841). The temporal setting is complicated, however, by the fact that Luke in this story also meets Walt Whitman, whose *Leaves of Grass* has been published only recently (the first edition appeared in 1855); the poet died in 1892.
26 For a discussion of anxiety about 'alien' women as surrogate parents see for example Barbara Ehrenreich and Arlie Hochschild (2003).
27 Some examples were TV reports and specials such as 'Wives and Mothers of Flight 93 Discuss Loved Ones,' *NBC Nightly News*, March 11, 2002; 'Families Left Behind, Effects of 9/11,' *ABC News*, September 11, 2002; and '63 Reasons to Hope,' *Primetime Live, ABC News*, August 29, 2002; as well as the many interviews with widowed Lisa Beamer. See also Susan Faludi (2007: 93–102).
28 For further discussion of children and 9/11, see Caroline Levander (2006), and Faludi (2007).
29 See Faludi (2007) on media representations of bereaved families and 'post-9/11-babies.'
30 For an interesting reading of the links between this character and escaped slaves, see Duggan (2010: 389).
31 See Simpson on 'self-orphaned' protagonists in the US canon (1988: 228–9).
32 For explorations of ideological links between childhood and innocence, see James Kincaid (1998), and Caroline Levander and Carol Singley (2005).
33 See also Philippe Ariès' study *Centuries of Childhood* (1962) for an in-depth discussion of such shifts.
34 For critiques of the uses of the Adamic figure in American literature see also Viorica Patea (2001).
35 While Lewis (1955) sees the Adamic self as linked to orphanhood in, for example, Hawthorne and Melville, he argues that orphanhood has no place in Whitman's work, since he created the world and the self in a way that needed no past.

36 The old woman called Walt Whitman also de-masculinizes the American Adam and alters the meaning of 'new beginnings' when she states that they are living in the beginning of *the end* of the world: 'it's starting ... [t]he end of days' (Cunningham, 2005: 168), thereby both reflecting and negating Cat's own dream of rebirth.
37 See, however, Tony Dokoupil for a discussion of an actual case of African American parents adopting a white child.
38 Joe Sutliff Sanders similarly notes that 'sentimental fiction and its descendants make a point of instructing their weak characters (and readers) in the art of being pleasant, of being *good* invalids, orphans, or waifs' (2008: 44).
39 We focus here on the narrative strand of Oskar's confessional narrative, and not on the chapters featuring his grandparents' perspectives. The grandfather's and grandmother's narratives have received scholarly attention; Ilka Saal's article (2011) on trauma transfer is particularly compelling.
40 This comforting function is also noted by Saal (2011: 470).
41 Chapman and Hendler go so far as to argue that 'work on sentimentality since 1985 has largely accepted the gendering of sentiment as feminine' (1999: 5).
42 The child does not, however, change the distribution of social power in the sentimental genre: 'although fictional children of [the nineteenth century] were imagined to exude influence over adults, this influence "does not fundamentally alter the structures of power"' (Sánchez-Eppler, quoted in Sanders, 2008: 48).
43 For a discussion of *Pollyanna*, see Sanders (2008).
44 On masculinity and sentimentality, see Chapman and Hendler (1999).
45 Chapman and Hendler refer to Raymond Williams's concept of the 'structure of feeling,' as do Shamir and Travis, who point out that Williams discusses feeling 'not *against* thought but *as* thought, not as *preceding* the social but *as* social ... [It] occupies a temporal present, an emergent or preemergent state before the procedure of classifying, defining, and fixing as cultural products (and relegating to the past) sets in' (2002: 7, original emphasis).
46 However, male tears can also be interpreted as 'the psychological-therapeutic *standing in for* political change' (Shamir and Travis, 2002: 17, original emphasis).
47 Oskar's father's innocence points in the direction of 'father-as-hero' in a post-9/11-context as discussed by Faludi in *The Terror Dream* (2007). However, when Oskar's grandfather envisions the father as a hero who went into the tower to save others, Oskar responds, 'That's what he was like' (Foer, 2005: 255–6), but states matter-of-factly that he knows this

was not what happened. Although heroics are rejected, Oskar nevertheless concludes that his father was 'the best person' (256).
48 In a sense it also repeats the pattern of 'salvation through motherly love' that Jane Tompkins finds being a recurring formula in nineteenth-century fiction (quoted in Chapman and Hendler, 1999: 4).
49 For further discussions see Aaron DeRosa (especially 2011: 616), and Duvall and Marzec (especially 2011: 383).
50 Ingersoll describes Foer's novel as offering 'a powerful vision of how "a child shall lead us" through the passages of suffering, loss, survivor's guilt, and despair toward the promise of recuperation' (2009: 66).
51 The novel's multiple narrative perspectives also serve to complicate questions concerning US victimhood and culpability. Critics who focus primarily on the grandparents' narratives have argued both for the globalizing function of Foer's juxtaposition of the suffering of the American child with that of adult Euro-American immigrants (Mullins, 2009) and against it (Saal, 2011).
52 It is not certain that 'white, middle-class emotion, and a discourse on white, middle class masculine emotion [can] remake existing forms of power'; it might instead reinforce them (Shamir and Travis, 2002: 9). As Sanders points out regarding nineteenth-century novels, 'right feeling heads off the need for action allowing inequity to persist' (2008: 58).

4

Family matters: Euro-American orphans, the *bildungsroman*, and kinship building

> Implicit in a phrase like 'loved ones' is an open-ended notion of kinship that respects the principles of choice and self-determination in defining kin, with love spanning the ideologically contrasting domains of biological family and families we create. (Weston, 1997: 183)

As we have seen in Chapter 3, contemporary orphan tales typically foreground alternative, or non-normative, families. In this chapter we focus on John Irving's *The Cider House Rules* (1985), and Kaye Gibbons's *Ellen Foster* (1987) and *The Life All Around Me by Ellen Foster* (2006). These novels question widespread assumptions about the benefits of the nuclear family through their orphan protagonists' explorations of alternative kinship constellations. Because they are orphans, Irving's and Gibbons's protagonists are outsiders, but because they are white they may still lay claim to the dominant formulation of American identity; and the challenge they launch against the nuclear family ideal may be effectual precisely because they occupy a position of racial privilege.

While we discuss how ideas about childhood, orphanhood, and notions of kinship operate in these novels, the central concern is how such socio-historically grounded aspects of the narratives relate to their development of the *bildungsroman* genre.[1] Hence, this chapter continues a discussion begun in Chapter 3 about the possibilities for using the white orphan figure to reconfigure the cultural memory of genre and literary history. Irving's and Gibbons's novels foreground the conventions of the classic *bildungsroman*, but also question or revise them. Indeed, we argue that these novels trouble gendered genre conventions, and that they elaborate on the genre's convention of social inclusion in specifically familial terms. While they critique familial norms, they simultaneously engage intertextually with and, at times, 'write back' to earlier American and English novels in this genre.

Bildung should be understood in two ways. It refers to the formal or informal education of the orphan child or young adult. But *bildung* also denotes what we term *kinship building*: a development of kinship ties that furthers an understanding of family as processual and inclusive; it privileges an idea of family based on affinity and emotional investment that does not adhere to the nuclear family, defined by blood or law.[2] In this sense, Irving's and Gibbons's novels are fictional explorations of constructionist ideas about kinship as practice that have gained prominence in anthropology and interdisciplinary family studies. In representing kinship as processual, they also share common ground with the novels by Linda Hogan and Barbara Kingsolver examined in Chapter 2. Like them, they ultimately establish some limits to the inclusiveness of family, and in Irving's and Gibbons's novels these limits are both gendered and raced.

Interracial family relations, and especially parent–child relations, are central to many contemporary novels, predominantly by Southern authors, including John Gregory Brown's *The Wrecked Blessed Body of Shelton LaFleur* (1996), Connie May Fowler's *Before Women Had Wings* (1997), Sue Monk Kidd's *The Secret Life of Bees* (2002), and Lorrie Moore's *A Gate at the Stairs* (2009). Although different in terms of temporal and spatial setting, as well as central thematic concerns, these novels elaborate on racial difference and the capacity for parental love and care, as well as the material and political conditions under which kinship is formed. Kidd's novel, set in the 1960s, foregrounds black women's capacity for love and care of a white girl, which is contrasted with the abusive practices of her white father in ways that are strongly reminiscent of *Ellen Foster*. Fowler's *Before Women Had Wings*, set in the same decade, is narrated by a poor white girl, who, like her older sister, is abused by their alcoholic mother; the narrator and her sister are finally rescued by the caring and wise black woman named Zora. Brown's novel is set in the 1930s and is unusual in that it features a white family that 'adopts' – actually, buys – a black boy, who after a subsequent stint in a black orphanage returns to his birth father. Moore's work, set in a post-9/11 context, shares with Brown's a concern with the mechanisms behind privileged white parents adopting black children, and a representation of the white adoptive mother as inadequate and finally unable to care for the black child. Irving's and Gibbons's novels do not offer representations of interracial families, but interracial relations play a part in their protagonists' kinship building and, albeit variously, both authors use the idea of the 'black family' to relationally construct a 'white family.' We focus on Irving's and Gibbons's novels partly because of how the kinship of white Euro-American orphans is constructed both through gender difference and racial difference, but also in tension with the *bildungsroman* genre.

Through representations of diverse family arrangements, the novels engage with ongoing debates about the downfall or survival of the family in the USA, addressing issues like single parenting, foster care, adoption, and 'the child's best interest' that were circulating in the 1980s and into the early twenty-first century, but were differently inflected in different decades. The 1980s, the years of the Reagan administration, saw a republican slant to family values that included the President's clear stand against abortion, and intensified attacks on welfare in order to 'cut back on domestic government services and taxes, to let market forces deal with social problems, and to halt a perceived "breakdown of the American family"' (Ashby, 1997: 166). In the 1980s there was also 'notable evidence of the growing reaction to the idea of children's rights' that had made some progress in the preceding decades (*ibid*.: 149). For instance, the national conferences on children's needs convened approximately every ten years since 1909 were replaced in 1980 by smaller state conferences.

In the 1980s, then, the relative radicalism of the 1970s and the collective struggles of underprivileged groups were beginning to be overrun by conservatism and individualism; one sign of the backlash was the defeat of the Equal Rights Amendment in 1982. This turn away from radicalism occurred in an era marked by significant shifts in familial practices and family politics. For example, the domestic so-called 'adoption pool' continued to grow, but while especially children of color in need of families became steadily more numerous, white families in the USA became less likely to adopt domestically, while transnational adoption increased. As some critics have pointed out, the circumstance of more children staying in the domestic adoption pool may have served to facilitate the legitimacy, and in some states the legalization, of gay adoption, which became a real possibility in this decade.[3] Thus, the 1980s saw developments in child welfare and family practices that, in part, enabled new forms of family.

During the 1990s, under the Clinton administration, fatherlessness was defined as a major social problem, and 'father absence' gained prominence both as a political issue and a topic in scholarship; in both arenas it was often argued that children need a male parent for healthy development.[4] During this decade, too, the Adoption and Safe Families Act (ASFA) that was passed in 1997 replaced the 1980 Adoption Assistance and Child Welfare Act, which had been designed to shorten children's time in foster care and to effect the reunion of children and birth parents. In the 1990s, the ASFA shifted the focus away from family reunification towards the needs of children for permanent and stable situations. According to Dorothy Roberts, although the main aim of the ASFA was to facilitate the adoption of foster children, the termination of parental rights promoted by the Act resulted in growing racial imbalances in US foster care (2003: 104–13). African American children today remain over-represented in care, and scholars attribute this trend to multiple causes, predominantly higher poverty levels but also, in part, to cultural biases among child welfare authorities, including stigmatization of African American single-mother families.[5]

The failings of the foster care system and the dismal prospects for children in the system have mobilized the main arguments since the late 1980s for reintroducing group homes for children. Around 1990, commentators across the political spectrum[6] suggested orphanages would be the best solution to problems with, and outright scandals in, foster care.[7] In the mid-1990s, however, Republican Speaker of the House, Newt Gingrich, and Charles Murray (of 'bell curve' notoriety) suggested orphanages as a means to solve the social problem of 'illegitimacy' and 'welfare mothers.' Although primarily arguing for orphanages as a means to cut welfare costs, Gingrich and Murray – continuing the line of reasoning established in the Moynihan Report of blaming women for the 'crisis of the family' – also alluded to the idea of single mothers as undeserving and morally corrupt. Because reactionary commentators spotlighted illegitimacy and women's sexuality, people in other political camps who had initially been in favor of group homes for children were alienated, the debate faltered, and 'orphanage' soon became an 'impossible word' (London, 1999: 98).

In earlier and ongoing debates about the benefits and drawbacks of orphanages in the USA, cultural representations of orphans and orphanages have been invoked as immediately recognizable illustrations of children in need. In the 1990s orphanage debate, Gingrich suggested that Americans who felt reluctant about orphanages should watch the film *Boys Town* (1938), which, he was certain, would convince them about the merits of these institutions. Historian Timothy Hacsi conjures the most common images of orphans and orphanages by referring to *Oliver Twist* (1838) and the long-running comic strip *Little Orphan Annie* which began in 1894, only to argue that these representations are far from the truth of the social history of US orphanages. Hacsi also points out that, although children in foster care outnumbered children in institutions by the late 1950s, 'orphanages never completely went away' in the USA. And they continue to operate in the new millennium:

> Many institutions that function as homes for troubled children began as orphan asylums. And orphanages have never left the public's consciousness, though they are remembered in two different ways. Some see them as Dickensian warehouses where children are virtually starved and dressed in rags, while others remember them as idealized 'Boys Towns' where children are raised by a wise, loving father figure. (Hacsi, 1997: 219)

It is of course striking that, even as it makes claims for the orphanage as a contemporary phenomenon, Hacsi's study relies on cultural images from the past to convey its meanings. Indeed, the representations of orphans most often employed both by politicians and scholars are those of the nineteenth century or the 1920s and 1930s. In this way, the orphanage and, hence, the orphan can be remanded in the past, either to invoke nostalgia, or to frame orphans as a past rather than a contemporary concern. That the orphan child in these fictions and films is white effects a racialization of the orphan that is aligned with the cultural hegemony of whiteness as 'Americanness.' It is also clear that the orphanage in such symbolic renditions is typically a masculine space, run either by good father figures, as in the film *Boys Town*, or bad ones, as in novels by Charles Dickens. This patriarchal emphasis is marked in contemporary novels such as *The Cider House Rules* and Hannah Tinti's *The Good Thief* (2008), which draw in different ways on Dickens in their fictional depictions of American orphanages.

However, the twenty-first century has also witnessed a re-emergence of the white orphan child as a symbolically important figure in a historical moment that is a post-traumatic 'present': the aftermath of the attack on the World Trade Center, as noted in Chapter 3. As this brief sketch of the past few decades indicates, the whitening of the orphan child in the media occurred while the number of orphans in the USA who are children of color increased. Media representations make an investigation into the gendering and racialization of the white orphan in post-civil rights novels an important undertaking. Thus, here we address the signifying capabilites of white orphans, the kinds of narrative and ideological processes they are involved in, and the ways that the stories of these orphans can be understood as engaging with earlier literature, drawing upon and shaping cultural memory through literature, especially in their engagement with the *bildungsroman* genre.

Critics have suggested that the contemporary American *bildungsroman* balances between 'presenting its protagonist as a newborn who is innocent of history and depicting a protagonist whose coming of age consists principally of acquiring historical knowledge' (Millard, 2007: 7). The notion of initial innocence is critiqued rather than taken for granted in the novels we analyze, where the protagonists' development is related to achieving historical as well as social knowledge – including learning about racism – that works towards identification and empathy rather than towards individualism and independence. Although it is often true that '[t]he historical awareness that the adolescent acquires is at odds with the faith in the sovereign individual and the mythology of self-determination that the genre of coming-of-age might appear to endorse' (*ibid.*: 10), nonetheless, self-determination is crucial, particularly in *Ellen Foster*. However, the masculinism of this mythology is problematized both in Gibbons's novels and in *The Cider House Rules*. The following analyses draw out the tensions in these orphan tales between the individual and the group, and between autonomy and relationality. While *The Cider House Rules* and both Ellen Foster novels undertake a 'dialogue' with the genre in its traditional guise, the picture is complicated by their also engaging with the conventions of the female *bildungsroman*.

The classic English *bildungsroman* features a male protagonist, often an orphan, whose journey from childhood to adulthood involves both formal education and learning about life in general. Typical features of the genre are enumerated by Jerome Hamilton Buckley: 'childhood, the conflict of generations, provinciality, the larger society, self-education, alienation, ordeal by love, the search for a vocation and a working philosophy' (1974: 18). In Buckley's taxonomy, the hero of the *bildungsroman* is always a 'he,' who has typically lost his father or both birth parents (*ibid.*: 19), but the genre obtained different national inflections in Germany, England, and the USA: the German *bildungsroman* usually focused on 'the individual's cultivation' and not his 'responsibility for the national culture,' whereas the English tried to encompass both the individual's development and 'the affiliations one had with the people – family, friends, acquaintances, and strangers – who constituted and shared one's social environment' (Jeffers, 2005: 35). Thomas Jeffers asserts that the 'American note' was 'struck somewhere between the German and the English' (*ibid.*: 35). As we indicate in Chapter 1, the American note chimed differently, though, depending on the protagonist's gender: closer to the German *bildungsroman* in novels featuring a male protagonist and closer to the English when featuring a female heroine.

We noted in Chapter 3 that feminist critics of the 1980s examined women's appropriation of the *bildungsroman*, including Chicana and African American women writers' interventions in the genre.[8] One central argument was that female fictions of development 'reflect the tensions between the assumptions of a genre that embodies male norms and the values of its female protagonists' (Abel, Hirsch and Langland, 1983: 11). In *The Voyage In: Fictions of Female Development*, Elizabeth Abel, Marianne Hirsch, and Elizabeth Langland highlight the commonalities as well as the differences between the female and the classic *bildungsroman*:

> While emphasizing gender differences, our definition shares common ground with the presuppositions and generic features of the traditional *Bildungsroman*: belief in a coherent self (although not necessarily an autonomous one); faith in the possibility of development (although change may be frustrated, may occur at different stages and rates, and may be concealed in the narrative); insistence on a time span in which development occurs (although the time span may exist only in memory); and emphasis on social context (even as an adversary). (*ibid.*: 14)

By then, the *bildungsroman* was seen by these critics as having 'played out its possibilities for males,' while it was argued that 'female versions of the genre still offer a vital form' (*ibid.*: 13). Seen in this light, *The Cider House Rules* with its male orphan protagonist Homer Wells is something of an anachronism. However, time and explorations of the ethnic *bildungsroman* have demonstrated that the male *bildungsroman* hero is far from obsolete. Indeed, *The Cider House Rules* seems to draw on the growing awareness in the 1980s that the female *bildungsroman* had its own distinctive tradition, and that it could work to revitalize the genre also in novels with a male protagonist.

In the nineteenth-century American *bildungsroman* the differences between the trajectories of a female and a male orphan protagonist – like Gerty in *The Lamplighter* (1854) and Huckleberry Finn – and the generic conventions of the novels in which they appear were even more marked than in the British tradition, as exemplified by Charles Dickens's *Great Expectations* (1861) and Charlotte Brontë's *Jane Eyre* (1847). In *The Cider House Rules*, Homer Wells grows up on a literary diet of classic English orphan tales by Dickens and Brontë, and makes them points of reference in his own life. The novels we examine also draw specifically upon white American orphans. Huck Finn is the most obvious orphan in this context, and, indeed, his intertextual presence is felt in Gibbons's *Ellen Foster*, which re-genders this character.[9] Ellen Foster echoes Twain's Huck in a quirky narration, its vernacular 'replete with southern speech patterns' (Monteith, 2000: 65), and in the key details of her story of escaping an abusive father, being white and poor, and having an African American character as her most intimate companion.[10] Thus, the gendering of national *bildungsroman* conventions is not upheld in the contemporary American novels that are our focus in this chapter. However, we see no simple re-gendering, but rather a troubling of gendered boundaries, a blending of genre conventions that were formerly more unambiguously gendered.

The Cider House Rules is largely set in an orphanage, whereas Ellen Foster, true to her name, becomes a foster child in a new family. As already suggested in the brief outline of the socio-historical context above, 'orphanage' and 'foster care' are heavily charged concepts in the contemporary US context. While as institutions and practices, orphanages and fostering have their own social histories that correspond to or deviate from the images and emotions that these terms typically conjure, they figure in specific ways in the novels under scrutiny here.

Depicting experiences of orphanages and foster care, the novels also draw upon debates on child abuse in the development of their protagonists. Homer Wells's placement in prospective adoptive families is often terminated due to physical or sexual abuse, whereas Ellen Foster flees her birth father who abuses her. Child abuse, which emerged in the media as a social problem in the USA in the

1960s, rapidly gained more attention in the 1980s when the issue of child sexual abuse was raised as a major concern, and in the 1990s, with debates about recovered memory.[11] While some advocated children's human rights, other commentators advocated parental rights, including parents' rights to use corporal punishment to discipline children. The problems addressed in these debates undermine the notion that living in a family is always in the child's best interest, and also temper the notion that 'father absence' is necessarily a major problem for all children. As Leroy Ashby points out, by 1996 'one of the leading advocates of family preservation programs, Richard Gelles, had concluded that the goals of protecting children and saving the family unit were in basic conflict' (Ahby, 1997: 175). The protagonists of *The Cider House Rules* and the Ellen Foster novels struggle to grow, develop, and learn in spite of growing up in an orphanage, being introduced to series of (potential) foster families, and/or being subject to abuse at home.

Shaped in part by contemporary discourses on, among other things, child abuse and trauma,[12] but also by their relations to literary forbears, the development of the protagonists involves – indeed their existence and survival depend upon – creating affiliations outside the nuclear family. Hence kinship building, envisioned largely in a context marked by racial and gendered difference, becomes essential to the white orphans' *bildung*. As we will show, Irving's and Gibbons's orphan characters make home, they create or accept shifting kinship arrangements, but the ways that families are racialized – by integrating or separating 'black family' and 'white family' – and gendered – for example in the presence or absence of mothers and fathers – are central to the understanding of kinship that the novels finally offer.

'We are an orphanage': John Irving's *The Cider House Rules*

> If you fail to withhold love at an orphanage, you will create an orphanage that no orphan will willingly leave. You will create a Homer Wells – a true orphan, because his only home will always be at St Cloud's. God (or whoever) forgive me. I have made an orphan; his name is Homer Wells and he will belong to St. Cloud's forever. (Irving, 1985: 39–40)

Since his debut in 1968, John Irving has published a dozen novels, many of which have been bestsellers, and his work has been critically acclaimed (Davis and Womack, 2004: 1). Some of Irving's novels, such as *The World According to Garp* (1978) and *A Widow for One Year* (1998), engage with central feminist issues such as reproductive rights, prostitution, and the sexual abuse of women, and feature memorable female characters. Others, like *A Prayer for Owen Meany* (1989) and *Last Night in Twisted River* (2009), focus more insistently on men's relationships with one another, pushing women firmly into the narrative margins. All his novels, though, may be termed family novels in that they explore the inner workings of families as well as the notion of American family, typically presenting readers with unconventional kinship formations that challenge the normative power of the American nuclear family ideal.[13] One prominent example of such explorations and challenges is Irving's bestseller *The Cider House Rules*.[14]

The Cider House Rules is a novel of development that spans the late nineteenth to the mid-twentieth century, and large parts of it are focalized through two male protagonists, the orphan Homer Wells and Dr Wilbur Larch. The novel is largely set in an orphanage, a milieu that in the 1980s would seem anachronistic to many. The first American orphanage was established in 1729, and numbers rose slowly until the Civil War and mass immigration from Europe resulted in a peak in numbers at approximately one thousand orphanages in 1923, housing as many as 143,000 children.[15] In addition, poor children with living parents increasingly populated orphanages in the early twentieth century. Beginning in the 1930s, however, foster care began to substitute for orphanages; behind this shift were economic factors, but also the argument that children needed home-like environments rather than institutions, and the increasing power of social workers to define the problem of child welfare. After the 1940s, there was also a shift in the population of orphan asylums from poor children to troubled children.[16] A small number of orphanages have continued to operate, although often under new names, such as residential education facilities.[17] Around 1960, the time when Irving's novel ends, orphanages were clearly in decline.[18]

Through its characters, plot, and the setting of St Cloud's orphanage, Irving's novel foregrounds orphanhood, and in the decades depicted in the novel, orphans are continuously 'produced' at St. Cloud's. Orphans are constructed relationally with aborted fetuses, adopted children, and biological kin, but also with racial 'others'. Orphanhood is also relationally constructed with orphan characters in canonical fiction. Direct references to specific characters and novels of development, as well as some of the genre conventions of the *bildungsroman*, figure prominently in *The Cider House Rules*. In this way, the novel is distinctly intertextual in its links to earlier orphan narratives, and it envisions orphans' identities as constructed with the help of 'symbolic representations and frames' (Misztal, 2003: 13).

Repeatedly referring to classic orphan novels, above all those by Charles Dickens, the narrative explicitly inserts itself into the tradition of the nineteenth-century English *bildungsroman*, and it has been seen by critics as one of Irving's 'immense Dickensian narratives' (Davis and Womack, 2004: 4).[19] Importantly, while calling the novel 'Dickensian' may point to potential common ground between US and English texts in terms of their reliance on 'Victorian values' (Booth, 2002), it also seems to place the significance of central issues in the narrative solely in the past. The author's own insistence that he is 'not a twentieth-century novelist' and his claim that 'I'm old-fashioned, a storyteller' (Hansen, quoted in *ibid.*: 18) also encourage such temporal displacement.

Nevertheless, the novel also raises questions of familial inclusion and exclusion that locate it firmly in the late twentieth-century context of the USA; for example, the relationship between orphans and abortion practices that Irving thematizes and treats in unusually explicit ways is clearly a late-twentieth-century concern. At the time of publication, little more than a decade after the landmark case of *Roe vs. Wade* (1973), abortion continued to be cast as a sign of the 'breakdown of the family.'[20] Moreover, the problematization of racism and interracial relations in the novel evokes concerns specific to the moment in which the novel was published. As one critic observed, 'Irving presses hot-button issues of abortion and race' (Booth, 2002: 303). However, the temporal arc that begins in the late nineteenth century and ends around 1960 locates these issues in a pre-civil rights and pre-women's liberation era. In this way, Irving employs the *bildungsroman* genre to construct a 'historical' narrative that addresses specific US family matters contemporary with its time of publication.

Born in the early 1920s at St Cloud's – a clinic, as well as an orphanage, where women come either to give birth or to have a safe, but illegal, abortion – Homer Wells does not know his birth parents. Despite repeated placements in supposedly 'normal' nuclear families, the boy keeps returning to the orphanage. When he enters his teens, he is the oldest orphan in the boy's division. At this point, Dr Larch trains Homer in obstetrics and gynecology in order for him to learn how to 'be of use' and to perform what Larch refers to as 'the Lord's work': the safe deliveries of babies, and safe abortion procedures. His medical apprenticeship coincides with a joyless sexual relationship with St Cloud's other overage orphan, Melony, whom he promises he will never abandon. At twenty, however, Homer breaks this promise when a young couple, Wally and Candy, invites him to Ocean View, an apple orchard run by Wally's mother. Homer is informally adopted by this new family and stays at Ocean View for a period of more than fifteen years, a place where issues of class and race surface in the interactions between the owners of the orchard, the white workers who are regular employees, and the black migrant workers who return there for each harvest. During his time at Ocean View, Homer has a child, Angel, with Candy. Together with Wally, who has been crippled in World War II, they raise Angel, but pretend that Homer has adopted him. Then, following the death of Dr Larch, Homer returns to St Cloud's to work as a gynecologist and obstetrician.

Unlike the conventional hero of the *bildungsroman*, Homer never gains access to his own familial past, but he attempts to orient himself as an orphan in the world by using alternative points of reference that include literary role models, as well as a succession of variously raced and gendered family constellations. The protagonist's path moves from the racial homogeneity of St. Cloud's to the relative, but always temporary, racial diversity at Ocean View, and from a patriarchal alternative family to other kinship formations. As one critic has pointed out, both the orphanage and the apple orchard are spaces that trouble boundaries between work and home (Booth, 2002: 293), positioning the characters in ways that also disturb any clean-cut distinction between public and private spaces. In both places, moreover, the families that are formed are set against the postwar nuclear family ideal in the USA. The tensions between the novel's temporal setting and its time of publication surface also in its representations of families. Homer's trajectory ends around 1960, that is, his adulthood is set during a time when the nuclear family ideal had unparalleled impact upon the lives of Americans and before significant social and familial shifts were brought on by the civil rights movement, the women's movement, as well as economic and demographic changes in the USA.[21] Irving's depiction of non-normative families therefore relates to the dominance of the nuclear family typical of the temporal setting, but also serves to contest claims concerning the dangers of the supposed downfall of the family in the 1980s.

The first family envisioned in the novel is the orphanage itself, a patriarchal and strictly hierarchical, but non-normative family headed by Dr. Larch, with nurses Edna and Angela and Mrs Grogan of the girls' division as more vaguely maternal figures, and the orphans as (transient) siblings. In the orphanage boys can be 'kings' and 'princes,' as they are called by Dr Larch in his nightly benediction. This contrasts sharply with his way of viewing girl orphans and women generally. Indeed, Larch's ability to see and love Homer is explicitly juxtaposed with his tendency to disregard women, a flaw in his character noted by Nurse Angela: 'He was not good at looking in women's eyes, Wilbur Larch; he had seen too much of them under the harsh lights. Nurse Angela at times wondered if Dr Larch even knew how he tended to overlook women' (Irving, 1985: 248). The only person he loves is Homer, to whom he is 'like a father' (ibid.: 147). Focusing his attention on the boy whom he grooms as his apprentice, Larch largely ignores the female orphan Melony.

Unlike Homer, who is liked by most and favored by Larch, Melony is a neglected and violent girl, disliked and feared by many. Her early sexual knowledge also marks her out as an aggressor. When she is around twenty, Larch realizes how little attention he has given Melony, but he still fails to see her as a person: 'he felt miserable for how neglected *the creature* before him was' (ibid.: 286, emphasis added), and his view of her as underdeveloped is emphasized when he thinks of her as a 'big child ... a baby thug' (ibid.: 286). His attempts to find her jobs outside the orphanage are too little, too late, and Melony runs away to make her own way, and initially to find Homer. After leaving St Cloud's, Melony works as a laborer and electrician, and develops a loving if difficult relationship with a woman named Lorna.

Although Melony is a significant character in the novel, she is auxiliary because there is no doubt that Homer is Irving's main character, with Larch as a second protagonist.[22] Irving's novel meets most of the criteria listed in Buckley's taxonomy of the *bildungsroman*, which refers explicitly to English nineteenth-century classics. Homer lives in rural Maine in places marked by the marginalization of provincial spaces; he ventures forth into 'larger society' when he leaves the orphanage for Ocean View in the 1940s; he continuously reflects upon what will become of him and comments self-consciously on his own personal development; he acquires formal and informal education; he has a frustrated love affair with Candy for over fifteen years while he also loves Wally as a brother, and they all love and raise

Angel together; he finally accepts his true vocation as a doctor and returns to St Cloud's; and he embraces his working philosophy, to 'be of use' to women and orphans. Like the classic male hero, whom Buckley (1974) describes as in need of substitute father figures, Homer, although an orphan, is not entirely fatherless, for he develops in relation to important father figures throughout the narrative: Dr Larch, Candy's father, and Mr Rose, the African American boss of the group of migrant workers.

The apparently strong alignment of the male orphan's development with the classic *bildungsroman*, however, is paralleled by what feminist critics at the time of the novel's publication defined as the female *bildungsroman*. Instead of the male protagonist's individualism and self-reliance, they suggested that a 'distinctive female "I" implies a distinctive value system and unorthodox developmental goals, defined in terms of community and empathy rather than achievement and autonomy' (Abel, Hirsch and Langland, 1983: 10). Since Homer affirms 'community and empathy' as key developmental goals, the trajectory of Irving's male protagonist draws on and combines conventions found in both varieties of the *bildungsroman*. This combination of gendered genre conventions is also emphasized in Homer's growing appreciation of Brontë's as well as Dickens's orphan stories.

At St Cloud's, classic English orphan tales are read to the children every evening, ostensibly to provide them points of identification and a vision of potential progress towards a brighter future. As soon as Homer is old enough to read to the other children, Dr. Larch engages him for the nightly reading installments:

> But Dr Larch decided that girl orphans should hear about girl orphans – in the same spirit that he believed boy orphans should hear about boy orphans – and so he assigned Homer the task of reading aloud to the girls' division from *Jane Eyre*. It struck Homer immediately that the girls were more attentive than the boys; they were an altogether better audience – except for the giggles upon his arrival and upon his departure. That they should be a better audience surprised Homer, for he found *Jane Eyre* not nearly so interesting as *David Copperfield*; he was convinced that Charlotte Brontë was not nearly as good a writer as Charles Dickens. Compared to little David, Homer thought, little Jane was something of a whiner – a sniveler – but the girls in the girls' division always cried for more, for just one more scene, when, every evening, Homer would stop and hurry away, out of the building and

into the night, racing for the boys' division and Dickens. (Irving, 1985: 102–3)

Larch's decision to match the gender of the audience of orphan children to the gender of the fictional orphan protagonist is grounded in conventional binary thinking, and Homer's childish dismissal of *Jane Eyre* certainly echoes such thinking. Nonetheless, he is the only boy at the orphanage who learns about Jane Eyre, and since he reads out loud he even functions as her mouthpiece in the girls' division.

While initially, Brontë's story of an orphan girl seemingly has nothing to offer Homer, Dickens's heroes function as inspiring models: 'Whether I shall turn out to be the hero of my own life, or whether that station will be held by anybody else, these pages must show. "Whether I shall turn out to be the hero of my own life," Homer whispered to himself' (*ibid.*: 98–9).[23] Later in the novel, however, Jane Eyre's words become his too: 'Homer Wells was tired of Melony making him anxious. He repeated the line, this time reading it as if he were personally delivering a threat. "It is vain to say human beings ought to be satisfied with tranquility: they must have action; and they will make it if they cannot find it"' (*ibid.*: 164). Gradually, Homer comes to identify with Jane Eyre as well as with David Copperfield and Pip. At the end of the novel,

> Homer Wells saw no end to the insights he perceived nightly, in his continuous reading from *Jane Eyre*, and from *David Copperfield* and *Great Expectations*. He would smile to remember how he had once thought Dickens was 'better than' Brontë. When they both gave such huge entertainment and instruction, what did it matter? he thought – and from where comes this childish business of 'better'? (*ibid.*: 716)

Homer incorporates both Brontë's and Dickens's narratives as instructive and entertaining reference points for his maturation, thereby seeing both the female and the male orphan protagonists' *bildung* as informing his own.

Indeed, Brontë's words inform *The Cider House Rules* in its entirety, because Irving uses a passage from her preface to the second edition of *Jane Eyre* as one of two epigraphs: 'Conventionality is not morality. Self-righteousness is not religion. To attack the first is not to assail the last.' He juxtaposes this epigraph with one by H.J. Boldt, MD from 1906: 'For practical purposes abortion may be defined as the interruption of gestation before viability of the child.' Thus, from the outset, Irving connects his novel's thematization of abortion to the female *bildungsroman* and a critique of conventions and self-righteousness through Brontë's preface.

The whiteness of Homer's English literary role models is paralleled by the whiteness of New England. Whereas racial difference is a non-issue in all-white St Cloud's, Ocean View is a spatial setting where, once a year, racial difference is made evident through the presence of the black migrant workers who come there for each apple-picking season. Homer, who has never seen a black person, is excited at the prospect of meeting them: '[H]e was curious about meeting the migrants, about seeing the Negroes. He didn't know why. Were they like orphans? Did they not quite belong?' (*ibid.*: 374). Having sensed 'dormitory anger and apprehension' (*ibid.*: 310) in the cider house that doubles as sleeping quarters for the migrant crew, Homer envisions the black workers as a family of orphans with whom he might identify. Unaware of racism, Homer takes the team boss, Mr Rose, to the fair. There, the unusual couple draws the attention of other pleasure seekers, to whom the very presence of a black man at a fair in white Maine is an anomaly. At first, Homer believes that he is the one whose otherness draws their gaze, but he soon realizes his mistake: 'as an orphan, he always suspected that people singled him out to stare at – and so he had not felt especially singled out in the company of Mr. Rose. But now he noticed more of the looks and realized that the looks an orphan might detect were only imagined, by comparison' (*ibid.*: 407–8). Later, Homer also realizes that the pickers adjust their speech for his comprehension; when they are speaking amongst themselves he does not understand them at all. As he learns about racism, but also about the interior workings of the picking crew, Homer begins to understand race and orphanhood as different existential dimensions, and his attitude shifts from one of initial potential identification to a sense of alienation.

Homer's interaction with the black picking crew does not, however, lead him to reflect upon his own racial privilege. While he sees both orphans and 'Negroes' as outsiders, he fails to regard himself in racial terms, even when Mr. Rose presents him with the idea. In a reference to the cider house rules compiled by the white employer, Olive Worthington, Mr Rose explains to Homer:

> 'We got our own rules, too, Homer,' he said.
> 'Your own rules,' said Homer Wells.
> ''Bout lots of things,' … ''Bout how much we can have to do with you, for one thing.'

'With me?' Homer said.
'With white people,' said Mr. Rose. 'We got our rules about that.'
'I see,' Homer said, but he didn't really see. (*ibid.*: 560)

Homer's response emphasizes that he does not see himself as part of a racial group; he has never thought of himself as part of the category 'white people.' Irving's narrative, then, underscores its protagonist's blindness to whiteness.

What finally leads to Homer's complete alienation from the crew boss is Mr Rose's incestuous relationship with his daughter Rose Rose, which is revealed when they arrive at Ocean View one fall, the girl pregnant by her father and wanting an abortion. The novel as a whole represents fathers across ethnic and racial boundaries as sexually abusing their daughters. An illegitimate practitioner (or 'quack') in Boston yells at the young Dr Larch that 'her father is the father!' (*ibid.*: 81), to explain a teenage girl's need for an abortion, and the problem of incest recurs throughout Larch's sections of the narrative.[24] However, Mr Rose's sexual abuse of Rose Rose is Homer's first encounter with father–daughter incest, and the only instance when he hears the utterance '[h]er father is the father' (*ibid.*: 694). Mr. Rose is also the only incestuous father in the novel who is a fully drawn character. In this way, incest becomes racialized in *The Cider House Rules*, and, seemingly in spite of itself, the novel thus reinforces the racial stereotypes of the morally deficient black father and the oversexed African American man.[25] In Irving's novel, the otherness of the African American father parallels that of the African American community, which follows a separate and distinctive set of 'rules' under the authority of its patriarchal and violent parent Mr Rose.

The novel is primarily and fundamentally concerned with the family lives of two white men, Homer Wells and Dr Larch, and the function of the black family, as of the black father, is to contribute to the relational construction of the white family, father, and child. Since both Dr Larch and Mr Rose can be termed patriarchal fathers, however, they both contribute to foregrounding the potentially detrimental effects of authoritarian and masculinist fathering, not least for (young) women.

Racial difference is also stressed through the uses of focalization in *The Cider House Rules*. While the classic *bildungsroman* focuses on an individual hero or heroine and is told in the first person, Irving introduces two protagonists, Homer Wells and Wilbur Larch, via a third-person narrative perspective, but incorporates other characters who also serve as focalizers. However, Mr Rose and Rose Rose are not among these; hence their perspective is never represented. Gender difference is ultimately a much more explicit and thoroughgoing focus in the novel, and this is also evident in its focalization.

Most importantly, Irving includes the perspective of Melony, who partly functions as Homer's shadow. However, Melony is not only a foil to the male orphan protagonist, a Magwitch to his Pip. She also foregrounds classed and gendered biases in configurations of the hero: she is a rewritten Bertha Mason to Homer's Jane Eyre, a re-envisioning of the violent and (partially) forgotten other who haunts the aspiring middle-class hero(ine). Melony's character may also be read as representing a critique of the heterosexism of the *bildungsroman* tradition. While Homer, like many female protagonists in that tradition, develops through his shifting familial relationships from childhood to maturity, Melony cannot develop as long as she stays in the orphanage, a milieu that does not recognize her needs or even her humanity. Nor does it integrate her into anything resembling a family. Whereas Homer has Larch as an attentive father figure and identifies with protagonists in literature, there is no parental figure to care about Melony's future, nor do orphans in literary classics function as sustaining models for her. In one passage, having escaped from St Cloud's, Melony reads *Jane Eyre*, which has previously 'helped her' (*ibid*.: 401), but now she responds differently:

> 'I must part with you for my whole life,' she read, with horror. 'I must begin a new existence amongst strange faces and strange scenes.' The truth of that closed the book for her, forever ... . Had she just read the passage from *David Copperfield* that Homer Wells so loved and repeated to himself as if it were a hopeful prayer, she would have discarded *David Copperfield*, too. 'I have stood aside to see the phantoms of those days go by me.' Fat chance! Melony would have thought. She knew that all the phantoms of those days were attached to her and Homer more securely than their shadows. (*ibid*.: 401)

In contrast to Homer, then, Melony rejects literary models of orphanhood, lives without any connection to parental figures, and makes her own way in the world without denying her history. After Homer's abandonment she is disillusioned with men, and forms a loving relationship with Lorna, forging a family of her own outside of all social conventions by completely rejecting heterosexual middle-class ideals.[26] Although their relationship is temporarily broken off when Lorna has a heterosexual affair, they later reunite and stay together until Melony's death in a work accident. It is in the context of this intimate relationship that she reveals her past to Lorna, and comments on Homer's development. In fact, it is Melony's visit to Ocean View that makes Homer realize that his life is based on dishonesty:

> 'You of all people – you, an orphan,' she reminded him.
> 'It's not quite like that,' he started to tell her, but she shook her huge head and looked away from him.
> 'I got eyes,' Melony said. 'I can see what it's like – it's like *shit*. It's ordinary, middle-class shit – bein' unfaithful and lyin' to the kids. You of all people!' (*ibid.*: 612)

Melony is a marginalized character at St Cloud's and elsewhere, and in many ways she is portrayed as a monstrous female; yet she also serves as the voice of honesty and reason in the narrative. She never denies her orphan status, nor is she ever represented as dwelling upon it.

Apart from Dr Larch's neglect of Melony, the orphanage is envisioned as a relatively functional familial setting, with caring if strict parental figures, an alternative to what Larch calls 'the rest of the world.' The world outside the orphanage is partly represented by the nuclear families of which the orphan children dream, but where they are often used and abused, and to which they remain outsiders. In the novel, adults who live in nuclear families or as conventional heterosexual couples are people whose actions are far from guided by ideas about the child's best interests, particularly in their dealings with orphans. The prospective adoptive parents that Homer encounters range from ineffectual or irresponsible to abusive or bigoted. The first couple returns him to St Cloud's because he is 'too quiet,' the second because he is 'too loud': he screams when they beat him. The third family, the Drapers, is one of such 'rare and championship qualities that to judge humanity by this family's example would have been foolish. They were that good a family' (*ibid.*: 26). However, Homer soon realizes that the Drapers are wholly uninterested in his well-being, while very convinced of their own superiority, favoring their blood kin as 'real family' but mistreating and disbelieving Homer. When he is subjected to 'buggery' by one of the Drapers' grandchildren, the blame is placed on Homer, and his status as an orphan outsider is thus maintained within this familial context. Hence, the novel exposes the limits and damaging effects of the normative nuclear family, and suggests that it cannot sustain the orphan child, whose kinship building must take place elsewhere.

Nevertheless, although Homer has never experienced a functional nuclear family, by the time he is to become a father, he has internalized certain conservative family values: 'He also possessed the self-righteousness of the young and wounded; Homer Wells had no doubts to soften his contempt for people who'd bungled their lives so badly that they didn't want the children they'd conceived ... *Homer was wielding an ideal of marriage and family like a club*' (ibid.: 518–19, emphasis added). Since the nuclear families he encounters as a child are inadequate or abusive, Homer cannot possibly base his family ideal on experience. One of the premises of his trajectory derives from having grown up in an orphanage where societal norms do not apply: he has not been exposed to the mores of the world outside, the romantic ideal of connecting love and sex, the link between marriage and childbearing, and the nuclear family ideal. Instead, his idealization of 'marriage and family' demonstrates the pervasiveness of the nuclear unit as an ideological and ideational presence, the power of which makes the protagonist favor this family pattern despite his experiences. That the American family ideal disturbs Homer's perception of his own family *as family* is illustrated by his thinking that they are '*like* a family' (ibid.: 563, emphasis added), mimicking family rather than actually being one, which highlights the power of the nuclear ideal to define 'real' families even in the face of actual familial diversity.[27] It seems, then, that whereas Homer as a child questions – or at least does not support – normative family values, as a young adult man he comes to incorporate such mainstream, middle-class values. At this point in the narrative, then, Homer is aligned with the conventional trajectory in the *bildungsroman* towards social integration, but his 'self-righteousness' and 'contempt' signal that there are problems with this ambition. Later, he will take a step away from this particular kind of social integration and instead orient himself towards a familial context that is outside both nuclear and patriarchal kinship constellations.

While Homer's biological paternity is initially cast as adoption, and while, on the level of the plot, hiding Angel's true parentage is explained as sparing everybody's – especially Wally's – feelings, the privileging of adoption also downplays the idea of blood relations as representing the only or 'real' kin. This de-privileging of blood relations becomes even more meaningful when read in relation to incestuous relationships between fathers and daughters as explored in the novel, including that between Mr Rose and his daughter. Against the 'bad' black father Mr Rose, Homer's white fatherhood is made to seem 'good,' as it also does when set against the abusive paternal practices of most men in the novel. Furthermore, in foregrounding his relationship with Angel over other familial relationships, Homer reproduces Larch's patriarchal relationship to himself as a favorite son without a mother, but Homer's loving and nurturing fatherhood is superior to the responsible, albeit emotionally stunted and rather possessive, fathering of Larch.

Whereas there are many prominent fathers in Irving's novel, it presents motherlessness as the primary figuration of parental loss. The birth mothers of the orphans at St Cloud's remain nameless, identified by geographical origin during their brief stays in the hospital, and erased as they leave, since Larch's policy is to keep no records of an orphan's parentage. For this reason, Homer cannot fulfill Melony's wish to learn about her birth mother. The lie that is told about Angel having been adopted by Homer alone also erases Candy's status both as the boy's birth and adoptive mother.

It is through Melony's agency that the identity of Angel's birth mother is revealed and Homer returns to St Cloud's to take up his vocation as a gynecologist, obstetrician, and head of the orphanage, as well as to build a family in the place where he was born. Melony confronts him with his lies, and accuses him of 'ballin' a poor cripple's wife and pretendin' [his] own child ain't [his] own' (*ibid.*: 612). Her harshness prompts Homer to finally tell Angel the truth, demanding honesty from himself and Candy, and returning to the orphanage in a shift that entails embracing his past, changing his stance on abortion, and re-establishing the centrality of his orphan status: 'He tightened his grip on Dr. Larch's bag ... Suddenly, it was clear to him – where he was going. He was only what he always was: an orphan who'd never been adopted. He had managed to steal some time away from the orphanage, but St. Cloud's had the only legitimate claim to him. In his forties, a man should know where he belongs' (*ibid.*: 626). St. Cloud's under Homer's leadership is the final expression of an 'alternative' family in the novel, but at this point, the legitimacy of their kin constellation is not questioned through the kind of 'as if' statements seen earlier in the narrative.

The orphanage as a family home with Homer as 'father' is also different than it was under Larch. Although, as Alison Booth observes, Homer's return emphasizes his expertise and, we would add, his move into a professional class of high status, it is not a nostalgic move. Unlike Larch, Homer is sexually active as well as a father, and he does not 'overlook women.' While Homer and Nurse Caroline take up 'the Lord's work' at St Cloud's – and enjoy an affair – they also integrate the Ocean View family into the orphanage, thereby creating an expanded and reconfigured familial space. As before, the orphanage is neither envisioned as a utopian space, nor as an American success story. It continues to be a marginal space, and the narrative stresses that the orphanage is much more a matter of necessity and duty than anything else. What nevertheless makes the orphanage an enabling space is that it remains detached from restricting social conventions pertaining to the nuclear family. However, the move back to St. Cloud's is also a move back into an entirely white context, which suggests that the difference embraced by the novel's representation of kinship building ultimately has definitive racialized limits. At this point, Mr. Rose is dead, Rose Rose has left New England, and it is clear that the African American family in *The Cider House Rules* figures mainly as an 'other' against which white parenthood and family can take form.

Although confirming the whiteness typical of the classic English *bildungsroman*, *The Cider House Rules* departs from another of its defining features: the orphan protagonist's integration into middle-class societal norms. For Homer, the pattern of social integration into middle-class family life is at first partially fulfilled, but then firmly rejected. Neither do the patterns of the classic American *bildungsroman* apply, patterns in which a boy fulfills an individualistic desire to 'light out for the Territory,' like Huck Finn, or advance through industry towards social and financial gain, like Ragged Dick. Rather, Homer rejects individualism when he finally embraces an alternative – the reconfigured orphanage – that combines various kinds of Euro-American kin. Melony, on the other hand, is socially integrated into working-class life as a manual laborer, and into a caring lesbian relationship with Lorna. Like Ruth in *Housekeeping*, she flouts middle-class standards conventionally linked to female coming-of-age, and middle-class femininity is never an option for her.

In this way, the kinship building of the central orphans in the novel moves away from models based on blood, law, and even authority, foregrounding instead choice, but also duty and necessity as driving forces behind family formation. Building kin networks, Homer Wells experiences the 'natural' pull of the nuclear family ideal even when it is at odds with his lived experience, but finally recognizes family as relatively diverse, jointly constructed, and built on emotion and codependency. Even while it emphasizes the differently gendered trajectories of Homer and Melony, the novel bridges female and male experience through the figure of Homer, not least through its intertextual uses of classic *bildungsroman* heroes and heroines. In Kaye Gibbons's novels about Ellen Foster, intertextuality also contributes to the protagonist's understandings of identity and belonging, but these novels, too, offer very specific envisionings of the relations between whiteness, blackness, gender difference, and possible kinship formations.

'The orphan American dream': Kaye Gibbons's *Ellen Foster* and *The Life All Around Me by Ellen Foster*

> Cast the bantling on the rocks,
> Suckle him with the she-wolf's teat,
> Wintered with the hawk and fox,
> Power and speed be hands and feet.
>
> (Ralph Waldo Emerson, 1841)[28]

In imagining and creating a national literature that would serve to underpin an American national identity, celebrating self-reliance as an important national and personal characteristic, Ralph Waldo Emerson has been pivotal. The epigraph to this section, which describes a young illegitimate child who is thrown out in the wilderness and has to fend for himself among wild animals, also serves as an epigraph for Kaye Gibbons's 1987 novel *Ellen Foster*. Gibbons's novel about a white orphan girl's trials and tribulations in her search for a home and a new family was published at the point when the 'classic' literary canon in the USA was beginning to be hotly debated in the 'culture wars' for its masculine, heterosexual, and Euro-American biases.[29] Seen against this background, the orphan in Gibbons's novel both draws upon and contrasts with Emerson's male 'bantling.' In particular, *Ellen Foster* activates cultural memory in its references to canonical American literature, while at the same time revising that memory in its use of a female protagonist. The novel also remembers nineteenth-century American orphan tales with white female protagonists, which were rediscovered and reassessed in the late 1970s and the 1980s.

Almost twenty years after the publication of Gibbons's first novel, *Ellen Foster*, its sequel *The Life All Around Me by Ellen Foster* (2006) appeared. Between the two novels about Ellen Foster, Gibbons published other works focusing on family relations and women's relationships across generations.[30] These themes are absolutely central to both Ellen Foster novels, which explore incest and other forms of child abuse, foster care, and adoption. Both novels depict interracial friendship and black family relationships that serve as models for the white protagonist's kinship building. As in *The Cider House Rules*, the African American characters are significant yet clearly subordinated to the white orphan's progress. However, they figure very differently in the first and the second Ellen Foster novel, and we will consider the significance of these differences.

Ellen Foster – who is eleven years old in the first novel and fourteen or fifteen in the second – is the first-person narrator of both, which are clear examples of the *bildungsroman*. They draw on male and female variations of this genre, but unlike Homer Wells, Ellen is firmly grounded in the American as well as the English *bildungsroman* traditions. In *Ellen Foster*, like many a hero and heroine in the nineteenth-century *bildungsroman*, Ellen is already an orphan when the novel opens. Her mother has committed suicide by taking an overdose of medicine and her father has killed himself by drinking himself to death. The narration shifts back and forth between her present situation at her foster mother's house (referred to as her 'new mama' throughout the first novel) and the problems in her recent past. From a relatively safe position, she works through her feelings about her mother's death, sexual abuse by her father, and a sequence of temporary homes, with a caring teacher and with various relatives, none of whom really want her. But her story also moves forward in the novel's present; it is not only told in retrospect. This double movement breaks the frame of the classic first-person *bildungsroman*, which is usually a retrospective narrative told from the perspective of a fixed but not always defined point in the narrator's present. Thus, Ellen's narration breaks up the linear progression of the *bildungsroman*; it is far from a smooth, chronological narrative, and it records trauma on different levels, as various critics have noted.[31]

Nevertheless, *Ellen Foster* is undoubtedly a *bildungsroman*, dealing with childhood, generational conflicts, and self-education, and so is its sequel, which, like *The Cider House Rules*, exhibits principal elements of a *bildungsroman*, according to Buckley's definition (1974: 18). *The*

Life All Around Me addresses provincial life in the South, its relation to larger society, and Ellen's alienation. It also introduces an 'ordeal by love' via Ellen's schoolmate Stuart's amorous attentions, but a more serious ordeal is the coming to terms with the apparent lack of love shown by her birth mother. A focus on formal education in *The Life All Around Me* is immediately emphasized as the novel opens with Ellen's letter to President Derek C. Bok of Harvard University to whom she applies at age fifteen to be admitted as a student 'because of all the surplus living that was jammed into the years' (Gibbons, 2006: 2). She is painfully aware that the schooling her rural southern environment offers is inadequate to her intellectual needs.

Much of *The Life All Around Me* revolves around Ellen's goals to obtain an education, and to finally come to terms with the loss of her birth mother and fully accept her new adoptive mother, the problems of which highlights emotional obstacles to kinship building. The narrative also features her interaction with schoolmates including African American Starletta, who is her only friend in *Ellen Foster*. One significant event in the sequel is Ellen's trip to Johns Hopkins University in Baltimore, which opens her eyes to how others outside her most immediate environment judge her according to their assumptions about class and region. Another is her confrontation with her Aunt Nadine, who has stolen Ellen's inheritance but finally returns it, and Ellen's reconciliation with her cousin Dora. The beginning of *The Life All Around Me* fills in what has happened in the intervening three years and qualifies Ellen's optimistic outlook at the end of *Ellen Foster*. Despite her positive qualities, her 'new mama,' who Ellen now calls Laura, has not been entirely able to fill the void of Ellen's birth mother, Shine. The peace in Laura's house, which appears to be an unqualified utopian haven in *Ellen Foster*, is threatened by the misbehavior of the other foster girls, which leads to Ellen reporting them to the child welfare authorities – to Laura's dismay. As is the case in *Ellen Foster*, legal and social authorities have the final say about where Ellen is to be placed, and both of them are distressed by the process Ellen has to go through in order for Laura to adopt her.

Ellen Foster's close relation to nineteenth-century novels and in particular the *bildungsroman* is obvious throughout the novel. Early on, Ellen observes, 'I myself prefer the old stories' (1987: 10). This comment is directly related to her reading *The Canterbury Tales*, but the phrase 'old stories' also refers to nineteenth-century works such as the Brontës' novels, which Ellen loves to read. Intertextually,

Gibbons's novel can be read according to what Peter Brooks calls the nineteenth-century hero's 'unifying quest.' In this era, Brooks argues, the hero's survival strategies typically take 'a more elaborated and socially defined form: [they] become ambition' (1984: 39). Ambition is both a 'typical novelistic theme' and 'a dominant dynamic of plot: a force that drives the protagonist forward, assuring that no incident or action is final or closed in itself until such a moment as the ends of ambition have been clarified, through success or else renunciation' (ibid.: 39). In *Ellen Foster*, the heroine is indeed an ambitious and self-reliant survivor, whose quest has a clear goal: a satisfactory, nurturing home. Ellen is looking for a functional family and home rather than trying, like Huck, to avoid being domesticated and 'sivilized.' She achieves this goal by unconventional means rather than by relying on blood relations.[32]

In its focus on the home as well as on an ambitious heroine, *Ellen Foster* is similar to those American nineteenth-century novels featuring a white orphan heroine that Nina Baym termed 'woman's fiction.' Like this fiction, *Ellen Foster* 'excoriate[s] an unhappy home as the basic source of human misery and imagines a happy home as the acme of human bliss' (Baym, 1993: 27). This kind of nineteenth-century literature highlights the struggles and success of 'a heroine who, beset with hardships, finds within herself the qualities of intelligence, will, resourcefulness, and courage sufficient to overcome them' (ibid.: 22). This heroine, as well as Ellen Foster, has much in common with Brooks's ambitious nineteenth-century hero. *Ellen Foster* is set one hundred years or more after the examples of woman's fiction that Baym discusses, but it is easy to recognize Ellen in the description of the heroine of this genre.

Although Ellen apparently reaches her goal of a nurturing home and can tell her story from a relatively safe place, in the first novel she is still in the process of working through her traumatic experiences and hardships. As she puts it towards the end of *Ellen Foster*, 'I have some other things to work on but at least I am somewhere friendly and nothing new bad has happened to me since I got here. That is something when you think about it' (Gibbons, 2006: 121). Ellen's is an American success story with modifications. This impression is further underscored in the first half of *The Life All Around Me*, when Ellen observes, 'After three years here, it's only loose ends left to manage, but when the list of things you have left to do on yourself includes items such as healing from terror that comes and goes and frequently gets in your way, it looks like the large job of work it still is' (*ibid*.: 54). Her observation on 'the list of things you have left to do on yourself' emphasizes her self-reliant, ambitious goal; what she talks about is self-improvement, in the manner outlined by Benjamin Franklin. Her attitude resembles Lucille's in *Housekeeping*, who, as discussed in Chapter 3, uses strategies similar to those of self-made men in American history in order to improve herself.

The socially inflected ambition that Brooks traces in the plots of nineteenth-century literature, and that Ellen subscribes to, is a prominent characteristic of the nineteenth-century *bildungsroman*. Indeed, Franco Moretti states that the genre is 'one of the most harmonious solutions ever offered to a dilemma conterminous with modern bourgeois civilization: the conflict between the ideal of *self-determination* and the equally imperious demands of *socialization*' (1987: 15). The ending of a classic *bildungsroman* often describes the (re)integration of the protagonist into society, and Ellen certainly aspires to familial and social integration even though her path is fraught with difficulties. She seeks a balance between individualism and belonging to functioning social groups or communities. In *The Life All Around Me*, whose title indicates a less absolute focus on the individual self, Ellen has come so far that when she writes to the president of Harvard she observes: 'If I had the job of selecting a well-rounded group of individuals to come to my college, I would worry about an underage orphan with a list of obstacles showing up and being a misfit, but I want to emphasize that I get along well both at school and at home' (Gibbons, 2006: 5). In contrast, in *Ellen Foster*, she tells the school psychologist, 'I was not social because I did not want to be but next year I might after I got my own business straight' (Gibbons, 1987: 87). Striving for and achievement of social integration outside her chosen family is much more pronounced in the second Ellen Foster novel than in the first.

Ellen Foster has been described as an 'attempt to rewrite the saga of the American hero by changing "him" to "her" and to rewrite the southern female *bildungsroman* by changing its privileged, sheltered, upper-class heroine to a poor, abused outcast' (Makowsky, 1992: 103). Sharon Monteith asserts that 'Kaye Gibbons unfixes some of the conventions of the form [the bourgeois *bildungsroman*] in her depiction of a poor white girl whose class and language clearly set her outside of a bourgeois formulation' (2000: 60–1). Nevertheless, as Monteith convincingly argues, the form of the first-person *bildungsroman* in *Ellen*

Foster with its focus on the individual's psychology and development, is 'monologic' and thereby 'silences other voices that might otherwise disrupt the monologue or deviate from its flow' (*ibid.*: 60). This totalizing trait of the genre relates to what Brooks says about ambition's role in nineteenth-century literature: 'Ambition is inherently totalizing, figuring the self's tendency to appropriation and aggrandizement, moving forward through the encompassment of more, striving to have, to do, and to be more' (1984: 39). Monteith traces the effects this choice of a monologic first-person narration has on the depiction of the black characters in *Ellen Foster*, and especially on Ellen's best friend, Starletta, who despite her importance to Ellen throughout the novel – like Jim's to Huck – remains voiceless and an object rather than a subject in her own right: 'Gibbons is clearly aware of the American literary tradition, most clearly explicated by Leslie Fiedler, in which African Americans and Native Americans have functioned as subordinate and peripheral sidekicks to white individualistic protagonists. In *Ellen Foster* she retains the basis of this binary intact as she negotiates such a relationship for her protagonist' (Monteith, 2000: 65). We see a similar dynamic between Ellen as the Euro-American first-person narrator and the voiceless African American Starletta to that we observed in Chapter 2 between Taylor, the first-person narrator in Barbara Kingsolver's *Bean Trees* (1988), and the silent Indian child, Turtle. Giavanna Munafo also feels that *Ellen Foster* 'can be faulted for this portrait [of Starletta] and for its habit of making black characters and homes serviceable vis-à-vis Ellen's tragic tale and heroic advances' and that 'Gibbons has not established adequate grounds for a truly mutual interaction between Ellen and Starletta ...' (1998: 58–9). At the end of the novel, when Ellen confesses to Starletta that she has been guilty of feeling superior because she is white, Starletta is not expected to respond in any significant way, because 'she hates to talk' (Gibbons, 1987: 125), and, as Taylor does with Turtle in *The Bean Trees*, it is Ellen who describes and defines both her own and Starletta's situation. During and after the confession, Ellen still refers to her black friend in a way that uncomfortably resonates with racial relationships under slavery: 'my Starletta' (*ibid.*: 126). Even if the ending of *Ellen Foster* presents Ellen ostensibly overcoming the racism that her society has inculcated in her and confessing her earlier feelings of white superiority to Starletta, the generic conventions and narrative strategies of Ellen's story work against a satisfying resolution in formal terms.[33]

In *The Life All Around Me*, also a first-person narrative, Ellen's voice reigns supreme to the point that dialogue is seamlessly integrated into her story without quotation marks. The narrator is older, though, and less traumatized than her younger self, and even though it is integrated into her narration, other characters' speech is sometimes reported in detail and at length. Nevertheless, while Laura's verbal responses to Ellen, in particular, are given much room, Laura observes, 'Other people notice it to me, but I'm just hearing it. I sound like you, I hear old Ellen in me. Do you hear it? Listen to us, amazing' (Gibbons, 2006: 53); Ellen's voice permeates Laura's speech. Starletta and her mother are also significant characters in *The Life All Around Me*, which ends with them moving into Ellen's house, which has now been restored to her.

There are some interesting discrepancies between the first and the second Ellen Foster novels that revolve around the characterization of and Ellen's relationship to the black characters, which we suggest could partly have to do with the different times of publication of the two novels. These discrepancies may also be related to Gibbons's attempts to make amends for the characterization of Starletta and the relationship between her and Ellen in *Ellen Foster*, as criticized by Monteith and Munafo, that is, much like Kingsolver writing *Pigs in Heaven* (1993) to make up for what happens in *The Bean Trees*.

In *Ellen Foster*, black families are the only examples of functional nuclear families.[34] When she stays at her grandmother's house and works in the fields with Mavis and other African Americans during the days, Ellen ends up walking up the 'colored path' and spying on Mavis's family at night: 'While I was easedropping at the colored house I started a list of all that a family should have. Of course there is the mama and the daddy but if one has to be missing then it is OK if the one left can count for two' (Gibbons, 1987: 67). According to Ellen's specifications, the family that she so ardently desires should however be 'white and with a little more money' (*ibid*.: 67). Despite all these caveats, the black family model serves as a blueprint for Ellen's kinship building as she actively looks for viable family relationships outside her birth family. In the case of Starletta's family, though, Ellen's racial mindset prevents her from recognizing them as a functional nuclear family, with both parents working and sharing the responsibility for Starletta's well-being. On Christmas when she sees Starletta's presents, Ellen observes that Starletta's father 'has never bothered me' and that 'he is the only colored man that does not buy liquor from my daddy' (ibid.: 30). In the novel, Starletta's father is figured as an image of the good father, whereas Ellen's father is an abusive and seriously flawed patriarchal figure. Ellen however concludes, 'I do not know what he spends his money on' (ibid.: 30), and seems incapable of making a conscious connection between Starletta's Christmas presents and her father's earnings. Although Ellen is unconditionally welcomed into Starletta's home and her best friend's parents show genuine concern and care for her, she is unable fully to see what they offer due to the dynamics of racism, which creates tension and anxiety in the narrator and leaves gaps, contradictions, and unintegrated traces in *Ellen Foster*.[35]

It is made clear in both Ellen Foster novels that it is unthinkable in the southern society in which Ellen grows up in the early 1970s that a black family should foster or adopt a white child.[36] In *Ellen Foster*, the teacher who finally helps her escape her abusive father gives Ellen clear signals that staying the night with Starletta's family could be deemed socially inappropriate: 'You could tell by the way she said colored that this would not do' (ibid.: 44). In *The Life All Around Me*, Starletta's mother says that 'the court wouldn't allow her and her husband to take [Ellen] ...' (Gibbons, 2006: 121), which emphasizes the racialized thinking that underpins the court's placement of a white orphan child in these two novels. As Dorothy Roberts has observed, in the USA, '[t]ransracial adoption advocates don't mention the possibility of Blacks adopting white children' (2003: 167).[37] The characterization of Starletta's mother in this novel, on the other hand, gives credibility to her assertion that she and her husband attempted to offer Ellen a home not only informally but also legally.

One glaring discrepancy between the two novels is the depiction of Ellen's attitude to staying overnight at Starletta's house. In *Ellen Foster*, after her mother's death, Ellen runs to Starletta's when her father has sexually abused her for the first time. There she tries to pay Starletta's mother a dollar to stay the night, indicating that she wants to regard the situation in terms of a business transaction with the African American woman providing a service for a white customer who is in social and emotional control of the event. Ellen sleeps in the bed with Starletta's mother since her husband is away for the night: 'When I got up in the morning I was surprised because it did not feel like I had slept in a colored house. I cannot say I officially slept in the bed because I stayed in my coat on top of the covers' (Gibbons, 1987: 39). Ellen has earlier refused to eat a biscuit in Starletta's house because '[n]o matter how good it looks to you it is still a colored biscuit,' and she takes pride in not eating and drinking in 'a colored house' (ibid.: 32, 33). In *Ellen Foster*, although Starletta is her only friend, Ellen only attempts to change her racist attitude at the very end of the novel. In *The Life All Around Me*, her memories of her relationship to Starletta's family are completely different. Here it is indicated that she stays over in Starletta's house whenever her own mother, named Shine in this novel, is in the hospital: 'I remembered days when I got home from school and she wasn't there, when Starletta's mother would be there to walk me across the yard and explain how everything was fine, she'd gone to the doctor and he said she'd feel better after a few days in the hospital, that's all, and she would've packed a grocery sack with clothes to spend the night at her house' (Gibbons, 2006: 190). In *The Life All Around Me*, then, spending the night at Starletta's house is made a frequent occurrence while Ellen's mother is still alive, and not a cause for racist anxiety, as it is in *Ellen Foster*.

It also appears that the interracial friendship between equals that, as Monteith and Munafo point out, Gibbons thwarts in *Ellen Foster* is suggested in the relationship between Ellen's foster mother Laura and Starletta's mother, who nevertheless remains unnamed, in *The Life All Around Me*. Laura and Starletta's mother are close and equal friends when the other foster girls are acting up in Laura's house: 'I heard [Laura] on the phone to Starletta's mother, saying the girls were growing up downhill and she was afraid, she said, on account of the quality and quantity of attention they were after' (ibid.: 43). Starletta's mother is also a frequent and vocal guest at Laura's house throughout *The Life All Around Me*. However, late in the novel, it is hinted that white and black women in the neighborhood are not usually close: 'As much as she [Starletta's mother] was looped into what took place on our road, people like Stuart's mother didn't phone up colored women with gossip' (ibid.: 115). At this point, Laura and Starletta's mother are both single mothers who live up to the standard that Ellen is looking for in a single parent in the first novel, a parent who can 'count for two' and who will do anything for her child's well-being.

If the depiction of Starletta makes her less of an equal friend than a cherished object in Ellen's narration in *Ellen Foster*, the differences are intensified in *The Life All Around Me*, where the portrayal of Starletta diverges from the previous characterization. In *Ellen Foster*, Ellen agonizes over Starletta's growth and development: she observes that Starletta no longer has her hair plaited, and that she 'has hit the growth spurt they talked about in [Ellen's] health book and she is getting tall' (Gibbons, 1987: 83). Moreover, Starletta tells her that she has a crush on a boy and points him out to Ellen, who believes that Starletta's interest in a white boy is due to ulterior motives such as cars and money: 'I know Starletta is getting a itch way down deep and low where a colored boy cannot afford to reach to scratch' (ibid.: 84). Here Starletta appears to be a girl of about the same age as Ellen who is developing physically, emotionally, and intellectually. In contrast, when Starletta finally enters Ellen's story in *The Life All Around Me* she is introduced as a twelve-year-old 'with the body of a six-year-old and the mind of a friendly older toddler. Although she goes around oblivious, she's stuck beside me through thick and thin. Everybody knows her and loves having her around' (Gibbons, 2006: 57). This physically stunted and mentally challenged version of Starletta is at least two years younger than Ellen, and she still plays with 'kooky windup tin toys' (ibid.: 39). Such characterization of Starletta effectively bars any possibility of an equal friendship between her and Ellen, and Starletta is a less important character in *The Life All Around Me* than she is in *Ellen Foster*.

While Starletta's role in Ellen's story is downplayed in *The Life All Around Me*, her mother plays a much larger and different role. Whereas in the first novel, Ellen states that Starletta's mother is illiterate and that Starletta is the only one in the family who can read (Gibbons, 1987: 30), in the second novel she is about to take college courses in social work (Gibbons, 2006: 117). It is to her that Laura and Ellen turn when they experience an imminent crisis: 'When Starletta's mother nodded her head down like a prayer and then lifted her eyes up and sighed, I knew she would say what I needed in my life' (ibid.: 119). Before she tells her what she needs, Ellen has managed to rattle off a list of possible ordeals that she imagines: 'The ordeal list is down to I'm adopted or my father's alive and married to a striptease, or maybe Starletta's my sister, and I'm way light, or my aunt broke the news that I'm an octoroon on her way out of town, which means paving my way stops being a fight, and I notify the United Negro College Fund' (ibid.: 118). Interestingly, half of this list of imagined ordeals has to do with Ellen imagining herself as African American, Starletta's sister, or an 'octoroon.' This fantasy makes her somewhat incongruously conclude that this would actually help her gain an education since she could then apply to the United Negro College Fund – a fund that she mentions in the letter to the president of Harvard (ibid.: 8).[38]

When Laura, Ellen, Starletta, and Stuart go on an outing to a fair, it is also Starletta's mother who is uppermost in Ellen's mind when Stuart wants the two of them to look at the sideshow of the house of Mrs Thumb, a midget: 'I'd be ashamed to tell Starletta's mother we inspected people like slavery' (ibid.: 106). She is sickened 'to hear the boy's tone when he'd said human and animal shows, but I kept looking because it felt interesting and I had to, despite what Starletta's family from another century had no doubt been put through on slave examining blocks, and what kind of impression I would've made on a human being in the market for another human being' (ibid.: 108). Here Ellen feels that she is placed in a similar position to whites who examined black slaves on the auction block while, at the same time, she imagines being examined on the block herself, thereby identifying with the slaves. In these contradictory contexts, Starletta's mother serves as a font of wisdom and a trigger of Ellen's conscience.

Another revealing fantasy on Ellen's list of imaginary ordeals is that she is adopted, which indeed she is at this point, and more or less happily so, by Laura. In *Ellen Foster*, a court decision removes Ellen from a satisfying home situation with her art teacher and her husband to a dysfunctional one at her grandmother's. This experience serves to diminish her trust in legal or government decisions made ostensibly to promote her best interests as a child. The first chapter of *The Life All Around Me* describes in some detail what Laura and Ellen have to go through to make their relationship permanent through adoption. As Ellen puts it, 'there's no way to avoid the government getting in on the decision' if one decides to make 'an underage change in life' (ibid.: 9), and the summer after the Christmas she moves in, Laura contacts the authorities to ask them to 'draw up her parental rights paperwork' (ibid.: 10). They receive a letter from Social Service that approves of the arrangement, according to Ellen, 'as long as I could pass the mental stability tests meant to prove whether I was too much of a damaged goods personality to live with a nice individual permanently or if I needed to be demoted into a more routine nightmare orphan home' (ibid.: 10). In addition to this test, Ellen has to take an intelligence test, which is sprung on her and Laura right after she has taken the first test. Waiting for the results of both tests takes months, and Ellen lives in a state of nervous suspension. When Laura calls the 'Social Service lady' after a month to enquire about the results, she is told that the tests are only formalities in any case, at which Ellen wants 'to shout and ask her if she'd ever needed permission to call her home a home ...' (*ibid.*: 15). In this chapter in *The Life All Around Me*, as in the letter to the president of Harvard, Ellen refers to herself as an orphan and imagines an orphanage as a possible fate should she fail the tests. She is dismayed when the other foster girls at Laura's house take so lightly her ordeal of having to wait for the test results: 'You'd think they would've sympathized with my fears of getting dragged off to some gnashing-teeth type of place and suffering to sleep on a spotted mattress, hunched over, holding my tennis shoes and clean socks with the blue dingleballs from getting robbed off my feet by some bloodthirsty orphans' (*ibid.*: 17). Ellen's image of a 'more routine nightmare orphan home' is based on cultural images of orphanages derived from sources such as Dickens and *Little Orphan Annie*.

Foster care is unsurprisingly a trope in both Ellen Foster novels because Laura takes in foster children who are usually 'referred to [her] through the court' (Gibbons, 1987: 118). The first time Ellen sees Laura and her foster girls is in church, and she later discovers that her 'new mama' receives part of the collection money every week for their support (*ibid.*: 56). At the time Ellen joins the household Laura fosters three girls – Jojo, Stella, and Francis – and Stella's baby Roger. The harmonious house that Ellen experiences in *Ellen Foster* seems to have quickly deteriorated in *The Life All Around Me*. The three named girls and the baby in the first novel have become 'two other girls living with us ...' (Gibbons, 2006: 16), and they are never mentioned by name in the second novel. Ellen has, however, reason to reflect on 'how things had corroded so darkly from where the girls had been the first day I saw them with Laura with a kind of bright light of bliss around them and thought they were set to live out the orphan American dream' (*ibid.*: 51). Unlike Ellen, these foster girls have living birth parents who have problems that have to be dealt with before the girls can return to them. These girls become increasingly disruptive to the domestic peace of Laura's house, and Ellen finally uses the pay phone in a store to tell the foster care services 'to come on back out here and load up because through no fault of their new mother's and the hoopla they'd created on their own, they were bordering on being out of hand, and if anyone needed evidence, they could be found drinking alcohol out of sacks outside a take-your-clothes-off place in town, where one or the both of them was nursing an ambition to work' (*ibid.*: 48). Immediately before she makes that call, Laura explains to Ellen that '[t]here aren't many people who'll take older girls, even briefly' (*ibid.*: 47), but – after the immediate crisis that Ellen's action causes in her and Laura's relationship – all ends well for both girls, who Laura helps to find another foster placement until their birth parents are ready to reunite with them (*ibid.*: 52). Hence, they do not 'age out' of foster care; they return to their families, go to school, hold part-time jobs, and conform to common standards for femininity.[39] This happy ending for the girls, which also means their convenient exit from Ellen's life and story, indicates that they are, first and foremost, present in her narrative in order to chart her own progress and development.

Laura's distressed reaction to Ellen's phone call is a result of the tension between Ellen's individualism and her having to acquire a more communal view. Kinship building implies a move toward a larger community than the immediate family, and in *The Life All Around Me*, this community consists entirely of women. Laura keeps her house open to women who need a break from their family lives: she lets them rest in her guest room, treats them to tea when they wake up, and washes their hair if that is what they need. She explains, 'Women hide women, Ellen' (*ibid.*: 37). That women may need to hide emphasizes the violence inherent in patriarchal social and familial structures that underpin Gibbons's stories. At one point, Starletta's mother tells Ellen that if her mother had lived closer to Laura's house she might have had a place to go instead of resorting to suicide (*ibid.*: 204). So, when Ellen contacts the foster care office, she worries Laura will conclude that 'I'd destroyed two girls to save myself, and I'd never be the kind of woman who shelters a friend if I was this conniving about putting them back in their pasts before people there were wholly healed and ready for them' (*ibid.*: 48). As Laura points out when Ellen endeavors to explain why she contacted the authorities, 'Your life, your life isn't the only one here' (*ibid.*: 50). Nevertheless, Ellen's anticipating and agonizing about Laura's reaction signals that she may well learn the lesson that Laura tries to teach her.

The focus on women's friendship and community as well as well-functioning families with single mothers in *The Life All Around Me* leaves little room for adult male characters. Ellen's abusive white father is dead, and so is Starletta's caring black father. Laura unambiguously connects the peaceful, open atmosphere in her house to the absence of men: 'There hasn't been a man here, not to stay, since my father left it, and that has to account for how bad it feels when there's a struggle, there's been nothing to accustom the place to fear' (*ibid.*: 128). The only male authority figure Ellen needs to negotiate with in this novel is the president of Harvard, who has the key to the education she craves, but it is Ellen who initiates communication with this distant male benefactor, who actually grants her requests by letter.

In *Ellen Foster*, the relationship between patriarchy and abuse – or men and fear, as Laura puts it – is depicted in the figures of Ellen's father and the school psychologist. Her father is characterized as a tyrant who demands that his wife cook even though she is gravely ill. He threatens Ellen with a knife when her mother takes an overdose and, in this way, prevents her from summoning help. He physically and sexually abuses her after her mother is dead. However, even though Ellen's father is white, incest in *Ellen Foster* remains associated with black men, as it is in *The Cider House Rules*, because it begins on the suggestion of one of her father's black drinking buddies. He tells Ellen's father that Ellen 'is just about ripe' when he hears that she is nine or ten: 'You gots to git em when they is still soff when you mashum' (Gibbons, 1987: 37). Racializing incest in this way underlines the tendency towards stereotypical depiction of black characters in this novel – here in the shape of the oversexed black man as potential rapist. In *Father–Daughter Incest*, which was first published in 1981 and deals exclusively with white American fathers and daughters, Judith Lewis Herman asserts that incest was 'rediscovered' by the women's liberation movement in the 1970s when *Ellen Foster* is set (Herman, 2000: 18).[40] She points out that – regardless of race or ethnicity – father–daughter incest is most common in a patriarchal family with an ill or absent mother.[41] Herman observes that '[f]ather-daughter incest is not only the type of incest most frequently reported but also represents a paradigm of female sexual victimization. The relationship between father and daughter, adult male and female child, is one of the most unequal relationships imaginable' (*ibid.*: 4).

In *Ellen Foster*, Ellen's interaction with the school psychologist – another unequal male–female and adult–child relationship – involves a struggle over her name that echoes her struggle with her father when he sexually abuses her and calls her by her mother's name:

> Do not oh you do not say her name to me. That was her name. You know that now stop no not my name.
> I am Ellen.
> I am Ellen.
> He pulls the evil back into his self and Lord I run. (Gibbons, 1987: 38)

Ellen desperately asserts her name and identity in the moment of abuse. Her self-assertion in the midst of a traumatic situation mirrors her attempt to create a coherent, self-reliant 'I' in her narrative. The conversation with the male psychologist concerns her last name, 'Foster,' which she has adopted in the belief that it is the last name of her new family: 'My old family wore the other name out and I figured I would take the name of my new family' (ibid.: 88). The psychologist laughs at Ellen's mistake: it is a foster family, not the Foster family. Although she can see her mistake, Ellen does not accept the psychologist's idea that she has taken a new name and assumed a new identity as a sign of traumatic dissociation. He, in turn, refuses to listen to what Ellen actually says to him, and his refusal echoes her father's insistence on calling her by her mother's name as he abuses her. It makes Ellen desperate: 'Not identity. Just a new name I wanted to write that big across the sky so he would understand and the picking into my head would stop' (ibid.: 89). Here the psychoanalytic situation is described as a site of physical assault, and the phrase 'picking into my head' suggests abuse. Ellen's selection of a new last name is a conscious move to mark her successful kinship building outside blood relationships; through taking the name Foster, she asserts that she belongs to a functional family that she has carefully chosen instead of a dysfunctional one to which she is born. It is obviously important in this context of patriarchal abuse that her new family is female-headed.

At the end of *The Life All Around Me*, after having read Shine's hospital admission records, Ellen is finally reconciled with the loss of her birth mother, whose love she realizes she will always carry with her. As a result, she comes to accept Laura as her mother, which is stressed in a scene where Starletta in the arms of her mother is mirrored by Laura opening her arms to Ellen: '[Laura] sat on the floor in front of Starletta and her mother arranged on the sofa, I told them, like a birthing' (Gibbons, 2006: 203); 'Laura called me over to where she was on the floor ... her arms and legs already opened ...' (ibid.: 205). This peaceful but pregnant scene suggests the strength of maternal lines, even beyond blood relations, and the adequacy of white and black single-mother families.

Whereas Homer and Melony retain their orphan status throughout *The Cider House Rules*, Ellen seems to overcome hers at the end of the second novel, integrating the memory of her birth mother into her life with her adoptive mother. Like *The Cider House Rules*, however, both Ellen Foster novels move beyond patriarchal and nuclear family norms insofar as a central aspect of the main orphan characters' development is kinship building: a relational process leading towards a progressive, affirmative stance on alternative families. While acknowledging the highly mythologized attraction of the nuclear family ideal, these novels depict dysfunctional and abusive white nuclear families and critique the ways that social service agents, school psychologists, politicians, and other officials interfere with the diverse family lives of orphans. The novels posit alternatives to the white nuclear family for the Euro-American orphans: a non-patriarchal version of the orphanage as family, a lesbian working-class family, and a foster or adoptive single-mother family, which serves as a node for a larger women's community.

Despite challenges to the continued idealization of the white nuclear family and the incorporation of contemporary debates on federal and states' roles in adoption, the depictions of gender and race connect these novels to classic texts in US literary history. Whereas women play crucial roles in Irving's narrative, it privileges the father–son relationship. In the Ellen Foster novels, as in *The Cider House Rules,* racial difference is introduced in ways that complicate notions of American family, but the principal function of racial 'others,' like that of the white women characters in Irving's novel, is to advance the trajectory of a single Euro-American orphan protagonist. Both Homer and Ellen develop in relation to black characters and black families, but these characters are more positively charged in the Ellen Foster novels. Despite Homer's initial identification and friendship with the African American picking crew, its boss Mr Rose eventually embodies abusive biological fatherhood. If Mr Rose epitomizes the incestuous father in Irving's novel, the white father takes that role in *Ellen Foster.* African American families serve as models for Ellen's kinship building in *Ellen Foster,* and at the end of *The Life All Around Me,* Starletta and her mother's loving relationship is mirrored in Laura and Ellen's. However, the black characters in the Ellen Foster novels are systematically subordinated to Ellen's progress. The explicit and implicit centrality of race in these novels, combined with their privileging of the white protagonists' development, locates them firmly within a literary tradition that has served to bolster hegemonic images of American family and of national identity.

Only partially challenging literary and cultural conventions, Irving's and Gibbons' novels nevertheless offer interesting opportunities for rethinking gender and genre as cultural memory. In these fictions, there is a troubling of gendered boundaries, and a mixing and loosening of generic conventions that were unambiguously gendered in the nineteenth-century American *bildungsroman*. Although Ellen Foster resembles the heroines of 'woman's fiction,' she has more in common with Huck Finn than does Irving's Homer. Despite her first-person narration and self-reliance against all odds, though, her main focus is finding kinship outside her birth family, whose members are either 'dead or crazy,' and integrating herself into a wider society through education. Homer Wells is neither modeled on Huck Finn nor on other American individualist boy orphans; his aim to 'be of use' points in the direction of a socially conscious community, as do the orphanage and the orchard as settings for alternative family formations. Even the structure of *The Cider House Rules* appears to favor community over individualism in the way that the novel employs third-person narration and the focalization moves between and across different characters. There are strong links, however, between Homer and the orphan hero and heroine of the English nineteenth-century *bildungsroman*, which is underscored by explicit references to Dickens and Brontë. Indeed, Irving draws on the female *bildungsroman* in the development of Homer, whereas Melony remains outside the bourgeois parameters of both the classics in the genre and more conventional fictions of female development. Irving and Gibbons use and reaffirm, but simultaneously contest many of the gendered conventions of the classic *bildungsroman*, and of traditional trajectories of young heroes in US literature, while launching a critique of the white nuclear family ideal through their orphan protagonists' experiences and successful kinship building outside this family model.

Notes

1. *Bildungsroman*, coming-of-age novel, and fiction of development are often used interchangeably, and we follow that practice. However, see Christy Rishoi for an attempt to distinguish between the *bildungsroman* and the coming-of-age narrative (2003: 67).
2. For example, Signe Howell (2007) has coined the term 'kinning' to refer to practices that create family bonds between adoptees and adoptive parents, and Kath Weston (1997) has explored the everyday emotive and material aspects of building kinship among gays and lesbians.

3   See Gerald P. Mallon (2004) on the shifting possibilities for gay parenthood in the USA since the 1980s.
4   See Helena Wahlström's *New Fathers?* for a discussion of how fatherhood figured in political, academic, and aesthetic discourses in the 1990s.
5   Sociologist and Senator Daniel Patrick Moynihan's report *The Negro Family: The Case for National Action* (1965) notoriously describes economic and social deprivation in the African American population, tracing these problems to the prevalence of non-normative family structures marked by 'father absence' and 'black matriarchy.' His argument has been criticized by scholars and activists as suffering from male and white bias, and as an example of 'blaming the victim.' Nevertheless, the idea that mother-headed households are the cause rather than the effect of social conditions, and that such households per definition are a problem, has proven persistent. See Roberts (2003: 8); see also Steve Estes (2005).
6   Including Senator Patrick Moynihan, Philadelphia Judge Lois Forer, and Senator Judy Barr Topinka.
7   Some claim that for many who grew up in such institutions in the USA, orphanages are 'success stories.' See, for instance, Richard MacKenzie (2009) for a discussion of the positive outcomes of life in orphanages.
8   See, for example, O'Neale (1982) and Braendlin (1983), as well as more recent work on the ethnic *bildungsroman* in the USA by Stella Bolaki (2011), Martin Japtok (2005), or Enrique Lima (2011).
9   *Adventures of Huckleberry Finn* (1884) has often been discussed as an example of *bildungsroman*, as well as coming-of-age novel; see for instance Millard (2007: 4–5) and Rishoi (2003: 66–73). Another example of a re-gendering of Twain's characters is Amy Denver and Sethe in Morrison's *Beloved* (Rody, 2001: 30).
10 See Monteith (2000: 65) for similarities but also differences between Huck and Ellen.
11 For two accounts from the late 1990s that outline and elaborate on the recovered vs. false memory debates, which often pivoted on memories of child abuse and incest, see Marita Sturken (1999) and Roger Luckhurst (1999). Luckhurst also examines the impact of these on selected American and British novels.
12 See Ian Hacking (1991) on the discourse of child abuse, and Herman (2000, 1992) on father–daughter incest and on trauma and recovery.
13 See Andersen (1991) or Coontz (2000) on the nuclear family ideal.
14 The reviews in 1985 were mixed; although many were favorable (DeMott, 1985), the controversial topic of abortion and the pro-choice narrative, while lauded by some, alienated others (Clemons (1985), Kramer (1985), Yardley (1985)); see also Josie Campbell (1998: 113). The book was a *New York Times* bestseller, as well as a book-of-the-month club selection; it was

dramatized for the stage in 1996, and filmed in 1999 (directed by Lasse Hallström) on the basis of Irving's own screenplay. See Irving (1999).
15 In 1800 there were about seven orphanages in the USA, by 1850 over 70. After the Civil War the number rose to over 600 in 1880, and mass immigration caused numbers to peak between the 1880s and the 1920s. For more detailed information about the history of orphanages, see Martin Olasky (1999).
16 'Troubled' is often used to refer to a combination of socio-economic and psychological problems, but also at times to disability. See Hacsi (1997: 50).
17 In the 1970s, too, it was revealed that some institutions that took in children made huge profits from them living in appalling conditions – the Meridell Center in Texas is one such case. See Ashby (1997: 138).
18 However, around 60,000 children still lived in institutions rather than, for example, in foster homes at that time. Most were boys in their teens or pre-teens, and typically they were from poor, single-mother families.
19 The novel has been discussed in terms of its specifically 'Dickensian' qualities; Alison Booth, for example, observes that 'Dickensian signals pervade the novel' (Booth, 2002: 284 fn 1), and Davis and Womack call it Irving's 'most Dickensian' novel 'in terms of its rich textual scope, wide range of characters, and expansive ideological vision' (2004: 14).
20 In 2012, the presidential campaign again raised the issues of abortion and family planning in ways that suggest that these issues are as topical as ever in US politics. As some feminist critics have observed, 'the breakdown of the family' has often been another term for 'independence for women' (Booth (2002: 287 fn 6); Andersen (1991)).
21 See Elaine Tyler May (1988) and Coontz (2000) for discussions of the dominance of the nuclear family in the postwar era.
22 Melony was actually written out of the film script for Lasse Hallström's *The Cider House Rules* by Irving, who has claimed that she was too powerful a character and would detract attention from the romantic plot between Homer and Candy. For a discussion of the adaptation, see Booth (2002); see also Irving (1999).
23 At thirteen, Homer discovers a tiny aborted fetus that has fallen from a wastebasket he has emptied into the incinerator at St Cloud's (Irving, 1985: 97) and is troubled by the fateful but – to him – unclear distinctions between being aborted or born into orphanhood: '"Whether I shall turn out to be the hero of my own life," Homer whispered to himself ... he remembered the cool, damp, curled-in-on-itself beginning that lay dead in his hand. (That thing he had held in his hand could not have been a hero)' (*ibid.*: 99). Here, the aborted fetus – a dead thing – has been acted upon, whereas Homer understands himself as a potentially heroic agent in the tradition of David Copperfield.

24 Susan Turell confirms, in an entry on incest in *Encyclopedia on Human Development* that, '[a]lthough stereotypes abound, incest crosses all ethnic groups, socioeconomic statuses, and is no more likely in rural areas than in urban ones' (2006: 684).
25 In *Exorcizing Blackness*, Trudier Harris discusses the myth of the black man's sexual prowess, and hence his animalization, in American history and literature in the context of lynching rituals. She demonstrates how the perpetuation of the myth in the cultural imagination was linked to white men's envy and fear of sexual competition (1984: 20–2).
26 See Monteith's *Advancing Sisterhood?* for an examination of white and black southern women characters in fictions from the 1970s, 1980s, and 1990s loving each other and forging alternative families (2000: 172–5). Jay Clayton also discusses explorations of family among women novelists of the late 1970s and 1980s (1993: 130–45).
27 For discussion of the power of the nuclear family ideal, see for example sociologists Margaret Andersen's (1991) and Patricia Hill Collins's crucial work (1998, 2000, 2005); see also Betty Farrell's historical investigation of 'family' as an American concept (1999), and Weston's (1997)and Valerie Lehr's (1999) studies of contemporary queer families.
28 Inscription to 'Self-Reliance.'
29 In *Pleasures of Babel*, Jay Clayton describes the concept of culture as 'a battleground, a field of contention, where assumptions about personal identity, the family, gender, class, education, technology, the environment, race, religion, and a host of other topics are debated' (1993: 8). Unlike conservative critics such as Allan Bloom, whose *The Closing of the American Mind* (1987) was published the same year as *Ellen Foster*, Clayton finds literary pleasure in oppositional narratives and in multicultural challenges to canon formation. In *American Literature and the Culture Wars* (1997), Gregory S. Jay makes a strong case for historicizing canon formation and conflicts about literary value, advocating a pedagogy of dialogue and self-awareness.
30 *A Virtuous Woman* (1989), *A Cure for Dreams* (1991), *Charms for the Easy Life* (1993), *Sights Unseen* (1995), *On the Occasion of My Last Afternoon* (1998), and *Divining Women* (2004).
31 For a discussion of these aspects, see Troy (2006). See also Linda Watts (2000) on survivor guilt in *Ellen Foster*.
32 Clayton argues that in *Ellen Foster*, 'the notion of "getting" a family implies that there may be a degree of agency involved in constituting this group. One is not simply born into family; one works for the privilege of membership' (1993: 140).
33 Both Munafo (1998) and Monteith (2000) end their discussions of the novel by concluding that Ellen's progress is compromised due to the

formal qualities of the novel which maintain Starletta's silence and leave Ellen to speak for her.
34 Black families are seldom regarded as models or ideal families in dominant social and political discourses in the USA. Ellen espouses stereotypes of black extended families in comparison to Starletta's family: 'They live regular but most colored people have a grandmamma or two and a couple dozen cousins in the same house' (Gibbons, 1987: 30).
35 See Troy (2006) for details.
36 There are, however, American novels set in the South in the 1960s that depict black women 'adopting' white girls, such as Fowler's *Before Women Had Wings* (1996) and Kidd's *The Secret Life of Bees* (2002).
37 Marianne Novy states, in an e-mail to the authors 19 Mar. 2012, that there are instances of black adults adopting white children in the US, but, as far as she knows, there are no available statistics, nor any research done in this area. See Tony Dokuopil for an example of black parents adopting a white child.
38 Ellen's repeated mention of this fund hints at another deleterious stereotype about Affirmative Action 'quotas' for African American students in Ivy league colleges.
39 In reality outcomes for foster children, many of whom have aged out of the foster system, are discouraging. In the early 1980s, Trudy Festinger observed that 'minimal attention has been paid to a small, but ever growing army of people who left foster care' as young adults and who 'did not return home to birth families, nor were they adopted' (1983: xiii).
40 Freud first (re)discovered incest in bourgeois families, but then denied it; the second time incest was rediscovered was when social scientists brought up incest in five studies published 1940–78, including the Kinsey report.
41 'If incestuous abuse is indeed an inevitable result of patriarchal family structure, then preventing sexual abuse will ultimately require a radical transformation of the family' (Herman, 2000: 202).

5

At home in the world? Orphans learn and remember in African American novels

> The single most compelling aspect of black women's writing today is its ability to envision transformed human social relationships and the alternative futures these might shape. (Willis, 1990: 159)

Novelists find the figure of the orphan useful for traversing and testing the literary terrains of family and nation, and such testing gained urgency, we argue, in the latter part of the twentieth century when multiple challenges to notions of unity erupted at different levels in the USA. In the work of several African American writers who gained recognition or came to prominence in the late twentieth century, literary orphans inhabit a site for artistic and sometimes political engagement through which to explore how race and gender figure in social discourses on family and nation. The 1965 publication of the Moynihan Report, which propagated the view that poverty and social decline among African Americans could be largely attributed to the pathology of 'matriarchal' family structures, spurred public controversy about African American families. Continuing through the 1980s and 1990s in debates concerning radical changes in welfare policy and in new attention to the legacy of slavery, and in the 2000s with attention to the growth of a black middle class, public scrutiny has continued unabated throughout the period we examine. As one scholar puts it, 'No system of family relations has received as much scholarly and public attention ... as that of the African American family' (K. Anderson, 1991: 259). Repeatedly linked to issues of national welfare, black family relations have been pathologized but sometimes extolled, and many African American writers have subjected these trends to artistic examination.[1] Among them are Ernest J. Gaines, Charles Johnson, Gayl Jones, Gloria Naylor, Ntozake Shange, Alice Walker, John Edgar Wideman, and Sarah E. Wright, as well as the writers we examine here: Octavia Butler, Jewelle Gomez, and Toni Morrison. Equally important for these writers, however, is their strong engagement in art, scholarship, and literary traditions, particularly those governing novelistic genres. Belonging to the generation that rediscovered slave narratives and Zora Neale Hurston, produced path-breaking historical scholarship on US slavery and black families, inaugurated affirmative action programs for university education, and contributed to the establishment of African American and other 'minority' studies programs in the US academy, intellectuals and writers such as Butler, Gomez, and Morrison have worked to release black-authored literature from purely sociological interpretive paradigms and to gain recognition for their own and others' intellectual and literary achievements.

Sociological issues concerning family life nevertheless hold sway in the public imagination as well as in the imaginations of the writers we examine here. While African American families have a history of persecution and denial from slavery times,[2] modern black family relations have been the subject of intense public debate ever since the Moynihan Report sought to affirm black patriarchy by discrediting an 'emasculating' black 'matriarchy.' While other commentators in the 1960s also disparaged female-headed black households, this government report by Senator Daniel Patrick Moynihan, *The Negro Family: The Case for National Action,* strongly suggested that an emasculated patriarchy was 'the underlying cause of racial oppression – rather than ... an unfortunate effect of it' (Jenkins, 2007: 65).[3] Though it is clear that, as Toni Morrison observes, 'everybody knows, deep down, that black men were emasculated by white men, period. And that black women didn't take any part in that' (1977: 17), deviation from the white nuclear family ideal in the form of African American extended family models continues to generate controversy and very real consequences. Dorothy Roberts, for example, analyzes how the 'powerful myth of the shiftless "welfare queen"' and the notion of a black 'culture of dependency' contributed to the 1996 passage of the Personal Responsibility and Work Opportunity Reconciliation Act which limited and regulated welfare benefits in ways that disadvantaged African American families with children (2003: 194). The effects of poverty, combined with deviation from a white nuclear family ideal, she argues, has also led to a disproportionate incidence of foster care placement for black children in the child welfare system and higher detention rates among black youth (*ibid.*: 219). While the reasons for the over-representation of African American children in care continue to spawn debate and inquiry, it is clear that over-representation exists, and that poverty is a risk factor.[4] Thomas J. Sugrue asserts that in the 1990s, the causes of poverty were misrepresented as cultural, rather than economic or political, by politicians, policy makers, influential public intellectuals, and writers, with dire consequences for poor people.[5] Patricia Hill Collins's *Black Sexual Politics* (2005) examines how media images of African Americans build upon previous white ideological constructions of black sexuality, recycling or revamping for our modern times conceptions that grew out of the periods of chattel slavery, the Jim Crow South, and urban ghettoization; as she puts it, the past is ever present, and is a feature of new forms of racism in the post-Civil Rights era.

At the same time, sociologists, including Collins, have drawn attention to how extended families in the black community provide the nurturance conventionally associated with the nuclear family. Children who have lost parents, temporarily or permanently, for a host of reasons ranging from death, to voluntary surrender, to state intervention (where figures indicate that African American children are removed from parental care at a much higher rate than non-black children), may be informally adopted or cared for by other family or community members. In *Black Feminist Thought* (2000), Collins discusses the role of 'othermothers' in African American families and communities, showing how women have supported 'bloodmothers' by alleviating or taking on parenting responsibilities for children who are not 'their own.'[6] Thus, in the late twentieth century, the 'pathology' of the black family became one dominant paradigm, while another model was that of strength and resiliency. Such dichotomous views have affected child welfare, adoption policies, and the practice of transracial adoption. These views have also, however, spawned thoughtful, complex academic and literary treatment of the African American family.[7]

In this chapter, we analyze orphans and family constellations in novels by prominent African American women writers. Though questions of family and nation are certainly taken up by male writers, and male-authored novels feature orphans – the albino Brother Tate of John Edgar Wideman's *Sent for You Yesterday* (1983) and Nathaniel Turner Witherspoon and the newborn baby in Leon Forrest's *The Bloodworth Orphans* (1977) are cases in point[8] – we focus on women writers who contributed to what Henry Louis Gates, Jr. describes as the 'efflorescence of black creativity' generated by 'the resurgence of black women's literature and criticism in the early eighties' (1997: 41). We have selected Octavia Butler's *Fledgling* (2005), Jewelle Gomez's *The Gilda Stories* (1991), and Toni Morrison's *A Mercy* (2008) because they epitomize the outspoken engagement with feminism, art, and racial equality that began in the 1970s but gained impetus in the 1990s and later.[9]

Throughout the 1990s, the institution and legacy of slavery were continuously under the public eye. President Clinton's and Pope John Paul II's public expressions of, respectively, regret and apology for American and Catholic involvement in the slave trade are prominent examples of such attention. The DNA testing in 1998 that confirmed that Thomas Jefferson did father at least one child with his enslaved servant Sally Hemings brought renewed attention to the effects of slavery on both the private and the national family Jefferson is said to have 'fathered.'[10] In their fictions Butler, Gomez, and Morrison explore the bloodlines of the national family and can be read as exemplifying the alternative concept of othermothering identified by Collins and Susan Willis's related idea of 'motherlines.' Willis asserts, 'For black women, history is a bridge defined along motherlines. It begins with a woman's particular genealogy and fans out to include all the female culture heroes, like the folk curers and shamans known as root workers and Obeah women, as well as political activists like Sojourner Truth and Ida B. Wells who have shaped the process and marked the periods of black history' (1990: 6). These motherlines encompass Collins's 'community othermothers,' who work as teachers, take on community responsibilities, and generate local activism, all in response to the needs of African American children and youth.

We view Butler, Gomez, and Morrison as literary othermothers, as representative of those black women writers whose commanding artistic visions derive in large part from their commitment to African American community and art. Their concern with a communal past, present, and future, as well as their profound exploration of the conditions for social and artistic belonging, are reflected in the use they make of orphan figures and the literary genres of speculative fiction and the historical novel – these are employed to negotiate dominant paradigms of American family and nation. In 'rememorying' the past through genre intervention, but above all by emphasizing how learning and literacies can yield empowering knowledge, they expand the 'American' literary canon to make a home for African American writing. At the same time, their work puts pressure on national boundaries, and positions national literatures in transnational or cosmopolitan contexts.

As indicated in Chapter 1, the concept of 'rememory' derives from Toni Morrison's 1987 historical novel of slavery, *Beloved*. This term, and the related one of 'disremembering,' further Morrison's deep concern with history, particularly the slave past, its destruction of family relations, and its legacy for contemporary America. Morrison's coinage of such terms has generated considerable commentary; rememory is often connected to trauma, stressing the difficulty of assimilating traumatic experience, but it is also a trope for imagining a black literary heritage, as Caroline Rody demonstrates, or a conceptual device that gives readers 'a way to understand how we can share in the prior experiences of others' (Rushdy, 2001: 6). The pronounced social valence of rememory, existing not only in individual consciousness but 'out there, in the world' (Morrison, 1987: 36), accounts for hauntings, such as that of Sethe by Beloved. Rememory, then, describes the contemporaneity and endurance of the past in the present: it invokes or instantiates historical consciousness. In our analyses, moreover, we emphasize the epistemological dimensions of rememory, its centrality to processing and transforming historical understanding. In contrast to 'disremembering' or losing family (members/memories), rememory can facilitate the reconstitution of family and community, the reclamation of a common past.

We see rememory as operating on a thematic and narrative level to transform traumatic memory into a 'property of consciousness with the heightened imaginative power sufficient to the ethnic historical novel's claim to retell the story of the past' (Rody, 2001: 28). In *A Mercy*, as well as in Butler's and Gomez's novels, rememory accesses and processes the cultural memory carried by foundational texts and literary traditions. Genres and literary devices have semantic aspects; formal conventions carry meanings that interact with formal innovations. Narrative devices such as intertextuality, plot, and constructions of subjectivity 'are semanticized to the extent that they implicitly convey culture-specific notions of the workings of individual and collective memory' (Neumann, 2010: 335). Gates's theory of signifyin(g) and Willis's of specifying help to account for an African American expressive tradition in which black-authored texts speak to other black-authored texts, or to mainstream canonical works. Angelyn

Mitchell, drawing explicitly on Gates, links intertextuality to the construction of rememory and the 'replaying of selected images' (2002: 12) in what she calls liberatory narratives – neo-slave narratives or historical novels of slavery. Processing the meanings held in literary techniques is an artistic endeavor, but, as Mitchell indicates, it is also an epistemological one, gaining and producing knowledge about self and other, about individual and shared pasts. For this reason, in discussing Morrison's *A Mercy*, as well as Butler's and Gomez's novels, we employ the notion of rememory to foreground the process of learning and the exercise of agency in fictions – speculative *and* historical – where orphans have an important role to play in learning about the past and in envisioning alternative futures.

Rememorying speculative fiction and the historical novel

> The speculative fiction genre is the product of dreams of what life might be. (Gomez, 1993: 954)

Butler and Gomez have each made explicit in interviews and essays, as well as in their novels, that speculative fiction has the potential to address pressing contemporary issues, features of the social imaginary, and paths to knowledge about the self and other.[11] Indeed, their fictions demonstrate that speculative literature may function as a component of political engagement for both readers and writers, not least because it can help to revise cultural images of the past and to imagine possible futures for marginalized groups.[12]

The term *speculative fiction* is one Gomez has used 'to encompass the broad range of writing that includes science fiction and fantasy' (*ibid.*: 948). Speculative fiction has often been associated with white writers: 'the term itself comes out of genre debates in US science fiction criticism of the 1940s and 1950s' (Thaler, 2010: 2).[13] However, in addition to Gomez and Butler, African American science-fiction and fantasy writers such as Steven Barnes, LeVar Burton, Samuel R. Delany, Tananarive Due, Nalo Hopkinson, and Charles R. Saunders have done significant work in this genre.[14] In our analyses of Butler's *Fledgling* and Gomez's *The Gilda Stories* we use speculative fiction according to Gomez's definition as an umbrella term that incorporates the two vampire novels, though they belong to different branches of speculative fiction. *The Gilda Stories* – which is part speculative, part historical – re-envisions the fantasy branch of the genre that includes horror and the gothic, whereas *Fledgling* belongs to the branch that grows out of science fiction in which the vampire is a different species from *homo sapiens* and is thus a natural rather than an undead or supernatural being (M. Carter, 2004: 3).[15] What Gomez's and Butler's vampire novels do have in common is a female African American orphan figure at the very center of the narratives; these novels combine the trope of the orphan with that of the vampire. This combination allows the writers to reinforce the connotation of the orphan as 'unfamiliar,' as an outsider to family, and to highlight other family constellations than the nuclear family and biologically grounded kinship.

The vampire as a subcultural and cultural trope has been circulating in different discourses in the English-speaking world for the past two centuries,[16] but it has recently enjoyed what seems to be an unprecedented mainstream popularity.[17] Its connotations have certainly changed and developed over time, but it shares an outsider status with the figure of the orphan that often serves to disrupt traditional family constellations and transgress national borders, or unsettle national identity.[18] As Ken Gelder observes in *Reading the Vampire*, 'the representation of the vampire as "unassimilated" – as a "cosmopolitan" or internationalised character who is excessive to national identities, whose lack of restraint threatens the very *notion* of identity – has been exploited by vampire fiction in one way or another for some time now' (1994: 23). Significantly, the lack of restraint Gelder describes also links the vampire to what society considers taboo and excessive or perverse sexuality. The vampire's powerful and often lethal presence, superhuman capabilities, and immortality or longevity, have further underscored its unsettling, if titillating, categorization as a national, social, and cultural other.[19]

Against the historical development of the vampire trope, Gomez's and Butler's work can be seen to complicate it in terms of sexuality and gender, ethnicity and race because their vampire protagonists are African American girls or women.[20] The orphan status of these two protagonists adds to the complications of sexuality, gender and race because the literary orphan – in stark contrast to the vampire – is often a vulnerable, exposed character, which is indeed the case for the main characters at the beginning of Butler's and Gomez's novels. This apparent vulnerability has everything to do with their embodiment as young black female orphans, whose agency is put to the test immediately; both characters' orphanhood is caused or exacerbated by American slavery and its after-effects in the form of racism.

The loss of the vampire protagonists' mothers has a lasting impact on their lives; in *The Gilda Stories* the Girl's memories of her mother are as important as Shori's amnesia and her consequent struggle to discover her heritage in *Fledgling*. Indeed, matriarchy plays an important part in both novels, especially as they explore the possibilities of powerful motherlines in the creation of new families and new kinship constellations. Models of sociality and equality are further problematized because vampires are sentient beings who are more powerful and live longer than humans but require their blood to survive. As powerful vampires, Butler's and Gomez's protagonists are forced to deal with the ethics of exploitation, survival, and sharing, which they do through memory, learning, and literacy.

The combination of the vampire and orphan tropes hinges on the significance of blood in both novels, where blood stands for sustenance, family, biotechnology, race, and sexuality and serves to unite the orphan and vampire.[21] Blood plays a part in genealogy and creates 'a conceptual link between family and race that reveals the family's role in creating and sustaining not only racial identities but racial categories,' as well as in trans- and intraracial and trans- and intra-species adoption in the two novels, where the practice of adoption challenges assumptions that 'kinship is based in "shared blood"' (Callahan, 2011: 17, 18). Belonging to an emergent trend in American fiction from the mid-1970s in which vampire families have taken precedence over the solitary vampire, Gomez's and Butler's novels imaginatively engage with the notion of sharing blood both for mutual sustenance and in the creation of kinship relations, but shared blood between parents and their biological offspring is only one of many kinship constellations explored. The novels also investigate the utopian and radical potential of the extended family in the form of 'queer consensual kinship.'[22]

Speculative fiction engages the past and Butler and Gomez, as well as Morrison, have all written historical novels set during slavery, featuring orphans. Butler's *Kindred* (1979) uses the device of time-travel to catapult her adult orphan characters, Dana and Kevin, as well as her readers, between California in the 1970s and antebellum Maryland.[23] Though here we analyze Butler's vampire novel, she shares with numerous African American writers a preoccupation with slavery. Gomez uses the vampire novel to traverse long vistas of time, beginning in a remembered African past, pushing forward into the era of American plantation slavery, and ending in the future of 2050. *The Gilda Stories* thus combines the genres of speculative and historical fiction,[24] with an orphaned child at the center. Morrison has written two novels set in times of chattel slavery: *Beloved*, which returns to the mid-nineteenth century, and *A Mercy*, which reconstructs a history of enslavement in the prenational United States. She casts enslavement as a condition of cultural orphanhood, but most of the characters also have direct and painful experiences of losing family and home. *A Mercy* explicitly engages the vocabulary of orphanhood, bringing this social condition to the fore.

The history of social conditions for African Americans plays a significant role in black-authored fiction of the post-Civil Rights era, and many writers demonstrate a renewed interest in the historical novel, particularly the historical novel of slavery or Abolition. For Georg Lukács, who first theorized the historical novel, this European genre was a renewal of the epic form portraying 'a much more differentiated social world' (1983: 46), in which 'the great transformations of history [are depicted] as transformations of popular life' (*ibid.*: 48–9) and historical heroes are humanized. Perry Anderson and Diana Wallace have divergent views on the traditional historical novel, but both consider it to have made a comeback in the postmodern age.[25] Anderson believes these changes to be radical departures, and to derive from new critical understandings of race and empire.[26] In contrast, Wallace argues that although historical fiction has 'always been central to women's attempts to reclaim their unrecorded past,' feminism is 'one of the major factors fuelling the interest in the historical novel from the late 1980s onwards' (2006). Anderson thus sees a more defined rupture and Wallace a stronger continuity with the genre in the post-Civil Rights and feminist eras. Both critics would, however, affirm Lukács's thesis that history is a process; as he puts it, history is 'the concrete precondition of the present' (1983: 21), and without 'a felt relationship to the present, a portrayal of history is impossible' (*ibid.*: 53).[27] Even conflicting theorizations of the historical novel agree on there being a crucial connection between the past that is imagined and the present that is imagining, so that the historical novel has the potential to 'make a clear contemporary political intervention' (de Groot, 2010: 140). Certainly, historical fiction dealing with slavery, especially that emerging in the 1960s, becomes an identifiable trend in the politicized climate of the 1980s.[28] Such fiction may be read as 'the inevitable literary outgrowth of both the civil rights movement and the feminist movement, the vehicle directly responsible for revising how we perceive black women and black family relations and for exposing and repositioning the role that gender plays in narrativizing history' (Beaulieu, 1999: 4), and it continues the work of revisioning.

Gomez and Morrison have each contributed to the renewal of the historical novel. Because they depart from or center on the slave past, however, their fictions have been variously categorized as neo-slave narratives (Bell, 1987), historical novels of slavery (Carby, 1989), postmodern slave narratives (Spaulding, 2005), and liberatory narratives (Mitchell, 2002).[29] Their modern stories of enslaved people have been compared, implicitly or explicitly, to the slave narratives that were written, or told to white recorders, from the 1770s to the Civil War. As we indicated in the Introduction, contemporary scholarship sees such narratives as constituting a uniquely American genre. Slave narratives gained status in the literary marketplace between the American Revolution and the Civil War as a result of efforts toward national cultural independence, with Philip Gould describing them as 'a form of increasingly popular, distinctly American autobiography' that 'further enabled this national cultural project' (2007: 26). Nevertheless, narratives such as Frederick Douglass's *Narrative of the Life of Frederick Douglass, An American Slave* (1845), which infuses Butler's *Kindred*, and Harriet A. Jacobs's *Incidents in the Life of a Slave Girl* (1861) only became established in the American literary canon during the period of culture wars over multiculturalism and canon debates in the 1980s and 1990s, a period in which creative writers also found in them inspiration for new novels of slavery.[30]

Hazel Carby's conceptualization of 'the historical novel of slavery' incorporates Lukács's insights, directing attention to Gomez's and Morrison's interest in repressed knowledge of the key roles the slave trade, slave economies, and racial oppression have had within and beyond national borders. Self-consciously aware of its relation to the genre of slave narrative, it concerns citizenship and the struggle for freedom and autonomy (1989: 4). Carby's term highlights historical forces and cultural memory, while Mitchell's idea of the liberatory narrative emphasizes literary tradition, intertextuality, and emancipatory politics.

Freedom and family are intimately connected in such stories. Historical accounts of slavery have dwelt extensively on the purposeful destruction of home and family relations under slavery, and literary works emphasize the hardships of slavery and family separation.[31] In such a context, freedom is sometimes conceived as family (McDowell, 2007: 153), as in Harriet Jacobs's narrative, when '[t]he question of an enslaved mother's relationship to her children poses perhaps the greatest contradiction of slavery' (Beaulieu, 1999: 10), because slavery induces a desire to escape through death, but parenting induces a desire to live. Both *The Gilda Stories* and *A Mercy* have a strong focus on the significance of the mother–daughter bond under slavery. The agency of the orphaned African American slave girls in these novels is clearly informed by their mothers; both interrogate perceptions of black family relations under slavery, drawing attention to orphanhood, motherlines, and practices of othermothering.

In our view, when such novels engage genres as forms of cultural memory, they involve counter-memories and counter-visions which vie for articulation, legitimacy, recognition, or dominance. Butler, Gomez, and Morrison bring to their writing counter-understandings or rememories of racial and national histories that are distinct from official ones, and make changes to genre conventions in the process of making a home in the American literary canon. Their fiction critiques national social norms and intervenes in a national literary tradition in part by emphasizing the place of nation in a transnational context, but also by unsettling naturalized boundaries and forging a wider imaginative horizon for imagining futures as well as reimagining the past. The works we examine here use orphan figures who learn and remember in order to imagine alternative family relations in and beyond the USA, as they intervene in the genres of speculative and historical fiction.

Revamping amnesia: Octavia Butler's *Fledgling*

> I remembered so little of my life that sometimes I thought I had never really existed, that I was nothing more than emptiness covered with skin. (Hogan, 1995b: 174)

Octavia Butler's final novel *Fledgling* (2005) is narrated by a black orphan protagonist, Shori. She is a present-day American vampire, or 'Ina,' as Butler's vampires call themselves, who suffers from amnesia due to a ferocious attack that eradicates her mother's family.[32] At the opening of the novel she is severely injured and does not even know her own name; she remembers nothing before she wakes up alone, starving, and in pain. As the story unfolds, Shori tries to learn who and what she is and, simultaneously, to discover who is determined to destroy her and those closest to her, after having annihilated her closest family members. She builds a new family in order to survive. *Fledgling* thus thematizes disremembering as the loss of family members and the destruction of family, and rememory as the process of building a new family, which involves gaining knowledge about the present as well as the past, and acquiring a form of collective memory through conscious strategies.

The first-person narrator in Butler's novel functions very differently from narrators such as Ellen Foster in Kaye Gibbons's novels, discussed in Chapter 4, and more like Hogan's narrator Angel Wing in *Solar Storms* (1995), discussed in Chapter 2. From the moment that Shori has healed sufficiently to recognize speech, her subjectivity is formed in interaction with other characters; because she cannot remember anything, she is dependent on others and on written sources to learn about who she is, particularly in relation to others, to family, and to culture. Memory work becomes an act of reconstruction: 'The person I had been was gone ... I could only learn what I could about the Ina, about my families. I would restore what could be restored' (Butler, 2005: 310). What becomes most important to Shori is cultural knowledge about the Ina and the restoration of her mothers' family, the Petrescus, not her own ambition or advancement as an individual. The first-person perspective encourages the reader to follow Shori: as she uncovers more about herself and the Ina, so does the reader. This narrative strategy resembles that of *Kindred*, in which the black narrator and protagonist Dana is thrown back into the slave past in order to learn about her family's and the nation's history, thus involving the reader in uncovering their tangled histories. However, by employing an amnesiac, first-person orphan narrator, *Fledgling* lays bare the very processes by which individual memory is shaped by familial memory and is intimately connected to the cultural and collective memory of larger groups.

The biological premise in *Fledgling* is that Ina and human beings are different species that cannot interbreed, although they can and do have sexual relations. Shori is the successful result of genetic experiments carried out by her families in which human and Ina genes are combined to afford the Ina the opportunity to function during daylight hours. That the Ina are exclusively nocturnal and physically unable to tolerate sunlight draws on a convention originating in vampire films in the first half of the twentieth century that spread to vampire novels and was incorporated into vampire lore: the sun is the ultimate destroyer of vampires. In *Fledgling*, melanin is the solution to this dilemma: a solution that Butler's orphan protagonist embodies. Consequently, Shori is a relatively small, black Ina among a tall, pale species. As a human–Ina hybrid, her mere existence is regarded as an insult by some of the Ina, notably those who are also responsible for the slaughter of her families. A review of the novel points out that 'Shori's terrible predicament and the losses she suffers, allow Butler to direct our attention subtly to the themes and issues interwoven into her best tales – power, community, kin, mutuality, education, ethics, values, moral and immoral behaviors, and relationships among women as well as relationships between men and women' (Govan, 2006: 43). We suggest that through this orphaned black vampire protagonist and narrator Butler's novel also engages with a number of contemporary and intersecting issues and anxieties that have to do with family, sexuality, gender, and race. In this way, the novel realizes the potential of speculative fiction to address contemporary social issues.

The narrator in *Fledgling* is neither entirely human nor entirely Ina;[33] Shori is both black in a white world and a biological or genetic outsider, which is underscored by her status as an orphan. One critic has pointed out that Butler typically focuses on moments of transition and on 'a figure who embodies the splitting between old and new paradigms, who becomes the unwilling vehicle of transformation and bearer of the impossible ethical quandary it invests them with' (Luckhurst, 1996: 33–4). Shori fits this description, although due to her amnesia she is more of an unwitting than an unwilling vehicle of transformation. Without her memories her subjectivity is initially reduced to her injured body and her physical responses to light and other stimuli; she can thus be said to embody an abject state of orphanhood.

With the black vampire orphan as central figure and consciousness, the relationships between identity and family are pivotal in Butler's exploration of family patterns with multiple mothers and fathers, single-sex Ina communities and inter-species relationships between Ina and their human 'blood donors,' or 'symbionts.' In many ways, then, Butler's vampire novel could be said to support an American obsession with the family as *the* national institution. On the other hand, *Fledgling* challenges a number of cherished notions pertaining to the nuclear American family ideal, such as monogamy and heterosexual domesticity. One challenge to this family ideal is the depiction of Ina reproduction and family constellations. A group of Ina sisters mate with a group of Ina brothers, so that, typically, an Ina child has multiple mothers and fathers. The Ina live in communities with close family members of their own sex, rather than with their mates, which moves the focus away from nuclear family ideals and encourages strong intergenerational bonds between 'eldermothers' and 'youngerdaughters,' and between 'elderfathers' and 'youngersons,' in Ina kinship.

The symbiotic interspecies relationship between the Ina and their human symbionts moves the idea of family in *Fledgling* even further away from a restrictive nuclear family. Each Ina needs approximately seven symbionts as blood donors; in exchange, through the venom an Ina releases as he or she takes their blood, the symbionts live longer and healthier lives than they otherwise would as humans. In addition, when an Ina bites and sucks blood the human experiences the assault as extremely pleasurable, which causes an addiction to the venom. Each individual Ina enjoys close emotional and sexual relationships with symbionts of both sexes. As one symbiont explains to Shori: '"The relationship among an Ina and several symbionts is about the closest thing I've seen to a workable group marriage ..."' (Butler, 2005: 127). Symbionts are free to have sex with humans, to marry other symbionts, and to produce children, but life in the family community discourages them from compulsively repeating the heterosexual nuclear family pattern. Thus, in a vampire novel that engages with different kinds of biological drives, sexual preferences and family politics, Butler depicts a family pattern that offers human beings a more flexible lifestyle – albeit at the price of being bound to another species.

From the outside, to the symbionts' visiting relatives, the Ina-and-symbiont family communities appear to be surviving 1960s communes (*ibid.*: 151). Lauren J. Lacey has pointed out that '[t]he social structures of Ina communities – which emphasize cooperative living, community gatherings, and, of course, groups of symbionts coexisting with the Ina to whom they are bonded – reveal an alternative to the hierarchical and impersonal norms of the contemporary world' (2008: 387). There is indeed a utopian character to these communities in the cases when the powerful Ina generally respect humans and treat their own and others' symbionts as valued partners, but as the novel makes clear this is not always the case. That symbionts are made dependent on their Ina's venom for life also raises questions about the coercion and restriction that this community life entails. Yet, the novel does uphold ideas about interdependency, mutuality, and reciprocity which counteract ideas of individualism traditionally associated with orphanhood in American literature. Of equal importance is that the interspecies family pattern Butler envisions is a family model that does not repeat, to borrow Donna Haraway's words, 'the cyclopean story that collects up the people into the reproductive heterosexual nuclear family, the potent germ plasm for the Sacred Image of the Same' (1997: 243).[34]

Interspecies responsibility is something the amnesiac, orphaned Shori both instinctively feels and actively learns: she instinctively starts building a new family of male and female symbionts, who will be bound to her for the rest of their lives, but she also learns from both species about the 'mutualistic symbiosis' or 'mutualism' (Butler, 2005: 123) that exists between Ina and their symbionts.[35] Fairly late in the novel, a distant female relative explains to her: 'We need our symbionts more than most of them know. We need not only their blood, but physical contact with them and emotional reassurance from them. Companionship. I've never known even one of us to survive without symbionts ... We either weave ourselves a family of symbionts, or we die. Our bodies need theirs' (ibid.: 270). In spite of this biological and emotional interdependence, conflicting views about humans abound among the powerful, long-living Ina, and the symbionts receive different treatment: 'not everyone treats symbionts as people' (ibid.: 131). As so often in Butler's fiction, questions of power and ethics are of utmost importance; in a relationship of mutual dependence where one party is more powerful than the other, ethical behavior becomes a paramount concern, which Shori both feels and learns throughout *Fledgling*.

Gendered power relations, as well as compulsory heterosexuality, are placed under scrutiny, if not attack, in *Fledgling*, which sets it apart from the majority of vampire novels. Many vampires are 'polymorphously' sexual, which can be seen as a challenge to normative heterosexuality, but in most narratives the central vampire is still male. In Butler's vampire novel the Ina function as a matriarchy, with regard to religion, custom, and power. Although most present-day Ina appear to be secularized, the Ina divinity is a goddess, and, traditionally, groups of Ina sisters hunt groups of Ina brothers to mate. Intriguingly, females have stronger venom than males, with one symbiont telling Shori that 'Ina men are sort of like us, like symbionts. They become addicted to the venom of one group of sisters. That's what it means to be mated. Once they're addicted, they aren't fertile with other females, and from time to time, they need their females ... like I need [my Ina]' (*ibid*.: 109). The strength of Shori's venom ensures, for instance, that she can take over her brother's and her father's symbionts when her relatives are killed, which saves these symbionts from dying for lack of venom.

By extension, Shori's integration of symbionts who belonged to her murdered relatives into the new family she is building may be read as an act of adoption, or othermothering practice, in a novel where adoption plays an important part. In *Simians, Cyborgs, and Women*, Haraway argues that Butler's *Xenogenesis* trilogy – published in the late 1980s – is 'predicated on the natural status of adoption and the unnatural violence of kin' (1991: 226). In both the trilogy and *Fledgling*, the 'unnatural violence of kin' should be read as the unnatural violence inflicted by members of one's own species. Haraway also notes that '[o]rigins are precisely that to which Butler's people do not have access' (*ibid*.: 226–7). This statement rings true for the protagonist's situation in *Fledgling* as well as for the remnant of human survivors in the trilogy; Shori has to learn about her own and her families' history and create a new family. Commenting on the importance of family in an interview published in the mid-1990s, Butler said:

> Even though I don't have a husband and children, I have other family, and it seems to me our most important set of relationships. It is so much of what we are. Family does not have to mean purely biological relationships either. I know families that have adopted outside individuals: I don't mean legally adopted children but other adults, friends, people who simply came into the household and stayed. (1996: 333)

The adoption of unrelated adult humans is the basis of Ina-symbiont families in *Fledgling*. Since Shori is alone after the death of her sisters and does not want the name of her female family to disappear, one of her distant female relatives suggests that Shori adopt a young Ina girl as a sister with whom she could build a female Ina family. Through adoption, which includes transfusions of blood, new family ties are created. This type of adoption and the creation of Ina–symbiont family relationships ensure that the 'natural status of adoption' of

Butler's earlier science-fiction novels is reinforced in the final novel she published before her death in 2006.

In creating and maintaining family networks as well as enforcing Ina law, *Fledgling* also connects the cosmopolitanism of the vampire with contemporary technological developments. Cosmopolitanism has been defined as 'a process of "internal globalization" through which global concerns become part of local experiences of an increasing number of people' (Levy and Sznaider, 2002: 87), and, whether locally or internationally, Ina communities are in no sense cut off from each other. Ina communities are imagined as part of a twenty-first-century worldwide web of vampires, and modern communication technology plays a large part in that global network, not least in the last third of the novel, which explores Ina ways of justice, in the form of a Council of Judgment that establishes the guilt and the punishment of the Silks, the slayers of Shori's original families, who also attempt to kill Shori and her new symbionts. In order to find appropriate families to serve on the Council, there is 'a great deal of telephoning, conference calling, faxing, and e-mailing' (Butler, 2005: 197). These means of communication moreover constitute a link for Shori with one of her female relatives who serves on the Council (*ibid.*: 215). Butler's vampire novel illustrates how global forms of communication make global concerns a part of local experiences, and how familial and local concerns become part of global experience.[36]

Even though it places Ina migration in a world history context, *Fledgling* is also haunted by American history in the form of slavery and the racism it spawned; it is racism that causes Shori's orphanhood. The prejudice against the mixing of human and Ina genes resonates powerfully with racism in the USA, and particularly with racist ideas about 'miscegenation.' In a discussion of race, family and kinship in the USA from the end of the nineteenth century to the end of the twentieth, aptly entitled 'Universal Donors in a Vampire Culture: It's All in the Family,' Haraway observes that '*[m]iscegenation* is still a national racist synonym for infection, counterfeit issue unfit to carry the name of the father, and a spoiled future.' It harks back to the 'bitter history of the scientific and medical animalization of people of African descent ...' (Haraway, 1997: 258). Towards the end of *Fledgling*, one of the Silk family members loses control and calls Shori a 'black mongrel bitch' and taunts 'What will she give us all? Fur? Tails?' (Butler, 2005: 300), creating the image of her as an animal. At the Council meeting the question of Shori's suitability as an Ina mate and mother is framed in terms of race: 'You want your sons to mate with this person. You want them to get black, human children from her. Here in the United States, even most humans will look down on them. When I came to this country, such people were kept as property, as slaves' (*ibid.*: 272). In a context that is best described as speciesist, Butler's vampire novel exposes the legacy of the infected ties between race, family, and kinship in the USA, both in terms of violent actions, or hate crimes, and racist statements.

Fledgling explores the extent to which living in the present is tied to the past.[37] Through the rememory of its amnesiac and orphaned narrator – her rebuilding a family and acquiring knowledge of herself, her families, the Ina, myths, and history – the novel highlights how individual memory and identity are shaped by collective and cultural memory. Through its central orphan figure, Butler employs the potential of speculative fiction to address contemporary social issues that have to do with family, sexuality, gender, and race. That these issues are tied up with ethical concerns and power is emphasized throughout *Fledgling*, as well as in Gomez's *Gilda Stories*, to which we now turn.

Living to learn and remember: Jewelle Gomez's *The Gilda Stories*

> How could he stand to possess so many memories? Was he truly that powerful? (Carr, 1995: 128)

Jewelle Gomez's *The Gilda Stories* (1991) spans 200 years, from 1850 to 2050, with each chapter set in a different decade and a different location. The black orphan protagonist is a runaway slave girl who is doubly orphaned, first by the institution of slavery that made it impossible for so many African Americans to create lasting family bonds and then by the racism that makes her a cultural orphan long after slavery has been abolished. She is simply called the Girl until she is turned into a vampire and inherits the name Gilda from a 300-year-old Old-World vampire of what appears to be indeterminate Middle-Eastern origin. This original Gilda initiates the Girl's transformation into a vampire, which is completed by another woman, her Native American vampire companion, Bird. In this discussion, we follow Gomez's naming practices, respectively using 'the Girl' and 'Gilda' to refer to the slave girl before and after her transformation. The novel charts Gilda's adventures as an African American vampire, and her quest for family intersects with African American and women's history in the USA, as well as other and overlapping marginalized groups that have been cast as monstrous or 'other.' At the end of the novel, Gilda leaves an environmentally devastated USA – where vampires are hunted by humans for their blood – in order to create a new community with members of her vampire family beyond national borders.

The Gilda Stories is a hybrid text, both a speculative fiction and a historical novel. The unusual convergence of these two genres, together with Gomez's use of an orphan protagonist, creates the textual space and conditions for exploring connections between learning and memory, family and history, between looking to the future and revisiting the past. As we have noted, the historical novel has become an important genre for the imaginative recovery of marginalized and silenced histories, for it 'can engage in political rewriting, outline the traumas of the past, rescue the marginalised and give voice to those who were silenced' (de Groot, 2010: 150). Gomez engages with the histories of African Americans, Native Americans, prostitutes, and lesbian, gay, and transgendered people to conceive 'a new set of possibilities, outside of (or at least not defined by) patriarchal, heteronormative bounds and historiographic limits' (*ibid.*: 151).[38] In *The Gilda Stories*, the imaginative potential inherent in historical fiction is combined with and enhanced by the potential of speculative vampire fiction to express queer desire[39] and to envision learning and agency as spurs to the refashioning of affiliation and kinship in the USA and beyond.

The longevity of the vampire provides an extended historical perspective, allowing Gilda to experience great swathes of time, to witness the past, present and future.[40] Like other sympathetic vampire figures at the end of the twentieth and the beginning of the twenty-first century, she functions as a vehicle of memory. Somewhat perversely, the image of the undead vampire forges a link to a living memory that historian Pierre Nora, in 'Between Memory and History: *Les Lieux de Mémoire*,' laments as a feature of the past that has been replaced by sites of memory. In other words, the vampire's perspective collapses the dichotomy that Nora establishes between an authentic collective folk memory and history as a 'problematic and incomplete' representation of the past (1989: 8). Memory is made crucial for the black orphan protagonist in *The Gilda Stories* as a source of identity, strength, and survival. She embodies mis- or under-represented aspects of national history; she is herself 'a living history' (Gomez, 1991: 177).

It is clear from the very beginning of the novel that oral history and cultural memory in the form of her mother's storytelling play an important part in the Girl's sense of identity and her ability to imagine freedom and to successfully escape from slavery after her mother's death. After having traveled through Mississippi into Louisiana for fifteen hours without stopping, the runaway slave girl, not yet turned into a vampire, sleeps restlessly in an abandoned farmhouse and dreams of her mother, 'now dead,' remembering their life on the plantation and the stories her mother told her about her 'journey to this land' and 'the Fulani past – a natural rhythm of life without bondage' (*ibid*.: 10). The Girl's sleep is 'hemmed by fear,' and danger materializes in the form of a white man 'wearing the clothes of an overseer' (*ibid*.: 9). Still half-dreaming as the bounty hunter drags her away, the Girl determines she is 'not ready to give in to those whom her mother had sworn were not fully human' (*ibid*.: 10). So, when 'the beast from this other land' tries to rape the Girl, she uses her knife and 'enters' him, thus reversing the rape and the seeming powerlessness of her situation (*ibid*.: 11).[41] His warm blood washing over her as he dies is compared to her mother bathing her as a child, a deeply sensual memory. In this situation, as well as throughout her long life, memories of her mother's actions, assessments, and stories sustain her.

With their mixture of dream, memories, and violent physical events, these first few pages are the most evocative in the novel in terms of style and structure and do a great deal of cultural work in 'haunt[ing] back'[42] – to borrow Teresa A. Goddu's phrase for African American writers' 'reworking [of] the gothic's conventions to intervene in discourses that would demonize them' (1999: 138) – and in asserting the subjectivity, agency, and family bonds of African American slaves. As the bounty hunter attempts to rape her, the Girl remembers an observation her mother makes about white people's inability to tell fat from butter on a warm biscuit: 'They just barely human. Maybe not even. They suck up the world, don't taste it' (Gomez, 1991: 11), an apposite way of describing exploitation in a vampire novel. In the opening of Gomez's novel, then, it is white people, specifically white men, who are demonized or cast as other, 'in terms of the vampire mold so familiar from novels by Stoker and other white men' (K. Patterson,

2005: n.p.). The mother's descriptions of white people as beasts or barely human exemplifies the practice of 'specifying,' which could be seen as way of 'haunting back' that is not necessarily related to the gothic genre; as Willis points out, '[a]lthough name-calling unites the speaking subject and the community, it does so at the expense of the individual being made the object of the abuse' (Gomez, 1991: 16). In this case, the slave mother's agency through language unites her with her daughter through mockery of those whites who physically exploit them, thus lending the Girl courage.

Willis observes that there are numerous ways that history enters black women's fiction but she highlights that '[t]he black woman's relation to history is first of all a relationship to mother and grandmother' (1990: 5). She points out that as workers black women 'have sustained their families; as mothers, they have borne the oral histories from their grandmothers to their children' (ibid.: 7). In *The Gilda Stories*, in addition to giving her daughter emotional and physical sustenance as long as she lives, the Girl's mother provides her with a history that is outside the USA and outside slavery. Although the home across the water her mother tells her about seems distant and unreal to the Girl, 'always a dream place,' she can feel the rhythm of the dancing when she tells others about it:

> The Girl could close her eyes and almost hear the rhythmic shuffling of feet, the bells and gourds. All kept beat inside her body, and the feel of heat from an open fire made the dream place real. Talking of it now, her body rocked slightly as if she had been rewoven into that old circle of dancers. She poured out the images and names, proud of her own ability to weave a story. (Gomez, 1991: 39)

In this decisive scene, the Girl takes over her mother's role as a storyteller while 'Bird smiled at her pupil who claimed her past, reassuring her silently' (ibid.: 39). Claiming the past in this way is inextricably linked to the power of memory and imagination, the 'ability to weave a story.' Rememory is cast primarily in positive terms, as a form of memory that the African American storyteller can learn to actively share with women of different heritages, ethnicities, ages, and experiences. In this sense, rememory can be said to open the way to knowledge, which, as she moves through time, Gilda seeks to gain and to transmit in other forms such as letters, journals, and the literary genre of historical romance.

While the Girl's memories of her mother's stories primarily lend her strength and a sense of connection to her past, some rememories have debilitating effects. In particular, once the Girl has become a vampire, the visceral rememory of the Middle Passage is so powerful that it prevents her from travelling by sea or air. In fact, it prevents her from leaving the continent. While to members of her vampire family the ocean is 'only somewhat daunting,' to her it is 'paralyzing. It was as if she were being asked to make the Middle Passage as her ancestors had done' (*ibid.*: 198). Albeit debilitating in this instance, the force of rememory is a tribute to the power of her mother's passing on lived experience through storytelling.[43]

Although the Girl runs away from the plantation as soon as her mother dies, she remembers her mother's stories throughout her centuries-long life as the vampire Gilda; they assert the subjectivity, agency, and family ties of African Americans and, thus, serve as a commentary on assumptions that communal bonds were lacking under slavery, the basis of the pathologization of the twentieth-century African American family. Gomez's novel may be read as offering commentary on these issues, functioning as a kind of literary counter-memory according to George Lipsitz's definition of the term: 'Counter-memory is a way of remembering and forgetting that starts with the local, the immediate, and the personal ... [It] looks to the past for the hidden histories excluded from dominant narratives ... [and] forces revision of existing histories by supplying new perspectives about the past' (1990: 213). *The Gilda Stories* could thus be said to belong to an intellectual and literary tradition that Ann duCille calls the 'resistance school' that 'insist[s] that slaves found creative ways to be together, love each other, and forge enduring marital unions and family networks, despite the cruelties of the system that held them captive,' as opposed to the 'ruination school,' which maintains that slavery 'undermined and effectively destroyed not only the institutions of marriage and family but the morale and mores of bondsmen and women' (2009: 606). The emphasis upon creative revision and agency described by Lipsitz and duCille comes to characterize Gilda's increasingly deliberate efforts to learn and to make both family and family history.

In one scene, the activity of learning to read – a dangerous activity in the context of US slavery – offers the Girl an inroad into memories of her familial past. Normally somewhat reticent, the Girl talks about her family only to Bird, and this occurs when Bird teaches her to read and they exchange stories. The Girl realizes that she does not think of her sisters except before she falls asleep at night, 'their memory her nightly prayers.' In this scene that relates reading instruction and storytelling, explicitly compared to Native American storytelling traditions, 'the litany of [her sisters'] names served as memory: Minerva, small, full of energy and questions; Florine, two years older than the Girl, unable to ever meet anyone's eyes; and Martha, the oldest, broad-shouldered like their mother but more solemn' (Gomez, 1991: 39). In other words, the Girl is an excellent example of the orphan as an agent actively sustaining African American family bonds by storytelling in the way that Valérie Loichot explores in *Orphan Narratives* where she argues that '[t]he trope of the orphan does not ... maintain plantation or postplantation subjects in a perennial position of victims. On the contrary, orphans are active performers in family reconstruction' (2007: 3). Connected with both oral history and reading experiences, the ongoing importance of knowing African American familial connections under slavery is repeatedly emphasized in Gomez's novel.

As important as her rememories are of her maternal ancestry and her birth family, the Girl is initiated into another kind of family when she becomes a vampire: she is adopted into a queer, interracial vampire family. This family is a work in progress throughout the novel, but the orphaned Girl's inclusion begins with the establishment of new connections and the forging of new motherlines across racial boundaries when she is found, covered with the blood of her would-be rapist and bounty hunter, by the apparently white lesbian vampire Gilda. Parallels are drawn between Gilda and the Girl's mother, emphasizing the maternal relationship between Gilda and the Girl. For instance, when Gilda says, 'Wake up, gal!' (Gomez, 1991: 12), she echoes the Girl's mother's words: 'Come on. Get up, gal, time now, get up!' (*ibid.*: 10). Similarly, Gilda immediately prepares a bath for the Girl, which resonates with the dream of her mother she was enjoying before being assaulted. Thus, the 'white fear' (*ibid.*: 12) that the Girl experiences at the first sight of Gilda's face dissipates and is soon replaced by a sense of mutual recognition. While Gilda immediately sees 'a need for family that matched her own' in the runaway slave girl she has rescued, the Girl, in turn, recognizes that Gilda's 'face was not unlike her mother's despite the colors painted on it' (*ibid.*: 16). Similarly, Gilda's partner, the Lakota woman, Bird, exudes a 'pungent earthiness' that the Girl recognizes: 'The soft scent of brown soap mixed with the leather of her headband and necklace created a familiar aura. It reminded the Girl of her mother and the strong smell of her sweat dropping onto the logs under the burning cauldrons' (*ibid.*: 20). Bird's power over words and multiple languages, as well as her storytelling, connects her to the Girl's mother who 'had pieced together [stories] from many different languages to describe the journey to this land' (*ibid.*: 10). It is important that the vampire women do not displace the Girl's birth mother, but are instead figured as offering the Girl reasons to remember her mother as well as to journey along new motherlines as she becomes privy to their memories and histories: Gilda's nomadic past on another continent and Bird's Lakota heritage, including that of tribal decimation (*ibid.*: 17–18, 22).

Maturity and consent play an important part in the Girl's ultimate integration into Gilda and Bird's vampire family; as two critics of the novel argue, 'The blood bond, that is, the vampire's bite, literalizes their new relationship and the multiple connections of "family" they have already begun to form' (Brinks and Talley, 1996: 163). As a young adult, the Girl becomes entirely devoted to the vampire women, so when Gilda asks her if she is willing to trust them and to become one of them she is very happy to consent. Neither the word 'vampire' nor the word 'lesbian' is spelled out in this exchange,[44] although these are the identities that the Girl gladly accepts in order to confirm affiliation with Gilda and Bird.

The deepening of familial bonds through blood exchanges between women has multiple implications for multiculturalism and sexual politics as well as genre. On the one hand, there is a utopian dimension to the creation of family bonds for this orphaned protagonist. Beginning with her transformation into a vampire, Gilda enters into a variety of nontraditional living arrangements. Throughout the decades explored in the novel, Gilda searches for a sense of family and home in different US locations, sometimes among black mortals – particularly black women – sometimes among her multicultural, queer vampire family. Finally, in 2020, Gilda is living in New Hampshire with a black vampire woman, and she muses: 'The family she had hungered for as a child was hers now. It was spread across the globe but was closer to her than she had ever imagined possible' (Gomez, 1991: 223). Gilda's achievement of family, however, is hard won and vulnerable, suggesting that Gomez sees limits to the possibilities for transgressive kinship formation. Indeed, the initial family constellation – Gilda, Bird, and the Girl – is upset when Gilda wills her own destruction. While Bird 'can be mother, father, sister, lover ... she cannot create the family' for the Girl, who inherits Gilda's name (*ibid.*: 177). In 2050, thirty years after finding a true sense of family, Gilda is forced to leave an environmentally devastated USA, where vampires are hunted and killed for their blood, and to seek refuge with her dispersed vampire family in South America. This family consists of both male and female members, who are black, white, and Native American. Not only are they forced to leave the USA; there are no white women and no heterosexual white men included in Gilda's vampire family when the novel closes. If we see the ending of Gomez's novel as a speculative allegory of the future of queer kinship in a multicultural USA, the dystopian limits appear to outweigh the progressive possibilities.

These dystopian limits are based in greed and exploitation, both of which form a sinister undertow throughout the novel. For example, when asked to account for the meteorological disruptions and diseases that plague the USA in 2050, a character replies with force: 'The answer is greed. We are dying of greed. I don't know the cure for that' (*ibid.*: 241). The Girl's mother sees greed in white people who suck up the world without tasting it, and a bounty hunter almost manages to rape the runaway slave Girl at the beginning of the novel. In addition, all of the Euro-American vampires that figure in *The Gilda Stories* are ethically flawed.[45] In the 1890s, when she first meets the gay white vampire couple Sorel and Anthony, Gilda is courted by and falls in love with Eleanor, a white woman of 'homegrown royalty' (*ibid.*: 63). Sorel has turned Eleanor into a vampire, which he deeply regrets since she does not abide by the ethical rules that govern vampires in Gilda's family, specifically that they should not kill their 'victims' when feeding nor revel in their fear, nor turn others into vampires carelessly, and that they should always leave dreams and hope in exchange for life-sustaining blood. Eleanor turns out to be deceptive, thrill-seeking, and egotistical. She is stalked by jealous and unprincipled Samuel, a Euro-American heterosexual man she has turned into a vampire on a whim; he cannot stand the sight of Eleanor with Gilda. Against this egotistical greed and exploitation with origins in American slavery in Gomez's novel, Gilda's vampire family's foundational idea of sharing – life, blood, memories, and dreams – stands out in strong relief.

Storytelling and the writing of historical romances as forms of cultural memory contribute to the idea of sharing, both for Gomez and for her protagonist. As Miriam Jones summarizes, the novel 'can be read as a simultaneous sharing, and seeking, of personal and collective histories in the face of a monolithic, exclusionary discourse' (1997: 156). Gilda is writing historical romances as 'a way of sharing some of the many stories she had gathered through her long life' (Gomez, 1991: 220), and in this form she ties together the past and the future, the historical and the speculative. Drawing on her memories as recorded in her journal, Gilda selects a popular genre, the historical romance, and infuses it with mystical elements: 'Gilda had written the stories of their history, cloaking it in adventure and mysticism ...' (ibid.: 220).[46] For Gilda, writing history is an imaginative act of artistic agency, of creatively sharing what she has learned and what she remembers from her long life. The urgency with which Gilda shares her stories with the public gives them the weight of living collective memory: 'For her, the stories were ... a way of speaking with thousands of people in distant places, places she had been to or hoped to visit in the future' (ibid.: 220). She remembers back to 'her master's lash as well as her mother's face, legends of the Middle Passage, lynchings she had not been able to prevent, images of black women bent over scouring brushes,' and in the 1980s, '[t]he inattention of her contemporaries to some mortal questions, like race, didn't suit her. She didn't believe a past could, or should, be so easily discarded' (ibid.: 180). Such ideas form a meta-fictional commentary insofar as Gilda's and Gomez's projects appear to be very similar. In writing *The Gilda Stories*, Gomez writes and re-envisions a history of slave families, black women, lesbians, and feminists, among many others, cloaking her history as a vampire novel with the powerful, but ethically responsible, black vampire orphan Gilda as its hero.

Through re-inflections of speculative fiction and the historical novel, Gomez's fiction intervenes creatively in discussions of the African American family, queer relationships, multiculturalism, and an environmentally sustainable future in the USA. *The Gilda Stories* acts as a literary counter-memory that works forcefully against the pathologization of the black family, in the past, the present and for the future, and gives voice to the histories of marginalized groups. The novel's most controversial idea is that Euro-American greed and exploitation make it difficult, if not impossible, to include Euro-Americans in a mutually supportive and ethically responsible kinship network; this greed, Gomez suggests in this novel, risks making the USA uninhabitable in the future.

From the beginning of the novel, the orphaned runaway slave Girl is presented as a strong agent, whose memories of her mother and of her mother's stories of Africa help to define and shape her identity as well as commenting more discursively on African American family bonds under slavery. The transnational character of her mother's stories also serves an important function: they provide reference points, or rememories, outside of the slavery into which the Girl is born. Different modes of cultural memory, such as oral storytelling and the writing of historical romances, are highlighted through the continued agency of the protagonist, who also learns about the social conditions of different groups in American society and writes about them in *The Gilda Stories*.

'Orphans, each and all': historical currents and 'minor' transnationalism in Toni Morrison's *A Mercy*

One story is good till another is told.
(Aesop, 2012)[47]

Toni Morrison's *A Mercy* (2008), set in the Middle and Chesapeake colonies from roughly the 1670s to the 1690s, is a historical novel of bondage and freedom that highlights motherlines and that examines relations between people of different social classes, religious persuasions, races, and nations in the early, foundational moments of colonial history in North America, prior to the creation of a republic. As in some of her other fiction, most notably *Paradise* (1997), Morrison's novel explores the conditions and limits for community by gathering together in one place a diverse group of individuals unrelated by blood. On Jacob Vaark's farm in the colony of New York live or work Vaark's wife, Rebekka, acquired through advertisement from Europe; the mixed-race Sorrow, gotten through trade; two male indentured servants from a neighboring farm; and two slaves: Lina, a Native American woman, and Florens, a slavegirl Vaark accepts in payment for a bad debt.[48] The lack of biological kinship, and the questions about social kinship that this raises, are underscored by the fact that virtually all of the characters in *A Mercy* are orphans. The ways in which they have lost their birth families are marked by strong historical forces, including that which Morrison calls 'cultural orphanage,' the erasure of lineage through slavery's unnaming of family connection (quoted in Li, 2012: 51). Whether literal orphans or 'cultural orphans,' the figures in Morrison's novel are used to explore the transnational and multicultural mixing which will later be imagined as a national, American 'family' and culture. Rather than emphasizing the unity forged from plurality (*e pluribus unum*), the novel emphasizes the complexities of multiethnic, multicultural difference. As one character puts it, 'they were not a family – not even a like-minded group. They were orphans, each and all' (Morrison, 2008b: 57). Orphanhood in this novel challenges cherished notions of kinship and freedom, past and present, in US society.

In *A Mercy*, as in *The Gilda Stories*, learning, reading, writing, talking, imagining – in short, performing intellectual work – are shown to be necessary to attain freedom, whether that freedom is individual or social in character. *A Mercy* explores and advocates intellectual and imaginative engagement with multiple historical perspectives. It charts the orphan characters' struggles and dreams, and it simultaneously invites, cajoles, and exhorts readers to attend to the complex histories of a prenational America. Morrison, like the lion in Aesop's tale who questions the victorious man's representation of his struggle for dominance over the lion, suggests that history told from the perspective of the powerful is skewed, misleading or, at best, incomplete. Multiple perspectives on the history of the USA launch a deep and responsible inquiry into foundational ideas about freedom and bondage. In this concluding section, we examine Morrison's mobilization of literal and figurative orphans within the genre of historical fiction to critique the slow consolidation of power, privilege, and dominion along lines of race, class, gender, and religion prior to the founding of the republic. *A Mercy* suggests the contemporary importance of creative intellectual work in forging an ethic of diversity and a multicultural society capable of creating 'family' freely, across racial, gendered, genealogical, and even national boundaries.

In 'The Site of Memory', Morrison states that 'the matrix of the work I do is the wish to extend, fill in and complement slave autobiographical narratives' (1998: 199). She clearly envisions her art as driven by an intertextual engagement with the past, forging intimate connections between history, narrative, and cultural identity. This thematic concern runs through all of her novels to date – perhaps most obviously in *Beloved*, building as it does on the historical facts of Margaret Garner's 1856 infanticide, but also in *A Mercy*. In writing it, Morrison was inspired by Don Jordan and Michael Walsh's popular history *White Cargo* (2007), which traces the emergence of black slavery from white servitude (Li, 2012: 114). This work resonates with the findings of historians who have analyzed slavery and racial formation as historical processes, agreeing that servitude in pre-national America was an oppressive social practice to which class, gender, and religion contributed, only to gradually be replaced or supplemented by categories of race.[49] *White Cargo* claims that race and enslavement became firmly conjoined first after Bacon's Rebellion in Virginia in 1676, when poor Africans and Euro-Americans united in common cause. Jacob Vaark bemoans the result of this 'people's war' in *A Mercy*, for it led to the passage of 'lawless laws' that 'separated and protected all whites from all others forever' (Morrison, 2008b: 8–9), forging a privileged category of white and an inferior category of non-white. Bacon's Rebellion also incited the passage of laws against literacy for enslaved people. David Brion Davis confirms that in the early days of Anglo-European settlement, blacks were to some extent integrated in the Chesapeake societies where Morrison's text is set, with strong racial divisions emerging first in the latter half of the seventeenth century.[50]

A Mercy thus imaginatively explores a place and time before slavery became completely racially determined. Morrison has elsewhere observed the dangers of nostalgia for, as she puts it, 'the race-free home I never had' (2008a: 4). In the USA, she says, race structures every 'home,' rendering a non-racialized home a utopian concept, at best a project, for anti-racists and racialized groups.[51] Her decidedly critical, rather than nostalgic, treatment of a moment in colonial history prior to the formation of an American national identity allows Morrison to create, as Valerie Babb describes, an alternative 'American origins narrative.' This multivoiced novel diverges from the myths that legitimized colonial conquest, settlement, and bondage by restoring marginalized perspectives to historical narrative: 'narrative space must be made for those voices that once talked to and for themselves but have been muted by the historical record' (Babb, 2011: 159). Morrison's text counters or supplements foundational texts by Europeans such as William Bradford and John Winthrop, as well as later canonical narratives which 'erased the social plurality of prenational America' (*ibid*.: 148). But Morrison's novel does more than augment or correct the historical record of American origins. In showing the process of racialized thinking and enslavement, in problematizing freedom for her bonded protagonists, and in foregrounding their literal and figurative orphan status, Morrison asks her readers to rethink and consider: how can anyone make home in the USA today?

As a historical novel, *A Mercy* dramatizes relations between the past and the present, writ both large and small. In general, Rody argues, 'narratives of history always depend on the symbolic structure of the parental relation, the most immediate imaginable unit of history' (2001: 41). Yet, practices of orphanhood mark the very foundation of British settlement in North America, as outlined in the historical analysis in *White Cargo*. Children, many of them poor inhabitants of slums, were sent to the colonies to work, as were members of dispossessed groups of vagrants, criminals, religious rebels, the Irish, kidnapped whites, and indentured servants such as Willard in *A Mercy*. As much scholarship has shown, parent–child relations were profoundly disturbed under the slave system, which enforced a form of 'natal alienation' on Africans and African Americans. '[T]he loss of ties of birth in both ascending and descending generations' could be conceptualized as a kind of 'social death' resulting from the 'alienation of the slave from all formal, legally enforceable ties of "blood"' (O. Patterson, 1982: 7). Loichot observes: 'Slavery not only attempted to orphan children from their real parents but also to sever slave parents from their parental function' (2007: 2). Thus, enslavement and other forms of bondage functioned as 'orphaning practices' that broke generational relations, creating serious impediments to historical understandings of the individual self and of cultural identity.

The inaugurating moment of Morrison's historical novel dramatizes precisely this disruption of the parental relation – the transfer of the child, Florens, from her enslaved mother to the farmer-cum-rum trader Vaark. Orphaned in his youth and heirless as an adult, Vaark is in many ways the archetypal American Adam; his lack of ancestry ensures his self-reliance and exertion of industry, allowing him to eventually amass a fortune. Florens is the pubescent child of an unnamed slave woman owned by a Portuguese Catholic slave trader in the province of Maryland. Unable to repay his loan from Vaark, the slave trader offers him his choice of slave as payment. The mother, anxious to remove her daughter from the sexual predations of the owner and his sons, implores Vaark to take Florens instead of either her or her infant boy. Vaark does so, enacting the 'mercy' of the title in spite of his dislike of slavery, because he, like Florens, misunderstands the mother's action as an abandonment and because he knows first-hand the vulnerability of 'waifs and whelps' (Morrison, 2008b: 30), 'orphans and strays' (*ibid.*: 31). He also believes that the child will bring solace to his wife after the death of their own children; at some level, he imagines taking Florens as a form of adoption. The initial severance of ties between mother and child – the production of orphanhood by way of slave economics – constitutes the origin of Morrison's narrative and of Florens's as well.

The novel opens with Florens's first-person narrative, characterized by qualities of orality such as immediacy, direct address, linguistic switching, and informal and non-standard language use. This narrative gives over to third-person narrations focalized through the other characters, usually one per chapter, illuminating remembered and current events from various perspectives. While it is in some respects true that *A Mercy* does not privilege any one voice (Babb, 2011: 149), it is important not to overlook the structural and thematic importance of Florens's unique voice. Florens narrates every other chapter up to the penultimate one; her mother narrates the last. Florens's narration, readers eventually learn, is retrospective and, in spite of its oral qualities, it is written, the words of her story scratched into the walls of the house that Jacob built.

A Mercy dramatizes the problem of historical knowledge and cultural transmission in its narrative form, through the unanswered call and response of the slave mother and Florens. Florens's psyche and her tale are profoundly marked by her sense of betrayal and abandonment due to being 'given away' by her mother. Her mother's tale is equally marked by anguish over her hard choice, and by hope that Florens has indeed escaped the worst degradations of enslavement. In other words, the anxiety of an orphanhood exacted by the conditions of slavery generates boundless desire and ceaseless narration: Florens's writing in the house, addressed to the unlettered blacksmith, and her mother's longing to reach her daughter at the conclusion of the novel. *A Mercy* thus begins in separation, in dire anxiety about socially determined forms of orphanhood, and in the longing to tell and to have others hear an understandable history: 'Storytelling becomes the text's self-conscious task' (Rody, 2001: 26).

Florens's intense desire for stories is depicted from Lina's perspective. As in *The Gilda Stories*, an African American orphan is instructed and cared for by a Native woman who excels in relating histories.[52] Florens calls particularly for 'stories of mothers fighting to save their children from wolves and natural disasters' (Morrison, 2008b: 59), or of an eagle mother protecting her eggs. Such stories feed Lina's and Florens's '[m]other hunger – to be one or to have one' (*ibid.*: 61). The mention of wolves in Lina's story echoes Lina's childhood memory of the wolves that devoured her family and tribe, decimated by disease, subtly suggesting that, like Bird and the Girl in Gomez's novel, Lina brings her own memories and experiences to a storytelling tradition she passes on. Indeed, Lina's memory is explicitly portrayed as a resource for surviving her initial anger and isolation at Vaark's farm: 'she decided to fortify herself by piecing together scraps of what her mother had taught her before dying in agony. Relying on memory and her own resources, she cobbled together neglected rites, merged Europe medicine with native, scripture with lore, and recalled or invented the hidden meaning of things. Found, in other words, a way to be in the world' (*ibid.*: 46). Throughout the novel, storytelling and oral history offer orphan characters ways to relate to a fragmented cultural and a broken familial past.

Oral discourse is often considered a hallmark of African American literature. Willis, for instance, demonstrates that the 'strongest influence on the development of black women's narratives derives from the storytelling tradition' (1990: 15), particularly the practice of 'specifying,' which 'represents a form of narrative integrity' (*ibid.*: 16). DoVeanna S. Fulton comments on the creative synthesis of spoken and written forms, viewing black feminist orality as 'a form of empowerment' (2006: 2) and noting the special importance of cross-generational transmission of oral history as 'a vehicle for insight and reclamation of the self' (*ibid.*: 108). *A Mercy* certainly uses vernacular forms, and portrays the cross-generational relation of history as a potential resource for the characters. At the same time, however, it emphasizes that the telling of tales and the oral transmission of history between mother and daughter have been disrupted by practices that break parent–child bonds. Though Morrison avails herself of a call and response pattern in the frame of the story, neither Florens nor her mother – separated by space and time – can hear the other's response. Unlike Babb, who sees the tales of the two women as being in dialogue and as illustrating 'rememory's capacity to bend space and time' (2011: 156), we view the inability of the women to reach one another as the central tragedy of the novel. In our reading, Morrison's work suggests that the call and response pattern might be completed, that some fullness of understanding might be achieved, only through learning, and especially through learning to read and write.

Florens has 'multiple literacies' (*ibid.*: 150), but it is her ability to read and write that is emphasized by the narrative frame. She is taught to read by a clergyman who takes risks to instruct the family, at her mother's request: 'I hoped if we could learn letters somehow someday you could make your way' (Morrison, 2008b: 161). Florens's mother understands that 'there is magic in learning' (*ibid.*: 161), and Florens appears to Lina to be a good learner, for 'she learned quickly, was eager to know more ...' (*ibid.*: 61). Though Lina comes to consider Florens 'crippled with worship' (*ibid.*: 61) of the blacksmith, she nevertheless notes proudly that Florens uses both reason and courage to make the right decisions when her journey towards the blacksmith is interrupted by the escape of the indentured servants with whom she has travelled. Moreover, though Morrison certainly affirms the value of other types of interpretive skills, especially in relation to Lina, she also suggests that the interpretation of signs can be dangerous, as it is in the episode concerning the Puritan girl, Jane, and Florens, when they are humiliatingly inspected by Puritan leaders who suspect both young women of consorting with the devil.

The climax of Florens's relationship to the blacksmith suggests the importance of tempering the experience of rememory with thought. Florens falls passionately and desperately in love with the blacksmith, who leaves her and the farm when his work there is complete. When Jacob dies of smallpox and Rebekka takes sick, however, Florens is sent to retrieve the blacksmith so he may cure her. Florens finds him living with a foundling, Malaik. Charged with caring for the boy in his absence, Florens controls her jealousy of the orphan child, whose age, demeanor, and pride of place in the heart of the blacksmith activate rememories of her little brother, who her mother kept when she gave Florens away. Immediately upon seeing him, Florens is almost overcome: 'This happens twice before. The first time it is me peering around my mother's dress hoping for her hand that is only for her little boy. The second time it is a pointing screaming little girl hiding behind her mother and clinging to her skirts. Both times are full of danger and I am expel' (*ibid.*: 133–4). Although she masters her distress over her rememories of abandonment and degradation, Malaik displays resentment, and the antagonistic feelings between them intensify until they explode, just as the blacksmith returns. He sees Florens yanking the boy's arm, injuring him, and he runs to the boy's defense. As Florens sees it, he chooses the boy, just as her mother once chose her brother. In the angry repudiation of Florens which follows, the blacksmith contemptuously calls her 'a slave by choice.' 'Your head is empty and your body is wild,' he tells her (*ibid.*: 139).

The blacksmith's severe condemnation – 'a slave by choice' – resonates with the knowledge that her mother wants so urgently to share with Florens (but can only share with the readers): 'to be given dominion over another is a hard thing; to wrest dominion over another is a wrong thing; to give dominion of yourself to another is a wicked thing' (*ibid.*: 165). 'Dominion,' in addition to referring to a place or geographic terrain, means both 'sovereignty' and 'absolute ownership,' and thus, in reference to the self, is strongly opposed to the condition of chattel slavery, or absolute possession. It would seem, then, that the novel as a whole works to endorse freedom and autonomy, and to condemn the mindless, slavish character of Florens's desire. Indeed, Florens confesses she does not understand what freedom is: 'It is as though I am loose to do what I choose, ... I am a little scare of this looseness. Is that how free feels? I don't like it' (*ibid.*: 68). *A Mercy* thus realizes the key features of Mitchell's 'liberatory narrative,' for it engages the historical past in order to problematize freedom for the past and the present (2002: 4). Freedom, Morrison suggests, is a hard thing that entails experience and responsible learning.

Learning at the end of the novel that Florens's story is a retrospective account, written primarily for the blacksmith who has repudiated her, encourages readers to revisit the opening of the novel. Her opening words, we now understand, explicitly address the blacksmith, but they might initially have been interpreted as referring to or at least including the reader: 'Don't be afraid. My telling can't hurt you ...' (Morrison, 2008b: 1). Through Florens's ambiguous narrative address, the text creates overlapping positions for the blacksmith and the reader. In other words, *A Mercy* positions the reader to judge Florens and her actions as severely as the free blacksmith finally does. Florens's opening admonition, moreover, goes on to raise and implicitly link two central issues: 'One question is who is responsible? Another is can you read?' (*ibid.*: 1). This second question draws attention to an important difference between the blacksmith and Morrison's readers: the blacksmith is illiterate, but readers of *A Mercy* are not.

Reading, rereading, and placing the novel in a literary landscape opens up interpretive alternatives. It allows us, for instance, to detect Florens's criticism of the blacksmith and the issue of responsibility that Morrison thereby raises. The last two pages of Florens's story feature alternative interpretations of the judgment on voluntary enslavement. Florens recalls the blacksmith's discussion of 'slaves freer than free men. One is a lion in the skin of an ass. The other is an ass in the skin of a lion. That it is the withering inside that enslaves and opens the door for what is wild' (ibid.: 158). Florens analyzes her experience and, like most protagonists of liberatory narratives, she seems to 'recognize and accept responsibility' for her actions 'in spite of those forces that conspire against [her]' (Mitchell, 2002: 16). Although she says she 'knows' that her withering is a result of her encounter with the Puritans, she also 'knows' there is something else to consider: 'A lion who thinks his mane is all. A she-lion who does not. I learn this from Daughter Jane. Her bloody legs do not stop her. She risks. Risks all to save the slave you throw out' (Morrison, 2008b: 158). The implicit comparison between the free blacksmith and a lion returns the reader, via slave narratives, to Aesop's fable, 'The Man and the Lion.' Morrison has reworked Aesop's Fables in collaboration with her son, Slade Morrison, for the *Who's Got Game* series of children's books, and her knowledge of slave narratives is both deep and wide.[53] The letter from abolitionist Wendell Phillips that prefaces Douglass's *Narrative of the Life of Frederick Douglass, An American Slave, Written by Himself* (1845) opens with a reference to this fable about the lion complaining that 'he should not be so misrepresented "when the lions wrote history"' (Phillips, 1973: xxi). Phillips – in language that casts enslaved people as figurative orphans, 'the most neglected of God's children' (ibid.) – approves of Douglass's narrative as an example of lions writing history. By way of this intertextual reference, *A Mercy* signifies on slave narratives written from a masculine perspective. As Mitchell observes, intertextuality in liberatory narratives is 'a strategy used to highlight the primary concerns of bondage and freedom' (2002: 14), and it is a strategy for creating rememory (ibid.: 12), paying tribute to but also transforming understandings of the past. Neither the point of view of the man, nor of the male lion, can ensure the reliability or fullness of a historical understanding. Morrison's work draws attention to multiple female perspectives across racial, religious, and other boundaries, and this multiplicity is a feature of the written form.

Reading and rereading allows us to share empathies and shift positions with all of the characters in the novel, and it allows readers to attend to the voice of the mother – the voice Florens cannot hear. In other words, the suggested call and response pattern that operates as the frame of the story is complete only in the communal space of written fiction, where readers become part of the narrative pattern. Morrison signifies on written narratives in ways that make it 'the duty of another agent, namely the reader, to relate these texts' (Loichot, 2007: 180). Thus, Morrison's text pays tribute to black orality, and its formal organization elicits the reader's participation in that tribute.

Nevertheless, as indicated, the oral relation of history dramatized in *A Mercy* does not concern African American memory alone, nor does it occur exclusively or even primarily within families related by blood. Instead, history is shared and transmitted across racial, cultural, and other divides, as is evident in the scenes of storytelling. It is also manifested in the complex structure of the novel, which opens up performative dimensions for readers, compelling readers to shift perspectives and to assume a variety of positions in relation to the characters, to history, and to the text as a whole. For Birgit Neumann, works that possess 'a multi-perspectival narration or focalization provide insight into the memories of several narrative instances or figures and in this way they can reveal the functioning and problems of collective memory-creation' (2010: 338), including questions about versions of the past. Readers of *A Mercy* must negotiate the orphan characters' different memories and accounts of freedom and bondage; as a result of this intellectual and imaginative work, the possibility emerges for readers to gain a fuller, more complex historical consciousness. In other words, the exercise of imagination, empathy, and thought becomes a dimension of rememory which is foregrounded in *A Mercy*.

Liberatory narratives, Mitchell argues, have precisely this pedagogical and civic value, for 'they can help to emancipate their readers from the cultural and historical amnesia that has surrounded the issue of slavery in the Unites States' (2002: 21). Moreover, 'By positing slavery as a site of memory and as a metaphor for contemporary race relations, the liberatory narrative allows for an examination of how race operated and operates in American history, society, and culture' (*ibid.*: 30). These critical and empowering dimensions of learning imaginatively about history affect readers who, given Morrison's status as a Nobel prize-winner and the numerous translations of her novels, should be envisaged as diverse in terms of race, gender, class, but also language and nationality. Mitchell's national focus is not undermined but is rather supplemented in *A Mercy* which puts the history of enslavement and servitude next to the founding national myth of freedom and equality, as Babb has described, but which also draws connections back to Europe and Africa, thus emphasizing the transnational character of the slave trade and colonial settlement in North America.

In its concern with 'spaces and practices acted upon by border-crossing agents,' the novel engages with what Francoise Lionnet and Shu-mei Shi have referred to as 'minor transnationalism' (2005: 5).[54] They focus on social relations between groupings, underscoring that 'the minor and the major participate in one shared transnational moment and space structured by uneven power relations' (*ibid.*: 7). An awareness of contemporaneousness and shared space makes visible uneven power relations of the sort that divide the gathering of orphaned individuals on Vaark's farm, and it underscores the hybrid, mixed character of cultures and their historical development.

Minor transnationalism also brings to recognition 'the creative interventions ... of minoritized cultures produce[d] within and across national boundaries,' as well as new 'expressions of allegiance' and ethical concerns (*ibid.*: 7, 8). Because they share the hardships of settler life, Lina and Rebekka become friends, 'mostly because neither knew precisely what they were doing or how. Together, by trial and error they learned ...' (Morrison, 2008b: 51). This novel, more than any of Morrison's previous fictions – with the possible exceptions of *Paradise* (1998) and 'Recitatif' (1983) – seeks out and represents provisional, cautious allegiances across many barriers and borders.[55] As in *Beloved*, when Amy Denver assists at Sethe's delivery, or here, when Scully and Willard help Sorrow give birth, or the Puritan Jane helps Florens escape, or even when Rebekka crosses the Atlantic in the company of women 'of and for men,' *A Mercy* envisages moments seemingly outside of time, 'where a past did not haunt nor a future beckon' (*ibid.*: 83), in which social hierarchies are temporarily suspended, social power achieves a delicate equilibrium, and the possibility for a muted reciprocity emerges through learning.

Moments outside of time would seem incompatible with a historical novel. Indeed, such moments appear utopian, and in all of Morrison's fiction, utopias are provisional, ad hoc affairs. For the most part, *A Mercy* shows that genuine exchange, border-crossing, and solidarity require the temporary suspension or surreptitious transgression of constraining social regimes, and they inevitably dissolve under other pressures, notably of religious or legal dictates which uphold unjust social stratification, but also due to pride.

In a passage which talks back to the dominant myth of American settlement, of the self-reliance of the American Adam and the American Eve, Lina identifies the 'folly' of Vaark's farm: 'Pride alone made [Jacob and Rebekka] think that they needed only themselves, could shape life that way, like Adam and Eve, like gods from nowhere beholden to nothing except their own creations' (*ibid.*: 56–7). Their lack of kinship is presented as a danger, and settler behavior is thought typical of orphans: 'Cut loose from the earth's soul, they insisted on purchase of its soil, and like all orphans they were insatiable. It was their destiny to chew up the world and spit out a horribleness that would destroy all primary peoples' (*ibid.*: 52). This passage resonates richly with Leslie Marmon Silko's comments on greedy Euro-American orphans in *Almanac of the Dead* (1991) and Gomez's depiction of greedy, devouring slave owners and Euro-American vampires in *The Gilda Stories*. Thus, like many of the works examined in *Making Home*, Morrison's novel suggests that the principles and characteristics lauded in American history – even in American literary history – produce not freedom, but greed, disproportionate desire, and a sense of righteous entitlement and privilege.

By relating diverse narrative perspectives of orphan characters on slavery and other forms of oppression in the colonial context, Morrison suggests the need to transform fundamental conceptions of the American nation, to rethink the history of making family, home, and nation in the USA and beyond. Rememorying orphans and orphaning practices helps envision ways of making kin and making home. Unlike *Beloved*, *A Mercy* offers no uncanny reunion between a once-enslaved mother and daughter. Instead, motherlines and other lines, the voices of mother, daughter, and other orphaned characters, are united only in the text and in the consciousnesses of its contemporary readers. *A Mercy* places recognition, responsibility, and understanding in the hands of an interracial and international readership, emphasizing the importance of crossing borders, of listening across transnational space, and, above all, of learning how to maintain dominion over one's self without wresting it from another.

This chapter opened with the question of apology for the historical crimes of enslavement and racial segregation raised in the 1990s. In 2008 the US House of Representatives finally passed such a bill,

H.Res.194, which apologizes 'for the enslavement and racial segregation of African-Americans.' Among those aspects of slavery that call for remorse is the fact that 'enslaved families were torn apart after having been sold separately from one another.' Although the bill has generated controversy and to our knowledge is yet to be ratified, the fact of its passage as late as 2008 eloquently attests to the profound relevance of slavery to the imagination of American 'family.' The speculative and historical fictions of Butler, Gomez, and Morrison, as we have shown, use orphan figures and the literary genres of speculative fiction and the historical novel to interrogate the parameters of national kinship. In engaging with the genres of the vampire novel or operating as 'liberatory' fictions, these texts rememory slavery and its legacies. In these narrative and generic contexts, the orphan trope enables authors to tell two stories at once: to narrate the destruction and disparagement of black family and culture in the USA at the same time as they relate their reconstitution and, to varying degrees, envision the possibility of a more diverse national, and even transnational, 'family.' The hybrid orphaned narrator in *Fledgling* discovers that family is both more local and more global than the conflation of family with nation usually implies. For the orphan protagonist of *The Gilda Stories*, Euro-American greed and exploitation foreclose the notion of family within national boundaries. Finally, in *A Mercy* orphaned protagonists find ways to make provisional filiations and ad hoc families, but any robust reconstitution of kinship and relatedness across boundaries, Morrison suggests, is the ethical responsibility of readers. By learning to read and by taking responsibility for our actions, past and present, readers may contribute imaginatively to making a home worth the name.

Notes

1 For example, in 'Reading Family Matters,' Deborah E. McDowell discusses the 1980s debate on the portrayal of black men by Toni Morrison, Gayl Jones, Ntozake Shange, and Alice Walker in terms of metaphorical and literal family matters in literature and the publishing business (McDowell, 1995: 118–37).
2 Alison Landsberg proposes that 'as slavery tore families apart, it produced a kind of orphaning whose effects lasted well beyond Emancipation' (2004: 86) and highlights the importance of the figure of the child in late twentieth-century texts about slavery.

3   Candice M. Jenkins contextualizes the Moynihan Report, calling attention to the class distinctions Moynihan made and relating these to her understanding of propriety in black women's fiction (2007: 64–70). See also Sharon Monteith's analysis of Sarah E. Wright's portrayal of a poor black family in *This Child's Gonna Live* (1969) as a way of challenging the Report (Monteith, 2006).
4   See Ruth McRoy and Amy Griffin (2012) on race and adoption and the effects of the Multiethnic Placement Act (MEPA); Roberts critiques the Adoption and Safe Families Act (2003: 105–16); Laura Briggs examines MEPA and the 'crack baby epidemic' of the late 1980s (2012: 95–125).
5   Sugrue considers the 'war on welfare' waged in the 1990s up until about 2004. Both conservative and liberal thinkers 'refocused the debate over poverty onto values and culture, shunting aside rigorous analyses of inequality and laying blame instead on individual characteristics. The new liberal emphasis on the behavioral origins of poverty came to fruition in the bipartisan consensus to abolish AFDS – and remains a prevailing framework shaping anti-poverty policy today' (2008: 331).
6   Collins writes, 'Children orphaned by sale or death of their parents under slavery, children conceived through rape, children of young mothers, children born into extreme poverty or to alcoholic or drug-addicted mothers, or children who for other reasons cannot remain with their bloodmothers have all been supported by othermothers ...' (2000: 180). She wonders whether this practice might be eroding today. The Fostering Connections to Success and Increasing Adoptions Act of 2008 aims to facilitate guardianship and kinship care.
7   For example, see Ann duCille (2009) and Jenkins (2007). See also Collins (1998) on how family rhetoric has been mobilized by both conservative groups and oppressed groups, and see Roberts's examination of 'the color of child welfare' (2003).
8   Toni Morrison was the editor of Forrest's trilogy of which *The Bloodworth Orphans* is the second novel. The other two were published in 1973 and 1984.
9   Earlier fictions that fall outside our period, but display similar thematic concerns are *This Child's Gonna Live* (1969), by Sarah E. Wright, and Octavia Butler's *Kindred* (1979).
10 In 1997, Annette Gordon-Reed's *Thomas Jefferson and Sally Hemings: An American Controversy* examined evidence about the paternity of Hemings's children. DNA testing the following year confirmed her conclusion that it is highly likely that Thomas Jefferson did father at least one of Hemings's children. See the second edition of Gordon-Reed's book.
11 Arjun Appadurai argues that 'contemporary literary fantasies tell us something about displacement, disorientation, and agency in the contemporary world' (1996: 58). Both Butler and Gomez have expressed

disappointment with science-fiction and fantasy writers who have not used the potential of speculative fiction to challenge conservative ideas about gender, race, and sexuality. See Butler (1980a: 60) and (1980b: 6); and Gomez (1997: 89).

12 See, for example, Sandra Grayson (2003: 4) and Hazel Carby (2003). See also Gregory Jerome Hampton on Butler's novels as 'political commentary (whether it is about religion, race, gender, the environment, or poverty)' (2010: 115).

13 Ingrid Thaler uses the term speculative fiction as 'an umbrella term for all kinds of fantastic writing' that 'deliberately and explicitly disturbs mimetic notions of "realistic" representation' (2010: 2). Joanna Russ argues conversely that much science fiction and fantasy rely on the conventions of straightforward realistic, or even naturalistic, narration (1995: 19).

14 Giulia M. Fabi discusses earlier African American utopian or speculative fiction as a context for writers to imagine alternative societies and launch a comprehensive social and political critique (2012: 113): 'Authors like Sutton E. Griggs, E. Pauline Hopkins, Charles W. Chestnutt, and Edward A. Johnson wrote works of speculative fiction in order to seize the literary and cultural power to articulate a restructuring of the very nation that was discriminating against them' (*ibid.*: 114).

15 Butler has called her vampire novel a 'science fantasy' (2004: 218) since her protagonist is a genetic experiment combining the genes of two separate species, while Gomez sees her vampire novel as an 'exploration of traditional form' in order to 'contribute to a new more feminist-grounded mythology' (1997: 92).

16 The literary origin of the Anglo-American vampire trope is John Polidori's 'The Vampyre' (1819). The vampire trope was so pervasive in nineteenth-century culture that Marx used it in Chapter 10 of *Capital*: 'Capital is dead labour which, vampire-like, lives only by sucking living labour, and lives the more, the more labour it sucks' (quoted in Gelder, 1994: 20).

17 Examples of popular, mainstream vampire narratives are the TV series *True Blood* (2008–13) and *The Vampire Diaries* (2009–13) as well as the *Twilight* films (2008–12).

18 Associated with geographic mobility, the vampire is sometimes read as an expression of capitalism, of an international or global system, or of anti-Semitism (Gelder, 1994: 23). Like many a vampire in earlier vampire fiction, Butler's and Gomez's vampires raise transnational concerns.

19 See M. Carter (2004: 135).

20 Gomez has observed that '[f]ilms like *Blacula* (1972) and the much more daring *Ganja and Hess* (1973) try to reinterpret the vampire myth for black culture, but they still adhere to the formulaic design: (black) woman as

handmaiden or (black) woman as temptress/bait' (1997: 89). Other films featuring black male vampires as main characters are *Vampire in Brooklyn* (1995), *Blade* (1998), *Blade II* (2002), and *Blade Trinity* (2004).

21 'In *The Gilda Stories*, blood loses the primary association with violence, pollution, and corruption so typical in the bulk of existing vampire fiction' (K. Patterson, 2005: n.p.). Thaler observes, '*The Gilda Stories* appropriates the vampire as a trope that fictionally negotiates the historical meanings of blood as a metaphor for race, family, and sexuality in the nineteenth century' (2010: 59).

22 In a discussion on kinship in *Buffy the Vampire Slayer* (1997–2003) and Octavia Butler's *Parable* novels (1993, 1998), Philip Wegner argues that the power of both of these narratives comes partly from 'drawing on the utopian content of the extended family and then inflecting it in new, politically radical directions' (2009: 205) – a displacement of hierarchical blood relationships and 'an increasing expansion and radicalization of new forms of queer consensual kinship …' (*ibid.*: 206).

23 Published in 1979, *Kindred* falls outside the purview of this study, but like Butler's *Wild Seed* (1980), it clearly displays Butler's interest in the US slave past. For discussions of *Kindred* see, for instance, Maria Holmgren Troy (1999: 149–79), Rushdy (2001: 99–127), and Tim A. Ryan (2008: 114–48).

24 See Thaler (2010) on Gomez's novel as a combination of neo-slave narrative and vampire novel. Rody calls *The Gilda Stories* a 'hybrid text' (2001: 79).

25 Perry Anderson (2011) focuses on the genre's relation to nationalism and progress, while Wallace contests accounts that disparage or ignore the work of female historical novelists.

26 'The persistent backdrops to the historical fiction of the postmodern period are at the antipodes of its classical forms. Not the emergence of the nation, but the ravages of empire; not progress as emancipation, but impending or consummated catastrophe' (P. Anderson, 2011: 28). See also Ernest E. Leisy (1950) on the genre's didactic and patriotic characteristics.

27 Jerome de Groot concurs: 'This clear sense of connection with the past, and an awareness that the events of history have an impact upon the contemporary, is something which has profound consequences for the way we live our lives and conceive of ourselves' (2010: 27).

28 Prominent examples of the genre are Margaret Walker's *Jubilee* (1966), Ernest J. Gaines's *The Diary of Miss Jane Pittman* (1971), Gayl Jones's *Corregidora* (1975), Alex Haley's *Roots* (1976), Ishmael Reed's *Flight to Canada* (1976), Butler's *Kindred* (1979), Sherley Anne Williams's *Dessa Rose* (1986), Morrison's *Beloved* (1987), Charles Johnson's *Middle Passage* (1990), and J. California Cooper's *Family* (1991). In a parallel fashion,

scholarly studies of slavery have proliferated. See Collins (2005) for a summary of how gender relations under slavery have been evaluated from the 1970s.

29 Mitchell prefers the term 'liberatory narrative,' because its focus on the past is undertaken 'in order to provide new models of liberation by problematizing the concept of freedom' (2002: 4).

30 See Christine Levecq on how Butler, in *Kindred*, signifies on the fugitive slave narrative genre; Levecq starts by comparing Dana and Frederick Douglass (2000: 542–6). Harriet Jacobs's narrative was authenticated in 1981 and often functions as an 'antecedent text' or 'Ur-text' for liberatory narratives by contemporary black women novelists (Mitchell, 2002: 22, 23). John Ernest observes that US public memory is partly shaped by racial ideologies; these narratives receive official attention 'only after the Civil Rights Movement and the Black Studies Movement began to force the issue of the need to recover the texts of African American intellectual, cultural, and literary history' (2007: 220).

31 See Orlando Patterson (1982), Gould (2007), and McDowell (2007: 151). By one count, 130 slave narratives were published before 1865, 16 of these by women (Mitchell, 2002: 9).

32 Named by her African American human mother, Shori's name is that of 'an East African crested nightingale' (Butler, 2005: 132). Her name resonates with the title of the novel and emphasizes learning and transformation. Moreover, in the context of vampire lore, a fledgling is a young vampire, or a human who has just been made a vampire.

33 That the narrator is not fully or exclusively human is significant for science fiction as a genre and its construction of the voice and agency of the un- or posthuman (Melzer, 2006: 39; Vint, 2007: 189).

34 Haraway has adopted the phrase 'Sacred Image of the Same' from Butler's 1978 novel *Survivor*, also featuring an orphan of color as the protagonist. For a discussion of this novel in terms of the Indian captivity narrative and science fiction, see Troy's 'Negotiating Genre and Captivity' (2010b).

35 As was observed prior to the publication of *Fledgling*, 'Butler's oeuvre ... is obsessed precisely with the tension between sociality and the necessity of acknowledging the biological imprint on identity' (Luckhurst, 1996: 33). Margaret Carter points out that generally the vampire which derives from natural, scientific causes 'allows the nonhuman characters free will and the possibility of moral choice, bounded by the limitations of flesh and blood' (2004: 3). Another critic, discussing the development of the sympathetic vampire in the 1980s, states that cross-species responsibility concerns ecology and human dynamics – 'the relationships between the sexes, among individuals, and among the many ethnic, racial, religious, and political groups of human beings' (Gordon, 1988: 231).

36 In the world at large, Appadurai suggests, 'Fax machines, electronic mail, and other forms of computer-mediated communication have created new possibilities for transnational forms of communication, often bypassing the intermediate surveillance of the nation-state ...' (1996: 194).
37 How much living in the present is tied to the past is one of the major themes in *Kindred*, but Butler's 1979 novel has a much narrower focus on the national past than *Fledgling* has.
38 For an analysis of Gomez's novel in the context of 're/writing queer histories,' see Scott Bravmann (1997: 113–20). In the USA and the UK, from the 1980s onwards, the lesbian historical novel has developed as a sub-genre in its own right. See, for instance, Wallace (2008: 7), Laura Doan and Sarah Waters (2000: 13), and Paulina Palmer (1998: 81).
39 As Sabine Meyer observes in a discussion of narratives of passing and the horrors of the normative in *The Gilda Stories*, 'The vampire has gained archetypal status for the representation of queer, social and sexual identities' (2002: n.p.).
40 There are few narratives in which the main vampire character is born in nineteenth-century America. For a discussion of Gomez's Gilda and *True Blood*'s Bill Compton as American vampires with their origins in a nineteenth-century USA, see Troy (2010a).
41 Bravmann suggests that, in stabbing the white man, the Girl reverses 'the phallic power of penetration within this particular kind of asymmetrical relationship that existed under patriarchal racial slavery' (1997: 114).
42 Drawing on Goddu's 'Vampire Gothic,' Kathy Davis Patterson (2005) accurately observes that Gomez's *The Gilda Stories* is an 'intriguing attempt' at haunting back.
43 This portrayal of the deep ambiguity of rememory is in keeping with Morrison's depiction of the intergenerational effects of history and memory on the inhabitants of 124 Bluestone.
44 In 1988, Richard Dyer compared vampirism and homosexuality in a much-quoted article: 'On the one hand, the point about sexual orientation is that it doesn't "show", you can't tell who is and who isn't just by looking; but on the other hand, there is also a widespread discourse that there *are* tell-tale signs that someone "is". The vampire myth reproduces this double view in its very structures of suspense' (1988: 58).
45 The only morally tainted or evil black vampire in *The Gilda Stories* is a pimp who Bird and Gilda manage to destroy in 1955.
46 This strategy, or magical realism, de Groot asserts, is often used 'by writers of historical fiction with a view to undermining mainstream models ... and to critique ideas of nationhood, identity and storytelling itself. In its attack on the supposed legitimacy of the realist mode it is part and parcel of the metafictional-postmodern project and its desire to undermine larger totalising narratives' (2010: 133).

47 'The Man and the Lion,' *Aesop's Fables: A New Revised Version from Original Sources*. Project Gutenberg.
48 Most of the geographical references in Morrison's text are to the Middle and Chesapeake colonies, though a reference to the Abenake trail might indicate New England. For a discussion of Sorrow, see Jessica Wells Cantiello (2011: 173–5).
49 See Orlando Patterson on categories of slave and servant, us and them (1982: 7). See also Pazicky's account (1998).
50 Davis attributes the gradual cementation of racial hierarchies to changes in demography and labor supply (2008: 132) and cites Edmund S. Morgan's thesis concerning colonial America: binary racial categories (not class oppositions or complex racial hierarchies) were formed in eighteenth-century Virginia and, because Virginia was home to many of the so-called founding fathers, US ideologies of independence and freedom became binarily racially inflected (*ibid.*: 135).
51 Maxine Montgomery finds this project successful in *A Mercy* which, she claims, 'destabilizes fixed notions of self and society, even as [it] works to create a transcendent realm leading to freedom, autonomy, and self-identity' (2011: 9). Our reading is somewhat bleaker.
52 Florens is also much like Denver in *Beloved*, who loves to hear the story of her birth repeated, but she is also like Beloved, who desires the same story from Denver.
53 See Rebecca Ferguson (2011) on adaptations of Aesop. Titles in the series include *The Lion or the Mouse* (2004), *The Ant or the Grasshopper* (2006), and *The Tortoise or the Hare* (2010).
54 Montgomery also observes that 'Despite the obvious concern with places of origin, [*A Mercy*] troubles the recognized historiography underlying the country's move toward nation building, Empire, and imperialist conquest, and it does so through a focus on the largely untold stories of a transnational assembly of outcasts' (2011: 628).
55 In *Advancing Sisterhood?* (2000), Monteith observes that the only critic who has provided a detailed reading of Morrison's 'Recitatif' by focusing on aesthetics is Elizabeth Abel in 'Black Writing, White Reading: Race and the Politics of Feminist Interpretation.' She notes how Abel 'pursues the means by which Morrison succeeds in undoing racial hierarchies' (Monteith, 2000: 48). See also Elizabeth Kella's *Beloved Communities* (2000) for a discussion of the formation of ad hoc communities in *Paradise*.

Coda

In American literature, the orphan embodies a radical doubleness: defined by loss of family, orphanhood nevertheless hinges on family connection. The orphan figure can signal exclusion from family, at the same time as it holds the possibility of familial inclusion. This doubleness, we have argued, endows the orphan with unique signifying capabilities, serving to advance both critiques of family and new visions of kinship. The doubleness and dynamism of the orphan figure allows writers to take a variety of positions in relation to American identity, questioning, challenging, affirming, or revisioning what it means to live in the USA.

In a similar fashion, orphan figures challenge, but also reaffirm ideas about American literature. One central idea advanced throughout *Making Home* has been that literary genres carry cultural memory and historically specific meanings. The genres we investigate are strongly connected to American nationhood, some because they are unique to this national context, like the captivity tale and the slave narrative; others because they have gained distinctive national inflections. All, however, are carriers of cultural memory in the USA. As writers of various ethnicities bring other genres and counter-memories – such as storytelling, signifying, specifying, and rememorying – to bear upon American literature, the limits of a hegemonic national collective memory are challenged.

As this study demonstrates, intertextual references to literary traditions function to complicate meanings of orphanhood and family in the novels. Plot and characterization in the captivity narrative exert a tremendous force on contemporary writing which activates this cultural form. The protagonists' gender, class, and race are revised in new versions of the *bildungsroman* as orphan characters reject or re-integrate with conventional families. Captivity narratives and the *bildungsroman* gain new significance in the contemporary context of a multicultural and multiply gendered national literature. In the forays African American women writers make into the realms of speculative and historical fiction, orphan figures are employed in order to 'rememory' these genres. In this way, these novels counter the semanticized features of Euro-American mainstream genres, and affirm and re-inflect the African American genre of the slave narrative. In this way, they also renegotiate American cultural myths with particular attention paid to those groups who have been marginalized or excluded from them.

One recurring feature in the novels is that they formulate an understanding of kinship as process: rather than a static, finished unit defined by blood or law, kinship is a complex and dynamic project, imagined in different ways. In *The Cider House Rules* and the Ellen Foster novels, kinship building is central, and the protagonists develop an understanding of alternative families as valuable, in contrast to the destruction, dysfunction, or restrictions that mark nuclear families. In *Solar Storms* and *Gardens in the Dunes*, Indian orphans signify regeneration through kinship, a dynamic indigenous concept of kinship that may unsettle the notion of America as multicultural, but also offers new visions for American community. *Fledgling* and *The Gilda Stories* represent kinship as a process formed through reconfigured and inclusive blood relations, and in *Specimen Days* it is radically unstable, moving beyond definitions based on blood, the law, and generational hierarchies.

Another feature that several of the novels share is a critique of masculinist notions of individualism, self-generation, historylessness, and independence, and the authors use orphan figures to advance this form of critique across different literary genres. Linda Hogan, for example, depicts a different type of agency placed in the orphan child, Barbara Kingsolver critiques entrenched, gendered ideas of individualism and independence, while John Irving and Michael Cunningham also highlight the ways that orphans carry history with them. These writers foreground the historical situatedness of orphans as yet another mode of countering historylessless, with memory often being desirable as well as ethically valuable.

This study has also demonstrated the continuing flexibility of fictional orphan figures. The orphan is at times – at least temporarily

– a self-made individualist, as in Kaye Gibbons's and Jonathan Safran Foer's novels, or a vulnerable but resilient survivor, as in *A Mercy*. But he or she may also be an uncanny 'other' as in *Specimen Days*, a resource or a life project for adults, as in Kingsolver's novels, or a bearer of the promise for change in the future, as in Linda Hogan's and Leslie Marmon Silko's works. In almost every novel, the orphan is also a kinship builder.

The regenerative aspects of kinship building depicted in novels from the 1980s to the 2000s open up feminist and multicultural possibilities for familial and national community. *Making Home* has focused on Native, African American and Euro-American writers, arguing that interactions between these groups have historically been decisive in shaping an American identity and literary imagination. In the era of US feminism and multiculturalism, women and minority groups increasingly gave voice to other histories, experiences, artistic values, and cultural traditions, bringing imagination and creativity to bear on national literary and critical traditions. Today, the demography of the US population continues to change, and with these changes come new contributions to all aspects of American life and culture. In this changing, increasingly global landscape, the dynamic, flexible trope of orphanhood appears to remain useful for writers. Parallel to, and sometimes overlapping with, the growing trend of adoption narratives, novels that feature orphan figures continue to be produced by writers with a variety of backgrounds. Prominent among these are Tim Gautreaux's *The Missing* (2009), Chang-Rae Lee's *The Surrendered* (2010), Sapphire's *The Kid* (2011), Eowyn Ivey's *The Snow Child* (2012), and Adam Johnson's *The Orphan Master's Son* (2012). These new works continue trends and expand the diverse ways that orphan figures can signify in US literature.

The prestigious Pulitzer Prize for Fiction is awarded each year to a fiction that explores American life. The 2013 winner, Adam Johnson's *The Orphan Master's Son* (2012), may at first sight seem an unlikely candidate because the novel is set mainly in North Korea, where the orphan protagonist Jun Do grows up in an orphanage called Long Tomorrows. Because he is an orphan, he suffers hardship and hunger, is scorned by and excluded from society, yet his expendability makes him useful to the regime. In his teens, Jun Do is trained as a tunnel soldier, and as an adult he becomes a Taekwondo expert, works as a kidnapper, learns English, and is stationed as a spy on board a fishing boat. He becomes a national hero when the authorities fabricate a story about him fighting a shark to save a shipmate, and because of his hero status and language skills he is assigned a political mission to the USA. He is subsequently taken to a North Korean prison camp, where he suffers a year of tremendous hardship, starvation, and violence, but manages to escape, later assuming the identity of the Minister of prison mines, Commander Ga, whom he has killed. In Pyongyang, he lives with Ga's wife, actress Sun Moon, and her two children until they disappear and he is captured and tortured by the secret police in an effort to get him to disclose what happened to Sun Moon and her children. He is killed in prison by an interrogator who wants to spare him a more painful public execution, but in a final ironic twist, his death is explained by the official national narrative as a result of his unrelenting resistance to the corrupting powers of the USA. This inventive narrative turns the marginalized and despised orphan into a North Korean hero.

Jun Do is thus violated by the nation he is expected to serve throughout the novel. Named for a martyr who gave his life to prove his loyalty to the nation, Jun Do dies as a consequence of his disloyalty to North Korea, and his loyalty to the family, whom he helps to defect to the USA. Johnson clearly establishes that the protagonist's actions run counter to the directive of the North Korean regime, which is to prioritize the entire people and the 'Dear Leader' Kim Jong Il at all times. Disrupted and corrupted familial bonds turn Johnson's fictional North Korea into a nation of orphans, where the horrific Dear Leader is the real orphan master. Widows are assigned replacement husbands and children are expected to report their parents for any disobedience to the regime. In many ways, the novel's insistence on the cruelty and distance of North Korean society results in an insistent othering of its people.

The protagonist, however, is different. Knowing English, he has heard voices from 'the outside' as a radio man at sea, and his encounters with Americans produce an understanding of the USA as a nation of saviors, disciplined soldiers, good strong women, and just men. During his picaresque journey Jun Do also develops from an 'everyman' (the novel plays explicitly with the meaning of 'John Doe') into a fully humanized individual. The orphan protagonist's inviolate mind and his ability to promote intimacy and independence contrast sharply with his repeatedly violated body and his suffering at the hands of authorities, but also contrasts with all other North Korean characters in the novel. Guided by a fundamental sense of decency, he tells Sun Moon late in the novel: 'I'm the good guy in this story ... Believe it or not, the hero is me' (Johnson, 2012: 552). The novel's structure – which includes the voice of an omniscient narrator, that of the secret police interrogator, and the 'official' voice of North Korean government via the nationalist daily newscasts that blare from loudspeakers everywhere – explicitly foregrounds *competing stories* about the orphan's heroism, and about his agency in working for national and familial inclusion.

Whereas the official North Korean narrative posthumously makes the protagonist a national hero, his 'true' story, as conveyed by Johnson, makes him hero material in American literature. His personal traits follow lines we have discussed in this study: an insistence on justice and independent thought, coupled with emotional attachment and longing for community. The picaresque is activated again, although with a setting that is relatively new to US fiction. However, while the protagonist's heroism is confirmed at the end of the novel, he dies, and his experiences of family are never more than fleeting.

The Surrendered (2010) by Korean-American Chang-Rae Lee is a novel that features a multitude of orphan characters, and that strenuously avoids adoption as a narrative outcome. Spanning several continents – Asia, Europe, and North America – and several periods – from the 1930s to the late 1980s – the novel appears to eschew family and, by extension, national community. This novel thus continues the move toward transnational concerns, particularly in its depiction of international warfare, but it also uses orphan figures for new purposes.

The story opens in war-torn Korea with one of the two main protagonists, the Korean child June, losing her entire family in horrific ways. June gradually makes her way to the ironically named New Hope orphanage in South Korea, where she meets Hector, whose young adult personality is strongly affected by childhood ambivalence toward his father and his early death, and Sylvie, a missionary wife herself orphaned during the violent prelude to the 1937–45 Sino-Japanese war. The separate and intricately interwoven pasts of these characters make up one narrative strand; the other concerns June's attempts, with Hector's help, many years later in the 1980s, to locate her adult son in Italy before she dies of cancer. Although at this point June has not seen Hector for several decades, since their brief marriage of convenience and the equally brief sexual act that, unbeknownst to Hector, produced a son, he agrees to help her on her international journey.

June is a survivor, and like orphans in earlier literature, her tenacity, determination, and hunger for life are crucial. At the orphanage, she is initially desperate for adoption: 'She told herself to keep disciplined, to stay the course she had laid out, to remake herself along the lines of an entirely different girl: someone who was not an orphan at all, had not lost anyone in her life, much less witnessed any horrors or degradation. She was a normal child, who would soon have a normal life' (ibid.: 382). June's desire to remake herself, to fashion an identity outside of her traumatic past, resonates with aspects of American mythology. Yet, when at last she is chosen by a couple for adoption, she is unable to go through with it: 'She could not be a part of any other family again' (ibid.: 391). Desiring to be taken by Sylvie, whom she loves as a mother, but also as a twin, June is devastated when Sylvie abandons her, and she orchestrates events that lead, perhaps unintentionally, to Sylvie's death. June burns down the orphanage, and as Sylvie rushes into the building to rescue June, she, her husband, and another orphan child are consumed by flames: 'And in a flash a plumed beast of flame leaped up from the flooring to enfold the couple and child, for a moment cradling them in an almost placid repose before swallowing them whole' (ibid.: 461). The novel never counters this powerful image of family destruction; instead it reinforces death, war, and orphanhood, and so becomes emblematic of a world in which family cannot provide shelter or salvation.

Somewhat conventionally, *The Surrendered* portrays orphans as survivors. More unusually, it also foregrounds survivors as orphans. In this anti-war novel, which eschews adoption and kinship building, regeneration is for the individual alone, and its secret lies in the orphan's strength, resilience, and unquenchable hunger for life – a hunger that is fed by the orphan's remembrance of things past.

Forgetting rather than memory is foregrounded throughout much of Sapphire's *The Kid* (2011), a sequel to *Push* (1996), filmed as *Precious* (2010), which features an African American orphan boy. Abdul Jones is the son of Precious, who bears two children by her own father. Raised by Precious alone, whose struggle for education and integrity is dramatized in Sapphire's first novel and the film, Abdul is unaware of his paternity until the end of the novel, when he applies for a birth certificate. At the opening, however, the nine-year-old protagonist's mother has just died of AIDS, and, because he cannot be immediately cared for by his mother's friend, he is sent, destitute, on a horrendous journey from foster home, to orphanage, to the care of a great-grandmother whom he has never met, to various arrangements with lovers and, finally, fellow dancers. In his first placement, he is harassed, raped, and severely beaten by an older boy. His injuries, including a head injury from which he never fully recovers, put him in hospital for several weeks, after which he is placed in a Catholic orphanage in Harlem, where routine sexual abuse continues at the hands of the Brothers, and where he himself becomes an abuser of younger boys. Narrated in the raw language of Abdul's increasingly disoriented consciousness, the novel challenges readers' abilities to sympathize with an orphan character who, though initially represented as a victim of poverty and the US child welfare system, becomes a victimizer as well.

Unlike *Push*, *The Kid* counters conventions of the *bildungsroman*, producing a narrative of reverse development, as Abdul's sense of personhood is ravaged. These attacks are represented by repeated sexual assaults and by the series of names forced on him by exploitative authority figures in the novel. As this orphan protagonist ages out of foster care, he enters into casual prostitution and a series of sexual liaisons with men and women, among them My Lai, who is sexually abused as a child by her adoptive father. Abdul becomes increasingly violent, aggressive, and disoriented. His talent and passion for dance constitute a potential source of empowerment that he works hard to develop, but the ambitions he finally embraces appear doomed to failure. The last section of the novel finds him incarcerated in a facility where he has been drugged, subjected to electric shock therapy, and battered by orderlies, after a suicide attempt that has apparently resulted in him being mistaken by police for a thirty-year-old Islamic terrorist, Abdul-Azi Ali. The conclusion is open-ended, with his psychologist doing all in his power to see that Abdul walks away from the facility and certain institutionalization, but with the orphan just beginning to struggle to remember and understand what has happened to him. Even before his incarceration, he has suffered from memory loss attributable to his early head injury or to repression of trauma. Throughout the novel, he is adamant in his refusal to be determined by history: 'I never think of my life as a story. I think of myself as a kid trying to make it. What fucking story? It ain't been written yet' (Sapphire, 2011: 257). He tears to shreds the notebooks left to him by his mother, violently rejecting knowledge about his origins and replacing his personal history with a fabricated story of normalcy.

In this counter-*bildungsroman*, rememory serves no purpose, and fiction offers greater consolation than fact.

In Tim Gautreaux's *The Missing* (2009), however, the orphan's search for knowledge and familial inclusion meets with some success. The novel is set in the 1920s, mainly in Louisiana and on the Mississippi River, a setting rife with racist tensions. The novel follows the adult Euro-American protagonist Sam Simoneaux, orphaned at six months of age, from the battlefields in France right after World War I, to New Orleans where his wife awaits, along with a job as a security guard in a department store. Sam loses this job when a blonde three-year-old girl, Lily, is kidnapped in the store on his watch. Determined to find the girl, he starts working on the steamboat on which Lily's parents work as musicians, reasoning that Lily was probably abducted by someone who had seen her sing and dance with her parents. Sam becomes an integral part of the steamboat crew, performing as a jazz pianist, and after half a year he discovers that Lily has been 'adopted' by a wealthy white couple who arranged her kidnapping. The hired kidnappers turn out to have been behind the murder of Sam's family when he was a baby. Lily has been told that her parents are dead, and she has begun to forget her birth family, embracing her adoptive family's name, lifestyle and values. In what ensues, her birth father is killed when pursuing the kidnappers, who have again abducted the child in the hope of extorting a ransom from her adoptive family; an alienated Lily is returned to what remains of her poverty-stricken birth family; her mother soon dies of influenza; and Lily and her older brother August end up in the care of Sam and his wife in New Orleans.

The Missing is a historical adventure novel filled with meditations on family and orphanhood. Apart from the central focus on Sam and Lily as orphaned characters, the novel touches on issues pertaining to orphanhood in the historical context of the setting: war orphans in France, the vulnerability of orphan train children, and the miserable conditions for orphans in orphanages. The wealthy couple who arrange for the abduction of Lily do so because they do not want an orphan but 'a child fortunate enough to be currently loved' (Gautreaux, 2009: 64), and their servant makes a similar distinction:

> She knew orphans, white and black, and every one would jerk back and cower if anybody raised a hand to them. Orphans wore no shoes, or wrong-sized shoes in which their feet grew crooked. Their feet bore

calluses, craters of sores, bite scars, toenails stobbed black, orange dirt stain, ankle meat clipped to white bone. Knees were crosshatched from working in crops or playing in common dirt, fingers stretched out by bucket or firewood chores. (*ibid.*: 104)

The ordeals of orphans in early twentieth-century American orphanages and their impact on the orphans' bodies and psyches are graphically depicted in this passage, which not only highlights the plight of white orphans, but also that of black orphans. Gautreaux's novel thus exhibits an awareness of the history of orphanhood in the USA that goes beyond popular cultural stereotypes.

The last few chapters of *The Missing* deal with Sam's and Lily's coming to terms with orphanhood and with their kinship building and familial integration. Visiting the pathetic remains of the criminal family who murdered his family, Sam presses the barely surviving criminals for details about his family, such as hair color and clothing, but leaves without exacting revenge. In the final chapter, Sam brings Lily to his uncle's farm where he grew up and, finally, to his parents' house, which he has never visited after his family was murdered. This journey to the bullet-riddled house, which Sam discovers that he owns and can sell to pay for the new family house in New Orleans, leads to Lily's emotional integration into Sam's new family, a creation of a strong bond between Sam and the girl whom he regards as 'a fellow orphan' (*ibid.*: 414) and his daughter. Their bond is sealed by Lily finding a keepsake in the house for Sam, a washboard, which as she assures him will help him create a 'memory' of his birth family's life before the murderous attack. Hence, somewhat surprisingly, *The Missing* combines two orphans' development beyond the trauma of loss of family with the genre of the picaresque historical adventure novel.

A finalist for the 2013 Pultizer Prize, Eowyn Ivey's *The Snow Child* (2012) takes its inspiration from outside US borders, but is nonetheless 'about American life.' This work is a beautifully wrought rendition of a Russian fairy tale about an older childless couple who make a child out of snow. In the fairy tale, the snow child comes to life and enriches the lives of the couple until their ungrateful and unloving behavior causes the snow child to leave them. Ivey's novel, by contrast, concerns a middle-aged couple, Mabel and Jack, who attempt to escape their grief over their infant child's death by homesteading in Alaska. In an unexpected, playful respite from their hard and lonely labor, they, too, fashion a snow girl, and the next morning they have their first glimpse of the enigmatic child, whose flesh-and-blood existence is doubted, in turn, by Jack, by their neighbors, by Mabel, and by readers of the novel. Generic uncertainty is created in the first part of the novel, as characters and readers ponder the nature of the child and of the text: is the child a figment of their imaginations, strained by the extreme isolation of the Alaskan winter, her existence to be finally explained by psychological realism? Or has the child really come to life, her existence to be affirmed in a work of magical realism? Mabel remembers hearing the fairy tale 'Little Daughter of the Snow' and muses: 'If there was such a book, could there be such a child? If an old man and woman conjured a little girl out of the snow and wilderness, what would she be to them? A daughter? A ghost?'(Ivey, 2012: 89–90). The intertext, which ends with the snow child leaving the old couple, creates anxiety for Mabel and suspense for readers. Even when the child, Faina, leads Jack to her dead father, confirming her orphan status, uncertainty remains about why she is so untroubled by cold, why she sweats profusely indoors, why she must leave them every summer.

From her first, fleeting appearance Faina is characterized as almost one with the landscape; Jack reflects that 'She moved through the forest with the grace of a wild creature. She knew the snow, and it carried her gently. She knew the spruce trees, how to slip among their limbs, and she knew the animals, the fox and ermine, the moose and songbirds. She knew this land by heart' (*ibid*.: 67). Faina clearly personifies the Alaskan wilderness. Moreover, in this novel of the American frontier, Faina – with her deep affinity with the land, her leather moccasins, her feather-covered wedding dress – replaces an indigenous presence. For Mabel and Jack, their neighbors Esther and George, settlement involves neither contact nor confrontation with Alaskan Natives; instead, it involves the gradual development of a respectful relation to a girl who stands in for a Native presence, and who, in spite of her exaggerated whiteness, is markedly different from the homesteaders, and whose difference must be accepted. It is tempting to see in Ivey's compelling novel a Euro-American fantasy or desire to revise colonial settlement along ethical lines, even as the narrative conforms to other Westerns in its depiction of absent, spectral, and always vanishing indigenous peoples. Ivey revises the story of settlement as a story of adoption, as Mabel and Jack develop parental relations with Faina, but also with Esther and George's son Garrett, and eventually with Garrett and Faina's child. Like Kingsolver in the novels we discuss, Ivey portrays adoption as involving complex emotional negotiations, love, and growth; when Faina suggests that Mabel take the child Faina is expecting, Mabel 'allows herself' a brief fantasy of adoption. Yet, Mabel quickly rejects that option: 'As much as she had ever wanted a baby, this one wasn't hers to take' (*ibid.*: 345). The child does eventually come to Mabel, however, confirming the bond with the land that Faina has helped establish: '[Mabel] was in love. Eight years she'd lived here, and at last the land had taken hold of her and she could comprehend some small part of Faina's wildness' (*ibid.*: 280). Faina's final disappearance, an uncanny displacement, coincides with the settler families making home on the frontier.

Employing the orphan figure in both traditional and innovative ways, this novel, together with work by Gautreaux, Sapphire, Johnson, and Lee, suggests that literary orphanhood will continue to generate diverse and far-reaching understandings of making home, in the USA and beyond its borders.

Bibliography

Abel, Elizabeth, Marianne Hirsch, and Elizabeth Langland. 1983. Introduction. *The Voyage In: Fictions of Female Development*. Eds Elizabeth Abel, Marianne Hirsch, and Elizabeth Langland. Hanover: University Press of New England. 3–19. Print.

Adamcyk, Valerie. 2001. 'Revising the Captivity Narrative: Lost Bird of Wounded Knee.' *Para-Doxa: Studies in World Literary Genres* 15: 38–48. Print.

Adams, David Wallace. 1995. *Education for Extinction: American Indians and the Boarding School Experience, 1875–1928*. Lawrence: University of Kansas Press. Print.

Adoption and Foster Care Analysis System (AFCARS). US Department of Health and Human Services. Children's Bureau. http://www.acf.hhs.gov/programs/cb/research-data-technology/reporting-systems/afcars. Web. Accessed 12 June 2013.

'Adoptions: Determining that a Child is an "Orphan."' Embassy of the United States. Skopje, Macedonia. http://macedonia.usembassy.gov/definition_of_orphan.html. Web. Accessed 23 October 2010.

Aesop. *Aesop's Fables: A New Revised Version from Original Sources*. Project Gutenberg. http://www.gutenberg.org/. Web. Accessed 3 March 2012.

Agtuca, Jacqueline. 2008. 'Beloved Women: Life Givers, Caretakers, Teachers of Future Generations.' *Sharing Our Stories of Survival: Native Women Surviving Violence*. Eds Sarah Deer, Bonnie Clairmont, Carrie A. Martell, and Maureen L. White Eagle. New York: Altamira, 3–37. Print.

Ahmed, Sara. 2007. 'A Phenomenology of Whiteness.' *Feminist Theory* 8.2: 149–68. Print.

Alcoff, Linda Martín. 1998. 'What Should White People Do?' *Hypatia* 13.3: 6–26. Print.

Aldrich, Elizabeth Kaspar. 1988. '"The Children of These Fathers": The Origins of an Autobiographical Tradition in America.' *First Person Singular: Studies in American Autobiography*. Ed. A. Robert Lee. London: Vision, 115–36. Print.

Andersen, Margaret L. 1991. 'Feminism and the American Family Ideal.' *Journal of Comparative Family Studies* 22.2: 235–46. Print.

Anderson, Benedict. 1991. *Imagined Communities: Reflections on the Origin and Spread of Nationalism*. London: Verso. Print.

Anderson, Eric Gary. 2000. 'States of Being in the Dark: Removal and Survival in Linda Hogan's *Mean Spirit*.' *Great Plains Quarterly* 20.1: 55–67. Print.

Anderson, Karen. 1991. 'African American Families.' *American Families: A Research Guide and Historical Handbook*. Eds Joseph M. Hawes and Elizabeth I. Nybakken. New York: Greenwood, 259–90. Print.

Anderson, Perry. 2011. 'From Progress to Catastrophe: Perry Anderson on the Historical Novel.' *London Review of Books* 28 July: 24–8. Print.

Appadurai, Arjun. 1996. *Modernity at Large: Cultural Dimensions of Globalization*. Minneapolis: University of Minnesota Press. Print.

Apte, Poornima. '*Extremely Loud and Incredibly Close*.' *Mostly Fiction*. MostlyFiction.com. http://mostlyfiction.com/contemp/foer.htm. Web. Accessed 10 February 2010.

Ariès, Philippe. 1962. *Centuries of Childhood: A Social History of Family Life*. New York: Vintage. Print.

Arnold, Ellen L. 2007. 'Through the Mirror: Re-Surfacing and Self-Articulation in Linda Hogan's *Solar Storms*.' *Cultural Sites of Critical Insight: Philosophy, Aesthetics, and African American and Native American Women's Writings*. Eds Angela L. Cotten and Christa Davis Acampora. Albany: State University of New York Press, 85–104. Print.

Ashby, Leroy. 1997. *Endangered Children: Dependency, Neglect and Abuse in American History*. New York: Twayne. Print.

Askeland, Lori, ed. 2006. *Children and Youth in Adoption, Orphanages, and Foster Care: A Historical Handbook and Guide*. Westport: Greenwood. Print.

Babb, Valerie. 2011. '*E Pluribus Unum*? The American Origins Narrative in Toni Morrison's *A Mercy*.' *MELUS* 36.2: 147–64. Print.

Bachinger, Katrina E. 1986. 'The Tao of *Housekeeping*: Reconnoitering the Utopian Ecological Frontier in Marilynne Robinson's "Feminist" Novel.' *Opening Up Literary Criticism: Essays on Prose and Poetry*. Ed. Leo Truchlar. Salzburg: Verlag Wolfgang Neugebauer. Print.

Bakhtin, M.M. 1981. 'Discourse in the Novel.' *The Dialogic Imagination*. Ed. Michael Holquist. Trans. Caryl Emerson and Michael Holquist. Austin: University of Texas Press, 259–422. Print.

—— 1984. *Problems of Dostoevsky's Poetics*. Ed. and trans. Caryl Emerson. Manchester: Manchester University Press. Print.

'Barbara Kingsolver.' 1988. *New York Times Book Review* 10 April: 15. Web. Accessed 15 October 2009. Print.

Bataille, Gretchen M. ed. 2001. *Native American Representations: First Encounters, Distorted Images, and Literary Appropriations*. Lincoln: University of Nebraska Press, Print.

—— and Charles L.P. Silet, eds. 1980. *The Pretend Indians: Images of Native Americans in the Movies*. Ames: Iowa State University Press. Print.

Baym, Nina. 1993. *Woman's Fiction: A Guide to Novels by and about Women in America 1820–70*. 2nd edn. Urbana: University of Illinois Press. Print.

Beaulieu, Elizabeth Ann. 1999. *Black Women Writers and the American Neo-Slave Narrative: Femininity Unfettered*. Westport: Greenwood. Print.

Bell, Bernard W. 1987. *The Afro-American Novel and Its Tradition*. Amherst: University of Massachusetts Press. Print.

Bensen, Robert, ed. 2001. *Children of the Dragonfly: Native American Voices on Child Custody and Education*. Tucson: The University of Arizona Press. Print.

Bloom, Allan. 1987. *The Closing of the American Mind*. New York: Simon. Print.

Bloom, Harold. 1994. *The Western Canon: The Books and School of the Ages*. New York: Harcourt. Print.

Bolaki, Stella. 2011. *Unsettling the Bildungsroman: Reading Contemporary Ethnic American Women's Fiction*. Amsterdam: Rodopi. Print.

Booth, Alison. 2002. 'Neo-Victorian Self-Help, or Cider House Rules.' *American Literary History* 14.2: 284–310. Muse. Web. Accessed 3 October 2011.

Bouvier, Tracey M. 2006. 'Examining the Interpretation and Application of the Indian Child Welfare Act of 1978.' *Native Americans and the Criminal Justice System*. Eds Jeffrey Ian Ross and Larry Gould. Boulder: Paradigm, 103–16. Print.

Braendlin, Bonnie Hoover. 1983. '*Bildung* in Ethnic Women Writers.' *Denver Quarterly* 17.4: 75–87. Print.

Bravmann, Scott. 1997. *Queer Fictions of the Past: History, Culture, and Difference*. Cambridge: Cambridge University Press. Print.

Breinig, Helmbrecht, ed. 2003. *Imaginary (Re-)Locations: Tradition, Modernity, and the Market in Contemporary Native American Literature and Culture*. Tübingen: Stauffenburg. Print.

Briggs, Laura. 2012. *Somebody's Children: The Politics of Transracial Adoption*. Durham: Duke University Press. Print.

Brinks, Ellen, and Lee Talley. 1996. 'Unfamiliar Ties: Lesbian Constructions of Home and Family in Jeanette Winterson's *Oranges Are Not the Only Fruit* and Jewelle Gomez's *The Gilda Stories*' *Homemaking: Women Writers and the Politics and Poetics of Home*. Eds Catherine Wiley and Fiona R. Barnes. New York: Garland, 145–71. Print.

Brooks, Peter. 1984. *Reading for the Plot: Design and Intention in Narrative*. Oxford: Clarendon. Print.

Brown, Gillian. 2002. 'Litigious Therapeutics: Recovering the Rights of Children.' *The Futures of American Studies*. Eds Donald E. Pease and Robyn Wiegman. Durham: Duke University Press, 371–86. Print.

Brown, John Gregory. 1996. *The Wrecked Blessed Body of Shelton LaFleur*. London: Sceptre. Print.

Buckley, Jerome Hamilton. 1974. *Season of Youth: The Bildungsroman from Dickens to Golding*. Cambridge, MA: Harvard University Press. Print.

Butler, Jack. 1988. 'She Hung the Moon and Plugged in All the Stars.' *New York Times* 10 April. http://www.nytimes.com/books/98/10/18/specials/kingsolver-bean.html. Web. Accessed 10 April 2012.

Butler, Octavia. 1980a. 'Future Forum.' *Future Life* 17: 60. Print.

—— 1980b. 'Sci-Fi Visions: An Interview with Octavia Butler.' Interview by Rosalie G. Harrison. *Equal Opportunity Magazine* November. Reprinted in *Conversations with Octavia Butler*. Ed. Consuela Francis. 2009. Jackson: University Press of Mississippi, 3–9. Print.

—— 1996. '"We Keep Playing the Same Record": A Conversation with Octavia E. Butler.' Interview by Stephen W. Potts. *Science-Fiction Studies* 23.3: 331–8. Print.

—— 2004. 'Interview: Octavia E. Butler.' Interview by John C. Snider. *SciFiDimensions*. Web. Reprinted in *Conversations with Octavia Butler*. Ed. Consuela Francis. 2009. Jackson: University Press of Mississippi, 213–18. Print.

—— 2007 [2005]. *Fledgling*. New York: Warner. Print.

Cain, Caleb. 2005. 'Fine Specimen.' *New York Magazine* 5 June. http://nymag.com/nymetro/arts/books/reviews/11940/Web. Accessed 19 October 2009.

Callahan, Cynthia. 2011. *Kin of Another Kind: Transracial Adoption in American Literature*. Ann Arbor: University of Michigan Press. Print.

Campbell, Josie P. *John Irving: A Critical Companion*. Westport: Greenwood, 1998. Print.

Cantiello, Jessica Wells. 2011. 'From Pre-Racial to Post-Racial? Reading and Reviewing *A Mercy* in the Age of Obama.' *MELUS* 36.2: 165–84. Print.

Carby, Hazel V. 1987. *Reconstructing Womanhood: The Emergence of the Afro-American Woman Novelist*. Oxford: Oxford University Press, Print.

—— 1989. 'Ideologies of Black Folk: The Historical Novel of Slavery.' *Slavery and the Literary Imagination*. Eds Deborah E. McDowell and Arnold Rampersad. Baltimore: Johns Hopkins University Press, 125–43. Print.

—— 2003. 'Figuring the Future in Los(t) Angeles.' *Comparative American Studies* 1.1: 19–34. Print.

Carr, A.A. 1995. *Eye Killers*. Norman: University of Oklahoma Press. Print.

Carter, Margaret L. 2004. *Different Blood: The Vampire as Alien*. n.p. [USA]: Amber Quill. Print.

Carter, Vernon B. 2009. 'Prediction of Placement into Out-of-Home Care for American Indian/Alaskan Natives Compared to Non-Indians.' *Children and Youth Services Review* 31: 840–6. Print.

—— 2010. 'Factors Predicting Placement of Urban American Indian/Alaskan Natives into Out-of-Home Care.' *Children and Youth Services Review* 32: 657–63. Print.

Casper, Lynne M. and Suzanne M. Bianchi. 2002. *Continuity and Change in the American Family.* Thousand Oaks: Sage. Print.

Castañeda, Claudia. 2002. *Figurations: Child, Bodies, Worlds.* Durham: Duke University Press. Print.

—— 2010. 'Incorporating the Transnational Adoptee.' *Imagining Adoption: Essays on Literature and Culture.* Ed. Marianne Novy. Ann Arbor: University of Michigan Press, 277–99. Print.

Castiglia, Christopher. 1996. *Bound and Determined: Captivity, Culture-Crossing, and White Womanhood from Mary Rowlandson to Patty Hearst.* Chicago: University of Chicago Press. Print.

Castor, Laura. 2006. 'Claiming Place in Wor(l)ds: Linda Hogan's *Solar Storms*.' *MELUS* 31.2: 157–80. Print.

Caver, Christine. 1996. 'Nothing Left to Lose: *Housekeeping*'s Strange Freedoms.' *American Literature* 68.1: 111–37. Print.

Chapman, Mary and Glenn Hendler. 1999. *Sentimental Men: Masculinity and the Politics of Affect in American Culture.* Berkeley: University of California Press. Print.

Child, Brenda. 2000. *Away From Home: American Indian Boarding School Experiences, 1879–2000.* Phoenix: Heard Museum. Print.

Clarke, Deborah. 2004. 'Domesticating the Car: Women's Road Trips.' *Studies in American Fiction* 32.1: 101–27. Print.

Clayton, Jay. 1993. *The Pleasures of Babel: Contemporary American Literature and Theory.* New York: Oxford University Press.

Clemons, Walter. 1985. 'Dr. Larch's Odd Orphanage.' *Newsweek.* 27 May: 80. Print.

Coffey, Michael. 1998. 'Michael Cunningham: New Family Outings.' *Publishers Weekly* 245.44: 53–5. Print.

Cogan, Frances B. 1989. *All-American Girl: The Ideal of Real Womanhood in Mid-Nineteenth-Century America.* Athens: University of Georgia Press. Print.

Collins, Patricia Hill. 1998. 'It's All in the Family: Intersections of Gender, Race, and Nation.' *Hypatia* 13.3: 62–82. Print.

—— 2000. *Black Feminist Thought: Knowledge, Consciousness, and the Politics of Empowerment.* 2nd edn. New York: Routledge. Print.

—— 2005. *Black Sexual Politics: African Americans, Gender, and the New Racism.* New York: Routledge. Print.

Coltelli, Laura, ed. 2007. *Reading Leslie Marmon Silko: Critical Perspectives through Gardens in the Dunes.* Pisa: Pisa University Press. Print.

Cook, Barbara J. 2003. 'Hogan's Historical Narratives: Bringing to Visibility the Interrelationship of Humanity and the Natural World.' *From the Center of Tradition: Critical Perspective on Linda Hogan.* Ed. Barbara J. Cook. Boulder: University Press of Colorado, 35–52. Print.

Cook, Jeanne F. 1995. 'A History of Placing: The Orphan Trains.' *Child Welfare* 74: 181–97. Print.

Coontz, Stephanie. 2000. *The Way We Never Were: American Families and the Nostalgia Trap.* 2nd edn. New York: Basic. Print.

—— 2008. Introduction. *American Families: A Multicultural Reader.* Eds Maya Parson and Gabrielle Raley. 2nd edn. New York: Routledge. Print.

—— Maya Parson, and Gabrielle Raley, eds. 2008. *American Families: A Multicultural Reader.* 2nd edn. New York: Routledge. Print.

Cunningham, Michael. 2006 [2005]. *Specimen Days.* New York: Harper. Print.

Davidson, Cathy N. and Jessamyn Hatcher, eds. 2002. *No More Separate Spheres! A Next Generation American Studies Reader.* Durham: Duke University Press. Print.

Davis, David Brion. 2008. *Inhuman Bondage: The Rise and Fall of Slavery in the New World.* Oxford: Oxford University Press. Print.

Davis, Todd F. and Kenneth Womack. 2004. *The Critical Response to John Irving.* London: Praeger. Print.

de Groot, Jerome. 2010. *The Historical Novel.* Abingdon: Routledge. Print.

Deloria, Vine, Jr. 1980a. 'American Fantasy.' Foreword. *The Pretend Indians: Images of Native Americans in the Movies.* Eds Gretchen M. Bataille and Charles L.P. Silet. Ames: Iowa State University Press, ix–xvi. Print.

—— 1980b. 'The American Indian Image in North America.' *The Pretend Indians: Images of Native Americans in the Movies.* Eds Gretchen M. Bataille and Charles L.P. Silet. Ames: Iowa State University Press, 46–54. Print.

DeMott, Benjamin. 1985. 'Guilt and Compassion.' *New York Times Book Review* 26 May: 1, 25. Print.

DeRosa, Aaron. 2011. 'Analyzing Literature After 9/11.' *Modern Fiction Studies* 57.3: 607–18. Print.

Derounian-Stodola, Kathryn Zabelle and James Arthur Levernier. 1993. *The Indian Captivity Narrative, 1550–1900.* New York: Twayne. Print.

Doan, Laura and Sarah Waters. 2000. 'Making Up Lost Time: Contemporary Lesbian Writing and the Invention of History.' *Territories of Desire in Queer Culture: Reconfiguring Contemporary Boundaries.* Eds David Alderson and Linda Anderson. Manchester: Manchester University Press, 12–28. Print.

Dokoupil, Tony. 2009. 'Raising Katie: What Adopting a White Girl Taught a Black Family about Race in the Obama Era.' *Newsweek* 22 April. *The Daily Beast.* www.newsweek.com/what-adopting-white-girl-taught-one-black-family-77335. Web. Accessed 17 April 2012.

Douglass, Christopher. 2009. *A Geneology of Literary Multiculturalism*. Ithaca: Cornell University Press. Print.

duCille, Ann. 2009. 'Marriage, Family, and Other "Peculiar Institutions" in African-American Literary History.' *American Literary History* 21.3: 604–17. Print.

Duggan, Robert. 2010. 'Ghosts of Gotham: 9/11 Mourning in Patrick McGrath's *Ghost Town* and Michael Cunningham's *Specimen Days*.' *Journal of Postcolonial Writing* 46.3–4: 381–93. Print.

DuPlessis, Rachel Blau. 1985. *Writing Beyond the Ending: Narrative Strategies of Twentieth-Century Women Writers*. Bloomington: Indiana University Press. Print.

Duthu, N. Bruce. 2008. *American Indians and the Law*. New York: Penguin. Print.

Duvall, John N. and Robert P. Marzec. 2011. 'Narrating 9/11.' *Modern Fiction Studies* 57.3: 381–400. Print.

Dyer, Richard. 1988. 'Children of the Night: Vampirism as Homosexuality, Homosexuality as Vampirism.' *Sweet Dreams: Sexuality, Gender and Popular Fiction*. Ed. Susannah Radstone. London: Lawrence, 47–72. Print.

—— 1997. *White: Essays on Race and Culture*. London: Routledge. Print.

Ehrenreich, Barbara, and Arlie Hochschild, eds. 2003. *Global Woman: Nannies, Maids, and Sex Workers in the New Economy*. New York: Metropolitan. Print.

Erdrich, Louise. 1990 [1984]. *Love Medicine*. London: Abacus. Print.

Erll, Astrid. 2010. 'Cultural Memory Studies: An Introduction.' *A Companion to Cultural Memory Studies*. Eds Erll Astrid and Ansgar Nünning. Berlin: De Gruyter, 1–15. Print.

—— 2011. 'Locating Family in Cultural Memory Studies.' *Journal of Contemporary Family Studies* 42.3: 303–18. Academic Search Elite. Web. Accessed 24 October 2011.

—— and Ansgar Nünning, eds. 2010. *A Companion to Cultural Memory Studies*. Berlin: De Gruyter. Print.

—— and Ann Rigney. 2006. 'Literature and the Production of Cultural Memory: Introduction.' *European Journal of English Studies* 10.2: 111–15. Academic Search Elite. Web. Accessed 15 May 2011.

Ernest, John. 2007. 'Beyond Douglass and Jacobs.' *The Cambridge Companion to the African American Slave Narrative*. Ed. Audrey Fisch. Cambridge: Cambridge University Press, 218–31. Print.

Estes, Steve. 2005. *I Am a Man: Race, Manhood, and the Civil Rights Movement*. Chapel Hill: University of North Carolina Press. Print.

Evan B. Donaldson Adoption Institute. 2008. *Finding Families for African American Children: The Role of Race and Law in Adoption from Foster Care: Policy and Practice Perspective*. The Evan B. Donaldson Adoption Institute. www.adoptioninstitute.org/research/2008_05_mepa.php. Web. Accessed 10 June 2009.

Fabi, Giulia M. 2012. 'Desegregating the Future: Sutton E. Griggs' *Pointing the Way* and American Utopian Fiction in the Age of Jim Crow.' *American Literary Realism* 44.2: 113–32. *Muse*. Web. Accessed 12 Apr. 2013.

Fagan, Kristina. 2001. 'Adoption as National Fantasy in Barbara Kingsolver's *Pigs in Heaven* and Margaret Laurence's *The Diviners*.' *Imagining Adoption: Essays on Literature and Culture*. Ed. Marianne Novy. Ann Arbor: University of Michigan Press, 251–66. Print.

Faludi, Susan. 2007. *The Terror Dream: Fear and Fantasy in Post-9/11 America*. New York: Metropolitan. Print.

Fanshel, David. 1972. *Far from the Reservation: The Transracial Adoption of American Indian Children*. Mutuchen: Scarecrow Press. Print.

Farrell, Betty G. 1999. *Family: The Making of an Idea, an Institution, and a Controversy in American Culture*. Boulder: Westview. Print.

Fergus, Charles. 1991. *Shadow Catcher*. New York: Soho. Print.

Ferguson, Rebecca. 2011. 'Of Snakes and Men: Toni and Slade Morrison's and Pascal Lemaître's Adaptations of Aesop in *Who's Got Game?*' *MELUS* 36.2: 53–70. Print.

Festinger, Trudy. 1983. *No One Ever Asked Us …: A Postscript on Foster Care*. New York: Columbia University Press. Print.

Fiedler, Leslie. 1962. A. *Love and Death in the American Novel*. Cleveland: Meridian. Print.

—— 1972. *The Return of the Vanishing American*. London: Paladin. Print.

Fisher-Wirth, Ann. 2003. 'Storied Earth, Storied Lives: Linda Hogan's *Solar Storms* and Rick Bass's *The Sky, the Stars, the Wilderness*.' *From the Center of Tradition: Critical Perspectives on Linda Hogan*. Ed. Barbara J. Cook. Boulder: University Press of Colorado, 53–66. Print.

Fishkin, Shelley Fisher. 1995. 'Interrogating "Whiteness," Complicating "Blackness": Remapping American Culture.' *American Quarterly* 47.3: 428–66. Print.

Flood, Renée Sansom. 1998. *Lost Bird of Wounded Knee*. New York: Da Capo. Print.

Foer, Jonathan Safran. 2006 [2005]. *Extremely Loud and Incredibly Close*. London: Penguin. Print.

Foster, Thomas. 1988. 'History, Critical Theory, and Women's Social Practices: "Women's Time" and *Housekeeping*.' *Signs: Journal of Women in Culture and Society* 14.1: 73–99. Print.

Fowler, Connie May. 1997. *Before Women Had Wings*. London: Black Swan. Print.

Francis, Consuela, ed. 2009. *Conversations with Octavia Butler*. Jackson: University Press of Mississippi. Print.

Frankenberg, Ruth. 1993. *White Women, Race Matters: The Social Construction of Whiteness*. London: Routledge. Print.

Franklin, Sarah and Susan McKinnon, eds. 2001. *Relative Values: Reconfiguring Kinship Studies*. Durham: Duke. Print.
Froehlich, Peter Alan, and Joy Harris Philpott. 2001. 'Leslie Marmon Silko's *Ceremony*: A Different Kind of Captivity Narrative.' *Paradoxa* 15: 98–113. Print.
Fuderer, Laura Sue. 1990. *The Female Bildungsroman in English: An Annotated Bibliography of Criticism*. New York: MLA. Print.
Fulton, DoVeanna S. 2006. *Speaking Power: Black Feminist Orality in Women's Narratives of Slavery*. Albany: State University of New York Press. Print.
Gailey, Christine Ward. 2006. '"Whatever They Think of Us, We're a Family": Single Mother Adopters.' *Adoptive Families in a Diverse Society*. Ed. Katarina Wegar. New Brunswick: Rutgers University Press. 162–74. Print.
Gates, Henry Louis, Jr. 1988. *The Signifying Monkey: A Theory of Afro-American Literary Criticism*. New York: Oxford University Press. Print.
—— 1997. 'Parable of the Talents.' *The Future of the Race*. Henry Louis Gates, Jr. and Cornel West. New York: Vintage, 1–52. Print.
Gautreaux, Tim. 2010 [2009]. *The Missing*. London: Sceptre. Print.
Gelder, Ken. 1994. *Reading the Vampire*. London: Routledge. Print.
Gernes, Sonia. 1991. 'Transcendent Women: Uses of the Mystical in Margaret Atwood's *Cat's Eye* and Marilynne Robinson's *Housekeeping*.' *Religion and Literature* 23.3: 143–65. Print.
Geyh, Paula E. 1993. 'Burning Down the House? Domestic Space and Feminine Subjectivity in Marilynne Robinson's *Housekeeping*.' *Contemporary Literature* 34.1: 103–22. Print.
Gibbons, Kaye. *Ellen Foster*. 1990 [1987]. New York: Vintage. Print.
—— 2006. *The Life All Around Me by Ellen Foster*. Orlando: Harcourt. Print.
Goddu, Teresa A. 1999. 'Vampire Gothic.' *American Literary History* 11.1: 125–41. Print.
Godfrey, Kathleen. 2001. 'Barbara Kingsolver's Cherokee Nation: Problems of Representation in *Pigs in Heaven*.' *Western American Literature* 36.3: 259–77. Print.
Goldberg, David Theo. 2004 [1994]. 'Introduction: Multicultural Conditions.' *Multiculturalism: A Critical Reader*. Ed. David Theo Goldberg. Oxford: Blackwell, 1–41. Print.
Gomez, Jewelle. 1986. 'Black Women Heroes: Here's Reality, Where's the Fiction?' *The Black Scholar* 17 (March–April): 8–13. Print.
—— 1991. *The Gilda Stories*. London: Sheba. Print.
—— 1993. 'Speculative Fiction and Black Lesbians.' *Signs* 18.4: 948–55. ProQuest Direct Complete. Web. Accessed 30 December 2010.
—— 1997. 'Recasting the Mythology: Writing Vampire Fiction.' *Blood Read: The Vampire as Metaphor in Contemporary Culture*. Eds Joan Gordon and Veronica Hollinger. Philadelphia: University of Pennsylvania Press, 85–92. Print.

Gordon, Joan. 1988. 'Rehabilitating Revenants, or Sympathetic Vampires in Recent Fiction.' *Extrapolation* 29.3: 227–34. Print.

Gordon-Reed, Annette. 1997. *Thomas Jefferson and Sally Hemmings: An American Controversy.* Charlottesville: University of Virginia Press. Print.

Gould, Phillip. 2007. 'The Rise, Development, and Circulation of the Slave Narrative.' *The Cambridge Companion to the African American Slave Narrative.* Ed. Audrey Fisch. Cambridge: Cambridge University Press, 11–27. Print.

Govan, Sandra Y. 2005/2006. '*Fledgling.*' *Obsidian III* 6.2/7.1: 40–3. *ProQuest Direct Complete.* Web. Accessed 31 December 2010.

Grabes, Herbert. 2010. 'Cultural Memory and the Literary Canon.' *A Companion to Cultural Memory Studies.* Eds Astrid Erll and Ansgar Nünning. Berlin: De Gruyter, 311–20. Print.

Gray, Paul. 1985. "An Orphan or an Abortion." *Time* 3 June: 81.

Grayson, Sandra M. 2003. *Visions of the Third Millennium: Black Science Fiction Novelists Write the Future.* Trenton: Africa World Press, Print.

Griffin, Edward M. 1986. 'Women in Trouble: The Predicament of Captivity and the Narratives of Mary Rowlandson, Mary Jemison, and Hannah Duncan.' *Opening Up Literary Criticism: Essays on American Prose and Poetry.* Ed. Leo Truchlar. Salzburg: Verlag Wolfgang Neugebauer, 41–51. Print.

Griswold, Jerry. 1992. *Audacious Kids: Coming of Age in America's Classic Children's Books.* New York: Oxford University Press. Print.

Guillen, Claudio. 1971. 'Toward a Definition of the Picaresque.' *Toward a Theory of Literary History.* Princeton: Princeton University Press, 71–106. Print.

H. Res. 194. 2008. *GovTrack.us.* Civic Impulse. www.govtrack.us/congress/bills/110/hres194/text. Web. Accessed 3 March 2012.

Hacking, Ian. 1991. 'The Making and Molding of Child Abuse.' *Critical Inquiry* 17.2: 253–88. Print.

Hacsi, Timothy. *Second Home: Orphan Asylums and Poor Families in America.* Cambridge: Harvard University Press, 1997. Print.

Halbwachs, Maurice. 1992. *On Collective Memory.* Ed. and trans. Lewis A. Coser. Chicago: University of Chicago Press. Print.

Hall, Joanne. 2006. 'The Wanderer Contained: Issues of "Inside" and "Outside" in Relation to Harold Gray's *Little Orphan Annie* and Marilynne Robinson's *Housekeeping.*' *Critical Survey* 18.3: 37–50. Print.

Hampton, Gregory Jerome. 2010. *Changing Bodies in the Fiction of Octavia Butler: Slaves, Aliens, and Vampires.* Lanham: Lexington. Print.

Haraway, Donna J. 1991. *Simians, Cyborgs, and Women: The Reinvention of Nature.* New York: Routledge. Print.

——— 1997. *Modest_Witness@Second_Millennium.FemaleMan©_Meets_OncoMouse™: Feminism and Technoscience.* New York: Routledge. Print.

Harde, Roxanne. 2008. '"One extra little girl": Elizabeth Stuart Phelps's Orphans.' *Enterprising Youth: Social Values and Acculturation in Nineteenth-Century Children's Literature*. Ed. Monika Elbert. New York: Routledge, 55–66. Print.
Harris, Trudier. 1984. *Exorcising Blackness: Historical and Literary Lynchings and Burning Rituals*. Bloomington: Indiana University Press. Print.
Hawes, Joseph M. and Elizabeth I. Nybakken, eds. 2001. *Family and Society in American History*. Urbana: University of Illinois Press. Print.
Hawkins-León, Cynthia G. 1997–98. 'The Indian Child Welfare Act and the African American Tribe: Facing the Adoption Crisis.' *Brandeis Journal of Family Law* 36: 201–18. Print.
Heller, Dana A. 1990. *The Feminization of the Quest-Romance: Radical Departures*. Austin: University of Texas Press. Print.
Herman, Judith Lewis. 1992. *Trauma and Recovery*. New York: Basic. Print.
—— 2000. *Father-Daughter Incest*. Cambridge: Harvard University Press. Print.
Himmelwright, Catherine. 2007. 'Gardens of Auto Parts: Kingsolver's Merger of American Western Myth and Native American Myth in *The Bean Trees*.' *Southern Literary Journal* 39.2: 119–39. Print.
Hogan, Linda. 1995a. *Dwellings: A Spiritual History of the Living World*. New York: Simon. Print.
—— 1995b. *Solar Storms*. New York: Scribner. Print.
—— 1999 [1998]. *Power*. New York: Norton. Print.
—— 2002 [2001]. *The Woman Who Watches Over the World*. New York: Norton, Print.
Hollinger, David. 1995. *Postethnic America: Beyond Multiculturalism*. New York: Harper Collins. Print.
Holt, Marilyn Irvin. 1994. *Orphan Trains: Placing Out in America*. Lincoln: University of Nebraska Press. Print.
—— 2001. *Indian Orphanages*. Lawrence: University Press of Kansas. Print.
Howard, June. 2001. *Publishing the Family*. Durham: Duke University Press. Print.
Howell, Signe. 2007. *The Kinning of Foreigners: Transnational Adoption in a Global Perspective*. Oxford: Berghahn. Print.
Huhndorf, Shari M. 2001. *Going Native: Indians in the American Cultural Imagination*. Ithaca: Cornell University Press. Print.
—— 2009. *Mapping the Americas: the Transnational Politics of Contemporary Native Culture*. Ithaca: Cornell University Press. Print.
Indian Child Welfare Act. 1978. Pub.L. 95-608. 93 Stat. 3069. 8 November. www.dshs.wa.gov/pdf/ca/ICWActof1978.pdf. Web. Accessed 4 June 2013.
Indian Child Welfare Program. Committee on Interior and Insular Affairs. 1974. Senate. 8–9 April, iv–531. *Native American Rights Fund*. www.narf.org/icwa/federal/lh.htm. Web. Accessed 1 May 2013.

Ingersoll, Earl J. 2009. 'One Boy's Passage, and his Nation's: Jonathan Safran Foer's *Extremely Loud and Incredibly Close*.' *CEA Critic* 71.3: 54–69. Print.
Irving, John. 1991 [1985]. *The Cider House Rules*. London: Black Swan. Print.
—— 1999. *My Movie Business: A Memoir*. New York: Random House. Print.
Isernhagen, Hartwig. 2003. 'From Identity to Exchange? Some Remarks on the Discursive Construction of Ethno-Cultural Difference and on Leslie Marmon Silko's *Gardens in the Dunes*.' *Imaginary (Re-)Locations: Tradition, Modernity, and the Market in Contemporary Native American Literature and Culture*. Ed. Helmbrecht Breinig. Tübingen: Stauffenburg, 107–37. Print.
Ivey, Eowyn. 2012. *The Snow Child*. New York: Reagan Arthur. Print.
Jacobs, Margaret D. 2006. 'Indian Boarding Schools in Comparative Perspective: The Removal of Indigenous Children in the United States and Australia, 1880–1940.' *Boarding School Blues: Revisiting American Indian Educational Experiences*. Eds Clifford E. Trafzer, Jean A. Keller, and Lerene Sisquoc. Lincoln: University of Nebraska Press, 188–231. Print.
Jacobson, Matthew Frye. 1999. *Whiteness of a Different Color: European Immigrants and the Alchemy of Race*. Cambridge: Harvard University Press. Print.
Jain, Priya. 2005. '*Extremely Loud and Incredibly Close* by Jonathan Safran Foer.' *Salon*. 20 March. www.salon.com/2005/03/20/foer_2/. Web. Accessed 4 November 2013.
Japtok, Martin. 2005. *Growing up Ethnic: Nationalism and the Bildungsroman in African American and Jewish American Fiction*. Iowa City: University of Iowa Press. Print.
Jay, Gregory S. 1997. *American Literature and the Culture Wars*. Ithaca: Cornell University Press. Print.
Jeffers, Thomas. 2005. *Apprenticeships: The Bildungsroman from Goethe to Santayana*. New York: Palgrave Macmillan. Print.
Jenkins, Candice M. 2007. *Private Lives, Proper Relations: Regulating Black Intimacy*. Minneapolis: University of Minnesota Press. Print.
Jerng, Mark C. 2010. *Claiming Others: Transracial Adoption and National Belonging*. Minneapolis: University of Minnesota Press. Print.
Johnson, Adam. 2012. *The Orphan Master's Son*. New York: Random House. Print.
Jones, Miriam. 1997. '*The Gilda Stories*: Revealing the Monsters at the Margins.' *Blood Read: The Vampire as Metaphor in Contemporary Culture*. Eds Jordan Gordon and Veronica Hollinger. Philadelphia: University of Pennsylvania Press. 151–67. Print.
Jordan, Don and Michael Walsh. 2007. *White Cargo: The Forgotten History of Britain's White Slaves in America*. New York: New York University Press. Print.
Justice, Daniel Heath. 2008. '"Go Away, Water!": Kinship Criticism and the Decolonization Imperative.' *Reasoning Together: The Native Critics*

Collective. Eds Craig Womack, Daniel Heath Justice, and Christopher B. Teuton. Norman: University of Oklahoma Press, 147–68. Print.

Kaivola, Karen. 1993. 'The Pleasures and Perils of Merging: Female Subjectivity in Marilynne Robinson's *Housekeeping*.' *Contemporary Literature* 34: 670–90. Print.

Kakutani, Michiko. 2005. 'A Poet as Guest at a Party of Misfits.' *New York Times Book Review*. 14 June. www.nytimes.com/2005/06/14/books/14kaku.html?_r=0. Web. Accessed 18 October 2010.

Kalaidjian, Walter. 2007. 'Incoming: Globalization, Disaster, Poetics.' *South Atlantic Quarterly* 106.4: 825–48. Print.

Kan, Sergei. 2001. Editor's Introduction. *Strangers to Relatives: The Adoption and Naming of Anthropologists in Native North American*. Ed. Sergei Kan. Lincoln: University of Nebraska Press, 1–10. Print.

Kella, Elizabeth. 2000. *Beloved Communities: Solidarity and Difference in Fiction by Michael Ondaatje, Toni Morrison, and Joy Kogawa*. Uppsala: Uppsala University. Print.

Kephart, Beth. 2005. 'Foer scores again with boy's touching, hilarious journey.' *Baltimore Sun*. 10 April. Print.

Keunen, Bart. 2000. 'Cultural Thematics and Cultural Memory: Towards a Socio-Cultural Approach to Literary Themes.' *Methods for the Study of Literature as Cultural Memory*. Eds Raymond Vervliet and Annemarie Estor. Amsterdam: Rodopi. Print.

Kidd, Sue Monk. 2002. *The Secret Life of Bees*. New York: Viking. Print.

Kimmel, Michael. 2006. *Manhood in America: A Cultural History*. 2nd edn. New York: Oxford University Press. Print.

Kincaid, James. 1998. *Erotic Innocence: The Culture of Child Molesting*. Durham: Duke University Press. Print.

King, Kristin. 1996. 'Resurfacings of the Deeps: Semiotic Balance in Marilynne Robinson's *Housekeeping*.' *Studies in the Novel* 28.4: 565–80. Print.

Kingsolver, Barbara. 1989 [1988]. *The Bean Trees*. London: Abacus. Print.

—— 1993. 'Barbara Kingsolver.' Interview by Donna Perry. *Backtalk: Women Writers Speak Out*. New Brunswick: Rutgers University Press, 143–69. Print.

—— 2007 [1993]. *Pigs in Heaven*. London: Faber. Print.

Kornfeld, Eve and Susan Jackson. 1987. 'The Female Bildungsroman in Nineteenth-Century America: Parameters of a Vision.' *Journal of American Culture* 10.4: 69–75. Print.

Kramer, Hilton. 1985. 'Abortion Gets the Best-Seller Treatment'. *Wall Street Journal* 15 July. Print.

Krupat, Arnold. 2002. 'The 'Rage Stage': Contextualizing Sherman Alexie's *Indian Killer*.' *Red Matters: Native American Studies*. Philadelphia: University of Pennsylvania Press, 98–122. Print.

―― 2003. 'Nationalism, Indigenism, Cosmopolitanism: Three Critical Perspectives on Native American Literatures.' *Imaginary (Re-)Locations: Tradition, Modernity, and the Market in Contemporary Native American Literature and Culture*. Ed. Helmbrecht Breinig. Tübingen: Stauffenburg, 87–106. Print.

Kushigan, Julia A. 2003. *Reconstructing Childhood: Strategies of Reading for Culture and Gender in the Spanish Bildungsroman*. London: Associated University Presses. Print.

Lacey, Lauren J. 2008. 'Octavia Butler on Coping with Power in *Parable of the Sower, Parable of the Talents*, and *Fledgling*.' *Critique* 49.4: 379–94. Print.

Lachmann, Renate. 2010. 'Mnemonic and Intertextual Aspects of Literature.' *A Companion to Cultural Memory Studies*. Eds Erll Astrid and Ansgar Nünning. Berlin: De Gruyter, 301–10. Print.

Lampert, Jo. 2010. *Children's Fiction About 9/11: Ethnic, Heroic and National Identities*. New York: Routledge. Print.

Landsberg, Alison. 2004. *Prosthetic Memory: The Transformation of American Remembrance in the Age of Mass Culture*. New York: Columbia University Press. Print.

LaRossa, Ralph. 1997. *The Modernization of Fatherhood: A Social and Political History*. Chicago: University of Chicago Press. Print.

Lassner, Phyllis. 1989. 'Escaping the Mirror of Sameness: Marilynne Robinson's *Housekeeping*.' *Mother Puzzles: Daughters and Mothers in Contemporary American Literature*. Ed. Mickey Pearlman. New York: Greenwood. Print.

Lee, Chang-Rae. 2010. *The Surrendered*. London: Abacus.

Lehr, Valerie. 1999. *Queer Family Values: Debunking the Myth of the Nuclear Family*. Philadelphia: Temple University Press.

Leisy, Ernest E. 1950. *The American Historical Novel*. Norman: University of Oklahoma Press. Print.

Levander, Caroline. 2006. *Cradle of Liberty: Race, the Child, and National Belonging from Thomas Jefferson to W.E.B. Du Bois*. Durham: Duke University Press. Print.

―― 2013. *Where is American Literature?* Chichester: Wiley-Blackwell. Print.

―― and Carol J. Singley, eds. 2005. *The American Child: A Cultural Studies Reader*. New Brunswick: Rutgers University Press. Print.

Levecq, Christine. 2000. 'Power and Repetition: Philosophies of (Literary) History in Octavia E. Butler's *Kindred*.' *Contemporary Literature* 41.3: 525–53. Print.

Levy, Daniel and Natan Sznaider. 2002. 'Memory Unbound: The Holocaust and the Formation of Cosmopolitan Memory.' *European Journal of Social Theory* 5.1: 87–106. Print.

Lewin, Ellen. 2006. 'Family Values: Gay Men and Adoption in America.' *Adoptive Families in a Diverse Society*. Ed. Katarina Wegar. New Brunswick: Rutgers, 129–45. Print.

—— 2009. *Gay Fatherhood: Narratives of Family and Citizenship in America*. Chicago: University of Chicago Press. Print.

Lewis, R.W.B. 1955. *The American Adam: Innocence, Tragedy and Tradition in the Nineteenth Century*. Chicago: University of Chicago Press. Print.

Li, Stephanie. 2012. *Toni Morrison: A Biography*. Santa Barbara: Greenwood. Print.

Lima, Enrique. 2011. 'The Uneven Development of the *Bildungsroman*: D'Arcy McNickle and Native American Modernity.' *Comparative Literature* 63.3: 291–306. Print.

Lionnet, Francoise and Shu-mei Shih. 2005. 'Introduction: Thinking through the Minor, Transnationally.' *Minor Transnationalism*. Eds Francoise Lionnet and Shu-mie Shih. Durham: Duke University Press, 1–15. Print.

Lipsitz, George. 1990. *Time Passages: Collective Memory and American Popular Culture*. Minneapolis: University of Minnesota Press. Print.

Loichot, Valérie. 2007. *Orphan Narratives: The Postplantation Literature of Faulkner, Glissant, Morrison and Saint-John Perse*. Charlottesville: University of Virginia Press. Print.

Lomawaima, K. Tsianina. 1994. *They Called it Prairie Light: The Story of Chilocco Indian School*. Lincoln: University of Nebraska Press. Print.

London, Ross D. 1999. 'The 1994 Orphanage Debate: A Study in the Politics of Annihilation.' *Rethinking Orphanages for the 21st Century*. Ed. Richard McKenzie. Thousand Oaks: Sage, 79–103. Print.

Luckhurst, Roger. 1996. '"Horror and Beauty in Rare Combination": The Miscegenate Fictions of Octavia Butler.' *Women: A Cultural Review* 7.1: 28–38. Print.

—— 1999. 'Memory Recovered/Recovered Memory.' *Literature and the Contemporary: Fictions and Theories of the Present*. Eds Roger Luckhurst and Peter Marks. Harlow: Longman, 80–93. Print.

Lukács, Georg. 1983. *The Historical Novel*. Lincoln: University of Nebraska Press. Print.

MacKenzie, Richard, ed. 1999. *Rethinking Orphanages for the 21st Century*. Thousand Oaks: Sage. Print.

—— 2009. *Home Away from Home*. New York: Encounter, Print.

Makowsky, Veronica. 1992. '"The Only Hard Part Was the Food": Recipes for Self-Nurture in Kaye Gibbons's Novels.' *Southern Quarterly* 30.2–3: 103–12. Print.

Mallon, Anne-Marie. 1989. 'Sojourning Women: Homelessness and Transcendence in *Housekeeping*.' *Critique* 30.2: 95–105. Print.

Mallon, Gerald P. 2004. *Gay Men Choosing Parenthood*. New York: Columbia University Press. Print.

Marsh, Margaret. 1990. *Suburban Lives*. New Brunswick: Rutgers University Press. Print.
McCarthy, Desmond F. 1997. *Reconstructing the Family in Contemporary American Fiction*. New York: Peter Lang. Print.
McDowell, Deborah E. 1995. *'The Changing Same': Black Women's Literature, Criticism, and Theory*. Bloomington: Indiana University Press. Print.
—— 2007. 'Telling Slavery in 'Freedom's' Time: Post-Reconstruction and the Harlem Renaissance.' *The Cambridge Companion to the African American Slave Narrative*. Ed. Audrey A. Fisch. Cambridge: Cambridge University Press, 150–67. Print.
McHugh, Kathleen Anne. 1999. *American Domesticity: From How-to Manual to Hollywood Melodrama*. New York: Oxford University Press. Print.
McRoy, Ruth and Amy Griffin. 2012. 'Transracial Adoption Policies and Practices: The US Experience.' *Adoption and Fostering* 36.3–4: 38–49. Sage Premier. Web. Accessed 1 October 2012.
Melnick, Jeffrey. 2009. *9/11 Culture: America under Construction*. Chichester: Wiley-Blackwell. Print.
Melzer, Patricia. 2006. *Alien Constructions: Science Fiction and Feminist Thought*. Austin: University of Texas Press. Print.
Meyer, Sabine. 2002. 'Passing Perverts, After All? Vampirism (In)Visibility, and the Horrors of the Normative in Jewell Gomez's *The Gilda Stories*.' *FEMSPEC* 4.1: 25–37 [n.p.] ProQuest. Web. Accessed 30 August 2009.
Michael, Magali Cornier. 2006. *New Visions of Community in Contemporary American Fiction: Tan, Kingsolver, Castillo, Morrison*. Iowa City: University of Iowa Press. Print.
Mile, Siân. 1990. 'Femme Foetal: The Construction/Destruction of Female Subjectivity in *Housekeeping*, or Nothing Gained.' *Genders* 8: 127–36. Print.
Millard, Kenneth. 2007. *Coming of Age in Contemporary American Fiction*. Edinburgh: Edinburgh University Press. Print.
Mills, Claudia. 1987. 'Children in Search of a Family: Orphan Novels Through the Century.' *Children's Literature in Education* 18.4: 227–39. Print.
Mintz, Steven. 2004. *Huck's Raft: A History of American Childhood*. Cambridge: Harvard University Press. Print.
Misztal, Barbara A. 2003. *Theories of Social Remembering*. Maidenhead: Open University Press. Print.
Mitchell, Angelyn. 2002. *The Freedom to Remember: Narrative, Slavery, and Gender in Contemporary Black Women's Fiction*. New Brunswick: Rutgers University Press. Print.
Monteith, Sharon. 2000. *Advancing Sisterhood?: Interracial Friendship in Contemporary Southern Fiction*. Athens: University of Georgia Press. Print.
—— 2006. 'The Never-Ending Cycle of Poverty: Sarah E. Wright's *This Child's Gonna Live*.' *Poverty and Progress in the U.S. South after 1920*. Eds Suzanne Jones and Mark Newman. Amsterdam: VU Press, 81–93. Print.

Montgomery. Maxine L. 2011. 'Got on My Traveling Shoes: Migration, Exile, and Home in Toni Morrison's *A Mercy.*' *Journal of Black Studies.* 42.4: 627–37. *Jstor.* Web. Accessed 28 April 2011.

Moore, David L. 2007. 'Ghost Dancing Through History in Silko's *Gardens in the Dunes* and *Almanac of the Dead.*' *Reading Leslie Marmon Silko: Critical Perspectives through Gardens in the Dunes.* Ed. Laura Coltelli. Pisa: Pisa University Press, 91–118. Print.

Moore, Lorrie. 2009. *A Gate at the Stairs.* London: Faber. Print.

Moretti, Franco. 1987. *The Way of the World: The* Bildungsroman *in European Culture.* London: Verso, 1987. Print.

Morrison, Toni. 1977. 'Intimate Things in Place: A Conversation with Toni Morrison.' Interview by Robert Stepto. *Massachusetts Review.* Reprinted in *Conversations with Toni Morrison.* Ed. Danille Taylor-Guthrie. University Press of Mississippi. 1994, 10–29. Print.

—— 1987. *Beloved.* New York: Knopf. Print.

—— 1992. *Playing in the Dark: Whiteness and the Literary Imagination.* Cambridge, MA: Harvard University Press. Print.

—— 1998. 'The Site of Memory.' *Inventing the Truth: The Art and Craft of Memoir.* Ed. William Zinsser. Revised edn. Boston: Mariner, 183–200. Print.

—— 2008a. 'Home.' *The House Race Built.* Ed. Wahneema Lubiano. New York: Vintage. 3–12. Print.

—— 2008b. *A Mercy.* New York: Knopf. Print.

Morson, Gary Saul and Caryl Emerson. 1990. *Mikhail Bakhtin: Creation of a Prosaics.* Stanford: Stanford University Press. Print.

Mousoutzanis, Aris. 2009. 'Uncanny Repetition, Trauma, and Displacement in Michael Cunningham's *Specimen Days.*' *Critical Survey* 21.2: 129–41. Print.

Moynihan, Daniel Patrick. 1965. *The Negro Family: A Case for National Action.* Washington DC: United States Department of Labor, Office of Policy Planning and Research. Print.

Mullins, Matthew. 2009. 'Boroughs and Neighbors: Traumatic Solidarity in Jonathan Safran Foer's *Extremely Loud and Incredibly Close.*' *Papers on Language and Literature* 45.3: 298–324. Print.

Munafo, Giavanna. 1998. '"Colored Biscuits": Reconstructing Whiteness and the Boundaries of "Home" in Kaye Gibbons's *Ellen Foster.*' *Women, America, and Movement.* Ed. Susan L. Roberson. Columbia: University of Missouri Press, 38–61. Print.

Murray, David. 2007. 'Old Comparisons, New Syncretisms and *Gardens in the Dunes.*' *Reading Leslie Marmon Silko: Critical Perspectives through Gardens in the Dunes.* Ed. Laura Coltelli. Pisa: Pisa University Press, 119–31. Print.

Murrey, Loretta Martin. 1994. 'The Loner and the Matriarchal Community in Barbara Kingsolver's *The Bean Trees* and *Pigs in Haven* [sic].' *Southern Studies* 5.1–2: 155–61. Print.

Nealon, Christopher. 2001. *Foundlings: Lesbian and Gay Historical Emotion before Stonewall.* Durham: Duke University Press. Print.
Nelson, Claudia. 2001. 'Drying the Orphan's Tears: Changing Representations of the Dependent Child in America, 1870–1930.' *Children's Literature* 29: 52–70. Print.
—— 2003. *Little Strangers: Portrayals of Adoption and Foster Care in America, 1850–1929.* Bloomington: Indiana University Press. Print.
—— 2006. 'The Orphan in American Children's Literature.' *Children and Youth in Adoption, Orphanages, and Foster Care: A Historical Handbook and Guide.* Ed. Lori Askeland. Westport: Greenwood, 79–91. Print.
Neumann, Birgit. 2010. 'The Literary Representation of Memory.' *A Companion to Cultural Memory Studies.* Eds Astrid Erll and Ansgar Nünning. Berlin: De Gruyter, 333–44. Print.
Newman, Judie. 2007. *Fictions of America: Narratives of Global Empire.* New York: Routledge. Print.
Nora, Pierre. 1989. 'Between Memory and History: Les Lieux de Mèmoire.' Trans. Marc Rodebush. *Representations* 26: 7–25. Print.
Novy, Marianne. 2005. *Reading Adoption: Family and Difference in Fiction and Drama.* Ann Arbor: University of Michigan Press. Print.
—— ed. 2001. *Imagining Adoption: Essays on Literature and Culture.* Ann Arbor: University of Michigan Press. Print.
O'Brien, Sheila Ruzycki. 1993. '*Housekeeping* in the Western Tradition: Remodeling Tales of Western Travelers.' *Women and the Journey: The Female Travel Experience.* Eds Bonnie Fredrick and Susan H. McLeod. Pullman: Washington State University Press, 217–34. Print.
O'Connor, Stephen. 2001. *Orphan Trains: The Story of Charles Loring Brace and the Children He Saved and Failed.* Chicago: University of Chicago Press. Print.
Olasky, Martin. 1999. 'The Rise and Fall of American Orphanages.' *Rethinking Orphanages for the 21st Century.* Ed. Richard MacKenzie. Thousand Oaks: Sage, 65–78. Print.
Omi, Michael and Howard Winant. 1986. *Racial Formation in the United States: From the 1960s to the 1980s.* New York: Routledge. Print.
O'Neale, Sondra. 1982. 'Race, Sex and Self: Aspects of *Bildung* in Select Novels by Black American Novelists.' *MELUS* 9.4: 25–37. Print.
O'Reilly, Andrea Herrera, Elizabeth Mahn Nollen, and Sheila Reitzel Foor, eds. 1997. *Family Matters in the British and American Novel.* Bowling Green: Bowling Green State University Popular Press. Print.
Owens, Louis. 2001. *Mixedblood Messages: Literature, Film, Family, Place.* Norman: University of Oklahoma Press. Print.
Paine, Thomas. *Common Sense.* 2004 [1776]. Ed. Edward Larkin. New York: Broadview. Print.

Palmer, Paulina. 1998. 'Representation of Sisterhood in Lesbian Fiction of the 1980s.' *Sisterhoods: Across the Literature/Media Divide.* Ed. Deborah Cartmell, I.Q. Hunter, Heidi Kaye and Imelda Whelehan. London: Pluto, 81–100. Print.

Patea, Viorica. 2001 'The Myth of the American Adam: A Reassessment.' *Critical Essays on the Myth of the American Adam.* Eds Viorica Patea and María Eugenia Díaz. Salamanca: Ediciones Universidad de Salamanca. Print.

Patterson, Kathy Davis. 2005 '"Haunting Back": Vampire Subjectivity in *The Gilda Stories.*' *FEMSPEC* 6.1: 35–57 [n.p. web]. *ProQuest.* Web. Accessed 30 August 2009.

Patterson, Orlando. 1982. *Slavery and Social Death: A Comparative Study.* Cambridge: Harvard University Press. Print

Pazicky, Diana Loercher. 1998. *Cultural Orphans in America.* Jackson: University Press of Mississippi. Print.

Pearce, Roy Harvey. 1947 . 'The Significances of the Captivity Narrative.' *American Literature* 19.1: 1–20. Print.

Pertman, Adam. 2011. *Adoption Nation.* 2nd edn. Boston: Harvard Common Press. Print.

Peters, Laura. 2000. *Orphan Texts: Victorian Orphans, Culture and Empire.* Manchester: Manchester University Press. Print.

Phillips, Wendell. 1973. 'Letter from Wendell Phillips, Esq.' *Narrative of the Life of Frederick Douglass, An American Slave: Written by Himself.* Frederick Douglass. New York: Doubleday, xxi–xxiv. Print.

Porte, Joel. 1969. *The Romance in America: Studies in Cooper, Poe, Hawthorne, Melville, and James.* Middletown: Wesleyan University Press. Print.

Porter, Laurin. 2003. *Orphan's Home: The Voice and Vision of Horton Foote.* Baton Rouge: Louisiana State University Press. Print.

Prosser, Jay. 2008. Introduction. *American Fictions of the 1990s: Reflections of History and Culture.* Ed. Jay Prosser. New York: Routledge. 1–13. Print.

Ravits, Martha. 1989. 'Extending the American Range: Marilynne Robinson's *Housekeeping.*' *American Literature* 61.4: 644–66. Print.

Regier, A.M. 2005. 'Revolutionary Enunciatory Spaces: Ghost Dancing, Transatlantic Travel, and Modernist Arson in *Gardens in the Dunes.*' *Modern Fiction Studies* 51.1: 134–57. Print.

Ress, Stella. 2010. 'Bridging the Generation Gap: Little Orphan Annie in the Great Depression.' *Journal of Popular Culture* 43.4: 782–800. Print.

Rigney, Ann. 2005. 'Plenitude, Scarcity and the Circulation of Cultural Memory.' *Journal of European Studies* 35.1: 11–28. *Ex Libris SFX.* Web. Accessed 20 April 2011.

Rishoi, Christy. 2003. *From Girl to Woman: American Women's Coming-of-Age Narratives.* Albany: State University of New York Press. Print.

Roberts, Dorothy. 2003. *Shattered Bonds: The Color of Child Welfare*. New York: Basic Civitas. Print.

Robinson, Marilynne. 1982 [1981]. *Housekeeping*. New York: Bantam. Print.

—— 1992. 'Interviews with Marilynne Robinson.' By Tace Hedrick, Eileen Bartos, Carolyn Jacobson and Ann E. Voss. *Iowa Review* 22.1: 1–28. Print.

—— 1993a. Interview by Allan Vorda. *Face to Face: Interviews with Contemporary Novelists*. Ed. Allan Vorda. Houston: Rice University Press. Print.

—— 1993b. 'My Western Roots.' *Old West – New West: Centennial Essays*. Ed. Barbara Howard Meldrum. Moscow, ID: University of Idaho Press. Print.

—— 1994. 'An Interview with Marilynne Robinson.' By Thomas Schaub. *Contemporary Literature* 35.2 (1994): 230–51. Print.

—— 2004. *Gilead*. New York: Farrar, Straus, Giroux. Print.

—— 2005. 'Family.' *The Death of Adam: Essays on Modern Thought*. New York: Picador, 87–107. Print.

—— 2008. *Home*. New York: Farrar, Straus, Giroux. Print.

Rody, Caroline. 2001. *The Daughter's Return: African-American and Caribbean Women's Fictions of History*. Oxford: Oxford University Press. Print.

Romero, Lora. 1997. *Home Fronts: Domesticity and Its Critics in the Antebellum United States*. Durham: Duke University Press. Print.

Rose, Jacqueline. 2005. 'Entryism.' *London Review of Books* 22 September: 25–6. www.lrb.co.uk/v27/n18/jacqueline-rose/entryism. Web. Accessed 26 October 2010.

Rubenstein, Roberta. 1987. *Boundaries of the Self*. Chicago: University of Illinois Press. Print.

Ruoff, A. LaVonne Brown. 2007. 'Leslie Marmon Silko's *Gardens in the Dunes*: Contact Zones and Cross Currents.' *Reading Leslie Marmon Silko: Critical Perspectives through Gardens in the Dunes*. Ed. Laura Coltelli. Pisa: Pisa University Press, 7–20. Print.

Rushdy, Ashraf H.A. 2001. *Remembering Generations: Race and Family in Contemporary African American Fiction*. Chapel Hill: University of North Carolina Press. Print.

Russ, Joanna. 1995. *To Write Like a Woman: Essays in Feminism and Science Fiction*. Bloomington: Indiana University Press. Print.

Ryan, Katy. 2005. 'Horizons of Grace: Marilynne Robinson and Simone Weil.' *Philosophy and Literature* 29.2: 349–64. Muse. Web. Accessed 4 October 2010.

Ryan, Maureen. 1991. 'Marilynne Robinson's *Housekeeping*: The Subversive Narrative and the New American Eve.' *South Atlantic Review* 56.1: 79–86. Print.

Ryan, Terre. 2007. 'The Nineteenth-Century Garden: Imperialism, Subsistence, and Subversion in Leslie Marmon Silko's *Gardens in the Dunes*.' *Studies in American Indian Literatures* 19.3: 115–32. Muse. Web. Accessed 28 May 2012.

Ryan, Tim A. 2008. *Calls and Responses: The American Novel of Slavery since Gone with the Wind*. Baton Rouge: Louisiana State University Press. Print.

Saal, Ilka. 2011. 'Regarding the Pain of Self and Other: Trauma Transfer and Narrative Framing in Jonathan Safran Foer's *Extremely Loud and Incredibly Close*.' *Modern Fiction Studies* 57.3: 453–75. Print.

Sánchez-Eppler, Karen. 2005. *Dependent States: The Child's Part in Nineteenth-Century American Culture*. Chicago: University of Chicago Press. Print.

Sanders, Joe Sutliff. 2008. 'Spinning Sympathy: Orphan Girl Novels and the Sentimental Tradition.' *Children's Literature Association Quarterly* 33.1: 41–61. Muse. Web. Accessed 28 April 2010.

Sapphire. 2011. *The Kid*. New York: Penguin. Print.

Satz, Martha, and Lori Askeland. 2006. 'Civil Rights, Adoption Rights: Domestic Adoption and Foster Care, 1970 to the Present.' *Children and Youth in Adoption, Orphanages, and Foster Care: A Historical Handbook and Guide*. Ed. Lori Askeland. Westport: Greenwood, 45–61. Print.

Seager, Joni. 2003. *The Atlas of Women*. 3rd edn. London: Women's Press. Print.

Seaver, James Everett. 2007 [1824]. *A Narrative of the Life of Mrs Mary Jemison*. n.p.: NuVision Publications. Print.

Shamir, Milette, and Jennifer Travis. 2002. *Boys Don't Cry? Rethinking Narratives of Masculinity and Emotion in the US*. New York: Columbia University Press. Print.

Shanley, Kathryn. 2001a. 'The Indians America Loves to Love and Read: American Indian Identity and Cultural Appropriation.' *Native American Representations: First Encounters, Distorted Images, and Literary Appropriations*. Ed. Gretchen M. Bataille. Lincoln: University of Nebraska Press, 26–51. Print.

—— 2001b 'Metacritical Frames of Reference in Studying American Indian Literature: An Afterword.' *Native American Representations: First Encounters, Distorted Images, and Literary Appropriations*. Ed. Gretchen M. Bataille. Lincoln: University of Nebraska Press, 224–6. Print.

—— 2012. 'The "Savage" Sublime in Novels by A.A. Carr and Joseph Boyden.' *American Indians and Popular Culture: Literature, Arts, and Resistance*. Ed. Elizabeth DeLaney Hoffman. Santa Barbara: Praeger.

Silko, Leslie Marmon. 1992 [1991]. *Almanac of the Dead*. New York: Penguin. Print.

—— 1996. 'The Indian with a Camera.' *Yellow Woman and a Beauty of the Spirit*. New York: Simon and Schuster, 175–9. Print.

—— 2005 [1999]. *Gardens in the Dunes*. New York: Simon and Schuster Paperbacks. Print.

Simpson, Eileen. 1988. *Orphans: Real and Imaginary*. London: Weidenfeld and Nicolson, Print.

'Single Parent Adoptions.' 2007. *The Adoption History Project*. University of Oregon. 7 November. http://pages.uoregon.edu/adoption/topics/singleparentadoptions.htm Web. Accessed 29 October 2010.

Singley, Carol J. 2011. *Adopting America: Childhood, Kinship, and National Identity in Literature*. New York: Oxford University Press. Print.

Skolnick, Sharon, and Manny Skolnick. 1997. *Where Courage is Like a Wild Horse: The World of an Indian Orphanage*. Lincoln: University of Nebraska Press. Print.

Slotkin, Richard. 2000 [1973]. *Regeneration Through Violence: The Mythology of the American Frontier 1600–1860*. Norman: University of Oklahoma Press. Print.

Smyth, Jacqui. 1999. 'Sheltered Vagrancy in Marilynne Robinson's *Housekeeping*.' *Critique* 40.3: 281–91. Print.

Snyder, Christina. 2010. *Slavery in Indian Country: The Changing Face of Captivity in Early America*. Cambridge: Harvard University Press. Print.

Sollors, Werner. 2009. 'The Word "Multicultural."' *A New Literary History of America*. Ed. Greil Marcus and Werner Sollors. Cambridge: Belknap Press, 757–61. Print.

Spaulding, Timothy. 2005. *Re-Forming the Past: History, the Fantastic, and the Postmodern Slave Narrative*. Columbus: Ohio State University Press. Print.

Stacey, Judith. 1998. *Brave New Families*. 2nd edn. Berkeley: University of California Press. Print.

Strach, Patricia. *All in the Family: The Private Roots of American Public Policy*. Stanford: Stanford University Press. 2007. Print.

Strong, Pauline Turner. 1999. *Captive Selves, Captivating Others: The Politics and Poetics of Colonial American Captivity Narratives*. Boulder: Westview. Print.

Sturken, Marita. 1999. 'Narratives of Recovery: Repressed Memory as Cultural Memory.' *Acts of Memory: Cultural Recall in the Present*. Ed. Mieke Bal, Jonathan Crewe and Leo Spitzer. Hanover: University Press of New England, 231–48. Print.

Sugrue, Thomas J. 2008. 'Poverty in the Era of Welfare Reform: The "Underclass" Family in Myth and Reality.' *American Families: A Multicultural Reader*. Eds Stephanie Coontz, Maya Parson, and Gabrielle Raley. 2nd edn. New York: Routledge, 325–37. Print.

Sundstrom, Ronald R. 2008. *The Browning of America and the Evasion of Social Justice*. Albany: State University of New York. Print.

Tarter, Jim. 2000. '"Dreams of Earth": Place, Multiethnicity, and Environmental Justice in Linda Hogan's *Solar Storms*.' *Reading under the Sign of Nature: New Essays in Ecocriticism*. Eds John Tallmadge and Henry Harrington. Salt Lake City: University of Utah Press. 128–47. Print.

Bibliography

Taylor, Kristin N. 2009. 'Home to Aunt Em: Sentimental Adoption in L. Frank Baum's *The Wonderful Wizard of Oz*.' *Children's Literature Association Quarterly* 34.4: 379–93. *Muse*. Web. Accessed 28 April 2010.

Taylor-Guthrie, Danille, ed. 1994. *Conversations with Toni Morrison*. Jackson: University Press of Mississippi. Print.

Templeton, Tom, and Tom Lumley. 2002. '9/11 in Numbers.' *The Observer* 18 August. www.theguardian.com/world/2002/aug/18/usa.terrorism. Web. Accessed 27 April 2013.

Thaler, Ingrid. 2010. *Black Atlantic Speculative Fictions: Octavia E. Butler, Jewelle Gomez, and Nalo Hopkinson*. New York: Routledge. Print.

Therborn, Göran. 2004. *Between Sex and Power: Family in the World, 1900–2000*. London: Routledge. Print.

'Thomas Jefferson and Sally Hemings: A Brief Account.' n.d. *Monticello.org*. Thomas Jefferson Foundation. www.monticello.org/site/plantation-and-slavery/thomas-jefferson-and-sally-hemings-brief-account. Web. Accessed 28 May 2012.

Thorne, Barrie and Marilyn Yalom eds. 1992. *Rethinking the Family: Some Feminist Questions*. Boston: Northeastern University Press. Print.

Thrall, William Flint, Addison Hibbard, and C. Hugh Holman. 1960. *A Handbook to Literature*. Revised edn. New York: Odyssey Press. Print.

Tinti, Hannah. 2008. *The Good Thief*. New York: Dial Press. Print.

Troy, Maria Holmgren. 1999. *In the First Person and in the House: The House Chronotope in Four Works by American Women Writers*. Uppsala: Uppsala University. Print.

—— 2006. 'Narrative and Trauma: Kaye Gibbons's *Ellen Foster* and Margaret Atwood's "Death by Landscape".' *Berätta för att förstå: sju essäer*. Eds Åke Bergvall, Anders Tyrberg and Elisabeth Wennö. Karlstad: Karlstad University Press, 125–52. Print.

—— 2010a. '"Between Memory and History": The Nineteenth Century in Jewelle Gomez's Vampire Novel *The Gilda Stories* and the TV Series *True Blood*.' *American Studies in Scandinavia* 42.2: 57–73. Print.

—— 2010b. 'Negotiating Genre and Captivity: Octavia Butler's *Survivor*.' *Callaloo* 33.4: 1116–31. Print.

Turell, Susan C. 2006. 'Incest.' *Encyclopedia of Human Development*, vol. 2. Eds Neil J. Salkind. Thousand Oaks: Sage, 684. Print.

Tyler May, Elaine. 1988. *Homeward Bound: American Families in the Cold War Era*. New York: Basic. Print.

Updike, John. 2005. 'Mixed Messages: *Extremely Loud and Incredibly Close*.' *The New Yorker* 14 March. www.newyorker.com/archive/2005/03/14/050314crbo_books1. Web. Accessed 10 February 2010.

VanDerBeets, Richard. 1984. *The Indian Captivity Narrative: An American Genre*. Lanham: University Press of America. Print.

Versluys, Kristiaan. 2009. *Out of the Blue: September 11 and the Novel*. New York: Columbia. Print.

Vint, Sherryl. 2007. *Bodies of Tomorrow: Technology, Subjectivity, Science Fiction*. Toronto: University of Toronto Press. Print.

Vizenor, Gerald. 1999 [1994]. *Manifest Manners: Narratives on PostIndian Survivance*. Lincoln: University of Nebraska Press. Print.

Voloshin, Beverly R. 1984. 'The Limits of Domesticity: The Female Bildungsroman in America, 1820–1870.' *Women's Studies* 10.3: 283–302. Print.

Wagner-Martin, Linda. 2003. *Barbara Kingsolver*. Philadelphia: Chelsea. Print.

Wahlström, Helena. 2010. *New Fathers? Contemporary American Stories of Masculinity, Domesticity, and Kinship*. Newcastle: Cambridge Scholars Publishing.

Wallace, Diana. 2006. 'Why Tulips?: A Case Study in Historicising the Historical Novel.' *Working Papers on the Web*. Sheffield Hallam University. http://extra.shu.ac.uk/wpw/historicising/Wallace.htm. Web. Accessed 20 March 2012.

—— 2008 [2005]. *The Woman's Historical Novel: British Women Writers, 1900–2000*. Basingstoke: Palgrave Macmillan. Print.

Warren, Joyce W. 1993. 'Introduction: Canons and Canon Fodder.' *The (Other) American Traditions: Nineteenth-Century Women Writers*. Ed. Joyce W. Warren. New Brunswick: Rutgers University Press, 1–25. Print.

Warrior, Robert. 1994. *Tribal Secrets: Recovering American Indian Intellectual Traditions*. Minneapolis: University of Minnesota Press. Print.

Watts, Linda. 2000. 'Stories Told by Their Survivors (and Other Sins of Memory): Survivor Guilt in Kaye Gibbons's *Ellen Foster*.' *The World Is Our Home: Society and Culture in Contemporary Southern Writing*. Eds Jeffrey J. Folks and Nancy Summers Folks. Lexington: University Press of Kentucky. Print.

Watts, Steven. 1994. *The Romance of Real Life: Charles Brockden Brown and the Origins of American Culture*. Baltimore: Johns Hopkins University Press. Print.

Weaver, Jace, Craig S. Womack, and Robert Warrior. 2005. *American Indian Literary Nationalism*. Albuquerque: University of New Mexico Press. Print.

Wegner, Philip E. 2009. *Life Between Two Deaths, 1989–2001: U.S. Culture in the Long Nineties*. Durham: Duke University Press. Print.

Weinstein, Cindy. 2004. *Family, Kinship and Sympathy in Nineteenth-Century American Literature*. Cambridge: Cambridge University Press. Print.

Welter, Barbara. 1966. 'The Cult of True Womanhood: 1820–1860.' *American Quarterly* 18 (Summer): 151–74. Print.

Weston, Kath. 1997. *Families We Choose: Gays, Lesbians, Kinship*. New York: Columba University Press. Print.

White, James G. and Sarah Michèle Martin. 2008. 'The Indian Child Welfare Act and Violence Against Women.' *Sharing Our Stories of Survival: Native Women Surviving Violence*. Eds Sarah Deer, Bonnie Clairmont, Carrie A. Martell, and Maureen L. White Eagle. New York: Altamira, 297–308. Print.

Whitman, Walt. 1963 [1887]. *Specimen Days in America*. New York: New York University Press. Print.

—— 1980 [1892]. *Leaves of Grass*. New York: New York University Press. Print.

Wilkins, David E., and K. Tsianina Lomawaima. 2001. *Uneven Ground: American Indian Sovereignty and Federal Law*. Norman: University of Oklahoma Press. Print.

Willis, Susan. 1990. *Specifying: Black Women Writing the American Experience*. London: Routledge. Print.

Wilson, Christine. 2008. 'Delinquent Housekeeping: Transforming the Regulations of Keeping House.' *Legacy* 25.2: 299–310. *Muse*. Web. Accessed 4 October 2010.

Wirth-Nesher, Hana. 1986. 'The Literary Orphan as National Hero: Huck and Pip.' *Dickens Studies Annual: Essays on Victorian Fiction* 15: 259–73. Print.

Womack, Craig. 2008. 'Book-Length Native Literary Criticism.' *Reasoning Together: The Native Critics Collective*. Eds Craig Womack, Daniel Heath Justice, and Christopher B. Teuton. Norman: University of Oklahoma Press, 3–104. Print.

—— Daniel Heath Justice, and Christopher B. Teuton, eds. 2008. *Reasoning Together: The Native Critics Collective*. Norman: University of Oklahoma Press. Print.

Yardley, Jonathan. 1985. 'John Irving's Odyssey of an Orphan.' *Washington Post* 19 May. Print.

Zaretsky, Natasha. 2007. *No Direction Home: The American Family and the Fear of National Decline, 1968–1980*. Chapel Hill: University of North Carolina Press. Print.

Zitkala-Sa. 1985 [1921] *American Indian Stories*. Lincoln: University of Nebraska Press. Print.

Index

Note: 'n.' after a page reference indicates the number of a note on that page.

9/11 23, 84, 99, 100, 101–11 passim, 113–18 passim

Abel, Elizabeth 213n.55
  Marianne Hirsch and Elizabeth Langland 120n.6, 132, 139
abortion 128, 136–7, 140, 142, 146, 165n.14, 166n.20
Adams, David Wallace 81n.26
adoption 4, 6–7, 23–5, 27, 30–2, 42, 43, 46, 64, 72, 80n.20, 81n.27, 109, 128–9, 145, 149, 155, 158, 163, 171, 176, 184, 199, 208n.4, 216, 218–19, 223–4
  captivity and 43, 48–61 passim
  transnational 7, 9n.8, 23, 128
  transracial 7, 9, 9n.8, 24–5, 30–2, 80n.21, 109, 155, 171
Ahmed, Sara 36
Alcoff, Linda Martin 33, 35
American Adam, the 3, 8, 17–21 passim, 45, 88, 90–1, 99, 100, 106, 108, 110, 118–19, 124n.36, 198, 206
Andersen, Margaret 9n.2, 38n.25, 39n.26, 39n.28, 165n.13, 166n.20, 167n.27
Anderson, Benedict 22
Anderson, Perry 177, 210n.25, 210n.26
Appadurai, Arjun 208n.11, 212n.36
Ariès, Philippe 25, 123n.33
Ashby, Leroy 26, 46, 80n.10, 123n.24, 128, 134, 166n.17

Askeland, Lori 24, 123n.22

Babb, Valerie 36, 197, 199, 200, 205
Bakhtin, M. M. 3, 9n.3, 12, 120n.1
Baym, Nina 9n.6, 16, 20, 90, 151
bildungsroman 5, 8, 12, 36, 37n.3, 85–8, 93, 98–9, 119, 120n.6, 126–52 passim, 164, 165n.8, 165n.9, 214–15, 220, 221
  American and English 131–2, 147
  class and 85, 152
  female 86–7, 98–9, 120n.6, 132
Briggs, Laura 38n.20, 38n.21, 38n.23, 80n.10, 80n.11, 208n.4
Brown, John Gregory
  The Wrecked Blessed Body of Shelton LaFleur 127
Buckley, Jerome Hamilton 131, 138, 139, 149
Butler, Octavia 170, 172–9 passim, 207, 208n.11, 209n.12, 209n.15
  Fledgling 13, 172, 179–86, 211n.35
  Kindred 176, 178, 180, 208n.9, 210n.28

Callahan, Cynthia 7, 31, 49, 52, 79n.7, 80n.20, 176
canon formation 3, 12, 18–20, 33, 83–4, 148, 167n.29, 178
captivity narrative 3, 5–7, 12, 36, 42–4, 63, 66–7, 69, 71, 79, 214–15
Carby, Hazel 17, 20, 178, 209n.12

Index

Castañeda, Claudia 32, 80n.21
Castiglia, Christopher 44, 59, 80n.14, 80n.15, 81n.30
Chapman, Mary and Glenn Hendler 19, 116, 117, 120n.5, 124n.41, 124n.44, 124n.45, 125n48
childhood, conceptions of 6, 10, 14, 25–6, 36, 81n.29, 102, 105, 123n.32
class 13, 15–17, 20, 34, 39n.29, 50, 75, 85–8, 98, 99, 101–2, 113, 118, 137, 143–5, 147, 150, 152, 169, 195–7, 208n.3, 213n.50, 214
Clayton, Jay 167n.26, 167n.29, 167n.32
collective memory *see* memory: collective
Collins, Patricia Hill 29, 167n.27, 171–2, 208n.6, 208n.7, 211n.28
Coontz, Stephanie 28–9, 39n.28, 165n.13, 166n.21
counter-memory *see* memory: counter-
cultural memory *see* memory: cultural
see also remembrance
cultural orphans 2, 41–2, 45, 64, 84, 93, 196
culture wars 2, 33, 83, 148, 167n.29, 178
Cummins, Maria
  The Lamplighter 16, 85, 97, 133
  Gerty 16, 85, 97, 133
Cunningham, Michael 215
  The Hours 99, 122n.19, 122n.20
  Specimen Days 18, 84, 88, 99–111, 118–19, 122n.19, 215–16

de Groot, Jerome 177, 187, 210n.27, 212n.46
domestic fiction 87, 99
Duvall, John N. and Robert P. Marzec 118, 120n.2, 125n.49
Dyer, Richard 36, 212n.44

Equal Rights Amendment 128
ERA *see* Equal Rights Amendment
Erdrich, Louise 1, 41
Erll, Astrid 11, 12, 37n.4, 37n.5

Fagan, Kristina 49, 56, 79n.6, 80n.20
Faludi, Susan 23, 38n.18, 123n.27, 123n.28, 123n.29, 124n.47

family
  African American family 29–30, 129, 165n.5, 169–73, 190–1, 194, 195, 198
  'alternative family' 8, 31, 137, 146, 164, 179
  American family ideal 29, 145, 182
  cross-species family *see* interspecies relationships
  extended families 168n.34, 171
  Native American family 30, 50
  nuclear family ideal 2, 27–8, 31, 84, 99, 126, 135, 137, 145, 148, 163–4, 170, 182
  queer family 99
  see also queer kinship
Farrell, Betty G. 9n.2, 38n.25, 167n.27
Fiedler, Leslie 153
  Love and Death in the American Novel 92, 120n.4
  The Return of the Vanishing American 92–5 passim
Foer, Jonathan Safran 13, 15, 20, 84
  Extremely Loud and Incredibly Close 111–20, 124n.47, 125n.50, 125n.51, 216
foster care 4, 24–5, 35, 51, 60–61, 80n.10, 128–30, 133, 135, 149, 159–60, 168n.39, 170, 220
Fowler, Connie May
  Before Women Had Wings 127, 168n.36
Frankenberg, Ruth 36
Froehlich, Peter Alan and Joy Harris Philpott 69, 81n.25
Fulton, DoVeanna 200

Gautreaux, Tim
  The Missing 216, 221–2, 224
Gelder, Ken 175, 209n.16, 209n.18
Gibbons, Kaye 13, 126–8, 131–4, 168n.34, 180, 216
  Ellen Foster 148–64
  The Life All Around Me by Ellen Foster 148–64
Goddu, Teresa 188, 212n.42
Gomez, Jewelle 11, 170, 172, 178–9, 207, 209n.15, 209n.18, 209n.20, 210n.24
  The Gilda Stories 172, 186–95, 212n.42, 212n.40, 212n.42

history and 176, 187–8, 212n.38
rememory and 173–4
speculative fiction and 174–6, 187, 208n.11
gothic 175, 188–9, 212n.42
Gould, Phillip 178, 211n.31
Griffin, Edward 54, 63, 81n.30

Hacsi, Timothy 130, 166n.16
Halbwachs, Maurice 37n.4
Haraway, Donna 183–5, 211n.34
Hawkins-León, Cynthia 30
Herman, Judith Lewis 161, 165n.12, 168n.41
historical fiction 72, 177, 179, 187, 196, 207, 210n.26, 212n.46, 215
historical novel 36, 172–8 passim, 187, 194–5, 198, 205, 207, 210n.25
historical romance 189, 193–5
Hogan, Linda 11, 41, 42, 45, 47, 59, 72, 76–8, 82n.35, 127, 215, 216
  Power 81n.31
  Solar Storms 13, 41–3, 60–72, 77, 79, 80n.18, 81n.24, 81n.26, 81n.27, 81n.28, 81n.29, 81n.31, 82n.32, 179, 180, 215
Holt, Marilyn Irvin 38n.16, 38n.20, 43, 50, 54, 60, 62, 79n.9, 80n.10
Huhndorf, Shari 40–1, 46, 81n.22, 82n.35

ICWA *see* Indian Child Welfare Act
incest 142, 146, 149, 161, 165n.11, 165n.12, 167n.24, 168n.41
Indian boarding schools 43, 50, 55, 72, 81n.26
Indian Child Welfare Act 24, 38n.20, 43, 51, 55, 80n.11
Interethnic Adoption Provisions 24, 80n.11
interspecies relationships 109, 180–3, 211n.35
intertext, intertextuality 3, 11–12, 84, 90, 93, 100, 110, 119, 126, 133, 136, 148, 150–1, 173
Irving, John 15, 134–5
  The Cider House Rules 31, 126–8, 134–48, 163–4, 215

Ivey, Eowyn
  The Snow Child 216, 222–4

Jacobson, Matthew Frye 35, 123n.23
Jenkins, Candice 29–30, 39n.29, 39n.30, 170, 208n.3, 208n.7
Jerng, Mark 7, 31–2
Johnson, Adam
  The Orphan Master's Son 216–18
Justice, Daniel Heath 61, 70–1, 77, 81n.23

Kella, Elizabeth 213n.55
Kidd, Sue Monk
  The Secret Life of Bees 127
Kincaid, James 9n.4, 26, 105, 123n.32
kinship building 8, 127–8, 134, 145, 147, 149, 150, 154, 160, 162–3, 164, 215–16
Kingsolver, Barbara 41–5, 47, 67, 72, 77, 79n.7, 80n.19, 80n.20, 127, 154, 215, 216, 224
  The Bean Trees 41–5 *passim*, 47–60, 78, 153
  Pigs in Heaven 41–5 *passim*, 47–60, 79
Kornfeld, Eve and Susan Jackson 87, 120n.7
Krupat, Arnold 81n.22, 82n.35, 82n.37

learning 111–12, 131, 172–6, 187, 196, 201–2, 204–7, 211n.32
Lee, Chang-Rae
  The Surrendered 216, 218–19
Levander, Caroline 9n.4, 25–6, 29, 31–2, 34, 36, 38n.17, 39n.33, 39n.35, 78, 118, 123n.28, 123n.32
Lewis, R.W.B. 9n.4, 17–20, 45, 88, 92, 100, 106, 110, 123n.35
liberatory narratives 174, 178, 203–4, 211n.30
  see also slave narratives
Lionnet, Françoise and Shu-mei Shih 205
Lipsitz, George 36, 37n.1, 190
literacy, literacies 172, 176, 197, 201
Loichot, Valérie 9n.7, 191, 198, 204
Lomawaima, Tsianina 40, 79n.8
Lukács, Georg 177–8

Index

Mallon, Gerald 165n.3
McDowell, Deborah 179, 207n.1, 211n.31
memory
　amnesia and 13, 52, 176, 179–86, 204
　collective 4, 11, 13, 37n.4, 83, 95, 173, 180, 194, 204, 214
　counter- 11, 37n.1, 190, 194
　cultural 3, 11–12, 83–5, 90–1, 107, 110, 118–19, 126, 131, 148, 163, 173, 178–9, 186, 188, 193, 195, 214
MEPA *see* Multiethnic Placement Act
Michael, Magali Cornier 49, 52, 56, 79n.6, 80n.18
Millard, Kenneth 88, 121n.12, 122n.14, 131, 165n.9
Mintz, Steven 22–3, 37n.15
Misztal, Barbara 11, 83, 136
Mitchell, Angelyn 37n.2, 174, 178, 202–5, 211n.29, 211n.30 211n.31
Monteith, Sharon 36, 133, 152–4, 156, 165n.10, 167n.26, 167n.33, 208n.3, 213n.55
Moore, David 73, 78
Moore, Lorrie
　A Gate at the Stairs 127
Moretti, Franco 152
Morrison, Toni 11, 36, 170, 172, 176, 207n.1, 208n.8
　Beloved 11, 165n.9, 173, 177, 178, 179, 196, 210n.28
　history and 178–9, 196–7
　A Mercy 13, 18, 31, 104, 172, 174, 177, 195–207, 213n.48
　Paradise 205, 213n.55
　Playing in the Dark 15
　'Recitatif' 205, 213n.55
　rememory and 173, 212n.43
motherlines 172, 176, 179, 191–2, 195, 206
Moynihan Report, the 29, 129, 169–70
multiculturalism 10, 32–4, 40–1, 55, 58–60, 75, 80n.20, 83–4, 178, 192, 194, 216
Multiethnic Placement Act 24, 25, 38n.23, 208n.4
Murray, David 72, 82n.37

Nelson, Claudia 9n.4, 9n.6, 13–14, 37n.7, 81n.29, 115, 123n.22
Neumann, Birgit 173, 204
Nora, Pierre 11, 187
nostalgia 29, 44, 58, 60, 79, 105, 130, 197
Novy, Marianne 6–7, 27, 38n.24, 49, 56, 80n.20, 168n.37

O'Connor, Stephen 38n.16, 39n.28
oral traditions 5, 12, 188–95 *passim*, 199–200, 204, 214
orphan
　definitions of 1–4, 7, 21–7
orphanage 6, 22–3, 50, 106, 127, 129–30, 133–48 *passim*, 159, 163–4, 165n.7, 166n.15, 216, 218–19, 220–2
othermothers 171–2, 208n.6
Owens, Louis 36, 39n.31, 44, 59

Pazicky, Diana Loercher 2, 13, 15–16, 22, 27, 36, 41, 45–6, 58, 64, 80n.13, 86–7, 93–4, 102
picaresque 85, 87–8, 93, 113, 118, 217–18, 222

queer family *see* family: queer
queer kinship 29, 176, 193, 210n.22

remembrance 11–13, 37n.5
rememory, rememorying 11, 37n.2, 172–4, 180, 186, 189–90, 200–7 *passim*, 214–15, 221
Roberts, Dorothy 25, 30, 38n.23, 129, 155, 165n.5, 170, 208n.4, 208n.7
Robinson, Marilynne 13, 84, 89
　Gilead 89–90
　Home 89–90
　Housekeeping 13, 18, 20, 31, 84, 88–99, 118–19, 147, 152
Rody, Caroline 165n.9, 173, 198–9, 210n.24
Roe vs. Wade 136

Sánchez-Eppler, Karen 9n.4, 25–6, 81n.29, 124n.42

Sapphire
  The Kid 216, 219–21
science fiction 101, 174–5, 185
sentimental novel 20, 84–5, 87, 111, 113, 118–19
Shamir, Milette and Jennifer Travis 85, 114, 116, 120n.5, 124n.45, 124n.46, 125n.52
Shanley, Kathryn 46–7, 55, 79n.4
Silko, Leslie Marmon 31, 41–9, 52, 59, 61, 82n.35, 93, 206, 216
  Gardens in the Dunes 31, 41, 43, 72–9, 82n.37, 82n.38, 82n.39, 93, 215
Simpson, Eileen 93, 96, 123n.31
Singley, Carol 9n.4, 9n.6, 9n.7, 25–6, 36, 37n.3, 37n.6, 123n.32
slave narratives 3, 170, 174, 178, 203, 211n.31, 214, 215
  see also liberatory narratives
Slotkin, Richard 18–19, 36, 44, 54, 59, 61, 80n.14
Snyder, Christina 42, 63–4, 81n.30
sovereignty 33, 40–4 *passim*, 60, 63, 68–70, 72, 81n.23, 202
speculative fiction 5, 36, 172, 174, 176, 181, 186–7, 194, 207, 209n.11, 209n.14
Strong, Pauline Turner 43, 54, 59, 63, 81n.30
survivance 45, 66, 69–71, 76–8

Thaler, Ingrid 174, 209n.13, 210n.21, 210n.24
Tinti, Hannah
  The Good Thief 6, 130
transnationalism 7, 34, 205

Troy, Maria Holmgren 79n.2, 121n.10, 167n.31, 168n.35, 210n.23, 211n.34, 212n.40
TTOF *see* Twin Towers Orphan Fund
Twain, Mark
  Adventures of Huckleberry Finn 3, 15, 87
  Huck Finn, Huckleberry Finn 6, 15–16, 45, 78, 93, 113, 120n.4, 133, 147, 164, 165n.9
Twin Towers Orphan Fund 6, 23, 103, 110

vampire novels 174–5, 181, 183
vanishing American 42, 44, 61, 67, 92, 94
Vizenor, Gerald 45, 59, 79n.5
Voloshin, Beverly 86, 98

Wahlström, Helena 165n.4
Wallace, Diana 177, 210n.25
Weaver, Jace 41, 81n.22
Weinstein, Cindy 9n.6, 30, 37n.10, 37n.14, 111–13, 118, 120n.3
Weston, Kath 29, 39n.26, 126, 164n.2, 167n.27
Whitman, Walt 18, 84, 110, 123n.35
  Specimen Days in America 100
  Leaves of Grass 106–7
Wilkins, David 40
Willis, Susan 169, 172–3, 189, 200
Wirth-Nesher, Hana 15
Womack, Craig 41, 62, 81n.22, 81n.23

Zaretsky, Natasha 9n.2, 27, 38n.25
Zitkala-Sa 79n.8

EU authorised representative for GPSR:
Easy Access System Europe, Mustamäe tee 50,
10621 Tallinn, Estonia
gpsr.requests@easproject.com

www.ingramcontent.com/pod-product-compliance
Lightning Source LLC
Chambersburg PA
CBHW070236240426
43673CB00044B/1819